# READING

# GENESIS ONE

Comparing Biblical Hebrew with English Translation

Rodney Whitefield

© **2003 by Rodney Whitefield**
6794 Heathfield Drive
San Jose, California 95120
email: whitefld@jps.net

All rights reserved. No part of this publication may be reproduced, stored in a retrieval system, or transmitted in any form or by any means, electronic or otherwise, without the prior written permission of the copyright holder.

ISBN 0-9728782-0-3

Library of Congress Control Number: 2003103221

Published by R. Whitefield Publisher
6794 Heathfield Drive
San Jose, California 95120
email: whitefld@jps.net

First printing 2003
Second printing 2004

IN THE BEGINNING GOD . . .

# Table of Contents

*Reading Genesis One* Comparing Biblical Hebrew with English Translation

| | |
|---|---|
| **Author's Foreword** | vi |
| | |
| ***Chapter One***        BIBLICAL HEBREW. | 2 |
| | |
| **IMPORTANT FACTS ABOUT BIBLICAL HEBREW.** | 2 |
|     How Words are Written in Biblical Hebrew | 4 |
|     Vocabulary: The Multiple Meanings of Words | 5 |
|     Word Meaning and the Translation of Genesis One | 6 |
|     Nouns, Prefixes, and Suffixes | 7 |
| | |
| **The Untranslated Word אֵת, The Direct Object Marker.** | 8 |
| | |
| **More About Verbs** | 8 |
|     The Biblical Hebrew Verb Does Not Have Tense | 8 |
|     The Hebrew Perfect (Completed Action) | 8 |
|     The Hebrew Imperfect and the "Waw-consecutive" | 10 |
|     The "Waw-consecutive" Verb Form | 11 |
|     An Example of Verb Translation | 12 |
| | |
| **Procedures Followed in the Study of Genesis 1:1 – 2:4.** | 13 |
| | |
| ***Chapter Two***       THE FIRST VERSES: Genesis 1:1-2. | 16 |
| | |
| **THE FIRST VERSE: GENESIS 1:1**     In the Beginning God. | 16 |
|     The Meaning of Genesis 1:1 | 18 |
| | |
| **THE SECOND VERSE: GENESIS 1:2**     Before the Start of the Story. | 21 |
|     The Meaning of תֹהוּ וָבֹהוּ "Tohu" and "Bohu". | 21 |
|     Genesis 1:1-2 Completed Before the "And God said" of Genesis 1:3 | 24 |
|     Genesis 1:2 Places No Restriction on the Age of Planet Earth | 26 |
|     Analysis Showing Genesis 1:3 is the Start of the First Creative יוֹם "Yom" | 27 |
|     Analysis of Exodus 20:11 | 28 |
|     "Young Earth" and Other Translation Issues | 30 |
|     More About "Bara," "Asah," and "Yatsar" | 32 |
|     More About "waw + noun --perfect verb," a Pluperfect Indicator | 37 |
|     More About "Tohu" and "Bohu" | 43 |
|     More About "Haya" Translated "Became" | 47 |
|     More About Ex Nihilo | 50 |
| | |
| ***Chapter Three***   THE FIRST CREATIVE "YOM": GENESIS 1:3-5 | 54 |
| | |
| **VERSE THREE: GENESIS 1:3**     The Start of the "Daytime". | 54 |
| | |
| **VERSE FOUR: GENESIS 1:4**     About the Separating. | 56 |

**VERSE FIVE: GENESIS 1:5**  The Naming and the Concluding Phrases. ................... 58
    The Use of יוֹם "Yom" in the Five Books of Moses and the Hebrew Bible ................. 60
    Translation and the Time Meaning of the Creative יוֹם "Yom" ....................................... 67
    Summary of Results for Genesis 1:1-5 and Comments Regarding 24-Hour "Day" Models ........... 70
    The Translation of Genesis 1:3-5 ................................................................... 74
    More About "Evening" and "Morning" ........................................................... 79
    "Yom" as a Marker of the Passage of Time ....................................................... 81
    When "Yom" Means 24 Hours ....................................................................... 84
    History of the English Genesis One Text .......................................................... 88

## *Chapter Four* THE REMAINING CREATIVE "YOM" ................................................ 90

**The Second Creative "Yom": Genesis 1:6-8**  The Sky and the Waters. ................... 90
    A Model of the Sky and the Waters .................................................................. 92
    The Translation of Genesis 1:6-8 ...................................................................... 94

**The Third Creative "Yom:" Genesis 1:9-13**  The Land and the Land Plants. ............ 96
    The "When" of Genesis 1:12: A Pluperfect Reference to Past Actions ..................... 97
    The Words Translated Grass and Tree ............................................................ 100

**The Fourth Creative "Yom": Genesis 1:14-19**  The Lights in the Sky ................... 102
    The "When" of the Actions of Genesis 1:14-18, the Pluperfect References to Past Actions ......... 106
    About the "Patterning" of Genesis One ............................................................ 108

**The Fifth Creative "Yom": Genesis 1:20-23**  Air Breathing Creatures in the Waters ....... 110
    Creatures in the Waters .................................................................................. 110
    The Methods Used by God to Introduce Plants, Air Breathing Life, and Fill the Waters .......... 116

**The Sixth Creative "Yom": Genesis 1:24-31**  Land Animals and the Creation of Adam. ..... 121
    The Land Animals ........................................................................................ 121
    Adam: Male and Female ................................................................................ 123

**The Seventh Creative "Yom": Genesis 2:1-4**  The Ceasing of the Seventh Time. ............ 130

**Concluding Remarks.** ................................................................................... 134

## *Chapter Five* THE TRANSLATIONS OF GENESIS ONE. ............................................ 139

    This Study's "Good English" Translation ........................................................ 140
    Modified KJV Translation (KJV-M) of Genesis One ........................................ 141
    This Study's "Good English" Translation of Genesis One with Strong's Numbers ........ 146

**Appendixes and Verse Indexes.** ..................................................................... 151

    Appendix 1: English Transliterations Used in the Text for Hebrew words ............... 152
    Table of Hebrew Letters with Name and Strong's Articulation ............................ 154
    Appendix 2: Strong's Numbers and Hebrew Root Word Phonetic Representations .......... 155
    **Index of the Hebrew Text of Genesis 1:1 - Genesis 2:4** .................................... 158
    **Index of Referenced Verses** (Not the verses of Genesis 1:1 - Genesis 2:4) ............ 159

**End Notes** ................................................................................................... 160

## Author's Foreword

Genesis Chapter One is a record of creation events. The accuracy of this record has long been the subject of much debate. Secular schools and universities teach a great deal of misinformation regarding Creation, the Bible, and Christianity. For many people, this secular criticism of Genesis One must be resolved before they will consider the truths of the Bible and the Good News of Jesus Christ.

Genesis One also divides the Christian community because of differing opinions regarding the age of the Universe and the length of the creative periods. This division is used by secular opponents to heap scorn on the Bible and on the believer. This scorn is a major impediment to Christian witness.

So, the question is this: "What does the Bible really say about creation?"

Since existing books and commentaries on Genesis One have not adequately answered this question, I undertook an intensive study of biblical Hebrew. My goal was to understand, by reading the Hebrew, what the Bible really says about creation events.

This book is a word-by-word study of Genesis Chapter One. The study uses the Bible itself as a dictionary to establish the meanings of words which are critical to understanding this chapter. By the end of the study the reader will understand the biblical text which is the basis for my conclusions regarding the correct interpretation of Genesis One. But the reader may not agree with these conclusions. In that case, differences can be discussed in terms of the biblical text itself, not the usual controversy of pitting one expert's opinion against another expert's opinion.

This study has increased my certainty regarding the truth of the Bible and Christianity. I believe that it will be of similar benefit to the reader.

The author wishes to acknowledge the invaluable assistance of Rose Whitefield, John Kulander, and Ed Harris; all of whom proofed and marked up many draft copies. There were also others who offered helpful comments about clarity of writing. To all these, I say "Thank you." Even with the considerable effort to achieve clear exposition, there will inevitably remain some difficult exposition and ordinary "typos."

Rodney Whitefield

6794 Heathfield Drive
San Jose, CA    95120      email: whitefld@jps.net
(408) 997-5463


About the author: Rodney Whitefield is a Ph.D. physicist who had the good fortune to retire early from IBM. Early retirement provided both the time and the resources with which to pursue the studies leading to the writing of this book.

# *CHAPTER ONE*

# BIBLICAL HEBREW

## Chapter One  BIBLICAL HEBREW

## IMPORTANT FACTS ABOUT BIBLICAL HEBREW

*"In the beginning God created the heavens and the earth." KJV Genesis 1:1*

## Introduction

Genesis 1:1 is the first verse of the Bible. It greatly influences how readers view the text which follows. Readers of the English Bible assume that they understand this verse simply because it is written in English. They assume that they understand the meanings of the word "created" and of the phrase "the heavens and the earth." These assumptions often overlook the fact that the English is a translation from the biblical Hebrew. The word "created" is a translation of the Hebrew word "bara." "Bara" has an additional sense of meaning not fully expressed by the English word "create." The meaning of the Hebrew word בָּרָא "bara" will be discussed extensively when Genesis 1:1 is considered.

Another Hebrew word which will be extensively discussed is בְּרֵאשִׁית translated "in the beginning." To people living after the year 2000, the Bible's statement that there was a "beginning" seems uncontroversial. Historically, this statement has been the source of great controversy and the basis of much opposition to the Genesis creation account. The "In the beginning" was considered by Christian and Hebrew scholars to indicate the creation of the matter which composes the universe. Science, until 1900, generally held that the universe was infinitely old and existed without a beginning. Since 1900 scientific evidence has accumulated to the extent that secular science now holds that there was a beginning to matter. In this change of scientific view, the "beginning" of the Bible has been vindicated.

Genesis One (i.e., the first 35 verses of the Bible) remains the subject of continuing controversy. There are differences of interpretation within the Christian community and continuing controversy between the Christian community and the secular world. The differences within the Christian community are primarily questions of "when." The questions are about the age of the earth as described by Genesis One and the amount of time attributed by Genesis One to the introduction of life. The questions of "when" and "amount of time" are questions which involve the meaning and translation of Hebrew verbs. These questions will be addressed by first preparing the reader to understand the translation issues. Then Genesis One will be studied using the preserved Hebrew text to examine the meaning. The first step in this preparation is to note that the verb in biblical Hebrew is very different from the verb in English.

**Verbs in biblical Hebrew do not express tense!**

Tense, in English, means that the form and placement of verbs tell the reader the "when" of the action, and often the "duration" of the action. For example, the English verb "walk" has the past tense form "walked" and the pluperfect form "had walked." Through the use of the past and the pluperfect verb forms, English indicates the order in time in which the separate actions represented by the verbs take place. A more complete discussion of the English past and pluperfect as it relates to the translation of the Hebrew will be given later.

In biblical Hebrew the verb does **not** specify the "duration" of verbal actions, and it does **not** convey the time ordering of verbal actions. This difference means that almost every English verb used in translation unintentionally adds some "when" information which was not included in the meaning of the Hebrew word. English verbs normally express some information about "when;" biblical Hebrew verbs do **not** express a "when."

A particularly clear statement regarding this issue is quoted below. The quotation is from *A Short Account of the Hebrew Tenses* by R. H. Kennett (Cambridge: At the University Press, 1901, page 1).[1]

> The 'name' tenses as applied to Hebrew verbs is misleading. The so-called Hebrew 'tenses' do not express the time but merely the state of the action. Indeed were it not for the confusion that would arise through the application of the term 'state' to both nouns and verbs, 'states' would be a far better designation than 'tenses.' It must always be born in mind that it is impossible to translate a Hebrew verb into English without employing a limitation (viz. of time) which is entirely absent in Hebrew. The ancient Hebrews never thought of an action as past, present, or future, but simply as perfect, i.e., complete, or imperfect, i.e., as in course of development.

Verbs in biblical Hebrew only indicate that an action is complete (finished) or incomplete (not finished). This limitation is very important when reading Genesis. The above quotation is a somewhat incomplete description. A completed action may be completed in the near past (an instant ago), the distant past, or the future. Also, biblical Hebrew does sometimes indicate the ordering of past actions. It does this not by the verb forms but by word order. This function of the word order will be discussed in detail in the discussion of Genesis 1:2. Note, verb forms in modern Hebrew do express tense; verb forms in Biblical Hebrew do not.[2]

The interpretation of Genesis One has also been influenced in some verses by gradual misunderstanding of the Hebrew meaning accumulated through the historic chain of translations. The English translation of Genesis One is derived primarily from the Latin Vulgate. The Vulgate is a translation derived in large measure from the Greek Septuagint. The Greek Septuagint is a translation from the Hebrew which was made about 250-300 B.C., after the conquests of Alexander the Great.

The chain of translation is thus:

Hebrew

Greek (Septuagint)

Latin (Vulgate)

English (The Wycliffe Bible to the Tyndale Bible to the King James Version Bible and then to later translations).

Each of the intermediary translations used grammar which did not perfectly express the Hebrew or the grammar of the preceding translation language. This was also true for words which did not perfectly express the Hebrew meaning or the meaning of the word used in the preceding translation language. The sequence of three translation steps has, in some cases, led to interpretations not supported by the Hebrew language itself. It is also for this reason that this study will proceed by considering the verses of Genesis One in Hebrew. The definitions of the Hebrew words will be investigated and determined based on the use of the Hebrew words in other verses of the Bible. In most cases the Hebrew, the KJV (King James Version), and the YLT (Young's Literal Translation) will all be presented for the verses being studied.

The next twelve pages are a preparation for this study. They are structured to give the reader an understanding of important differences between biblical Hebrew and English. These are differences which significantly effect the translation and the understanding of the text. It is not a complete course in biblical Hebrew but does provide a basis for the discussion and analysis of Genesis One. By studying Genesis One in Hebrew it is possible to avoid misunderstandings which have accumulated as a result of the historical chain of translation from the Hebrew to the English.

Differences of opinion about the duration and sequence of events in Genesis One are resolved by understanding the limitations on meaning imposed by biblical Hebrew verbs. Some interpretations which are based on English translations require verb tense meanings which the biblical Hebrew verb did not, and could not, express. This will be discussed in greater detail in the section "More About Verbs" as part of the preparation for the verse study. A number of other facts about biblical Hebrew words and their construction will be explained first, starting on the next page, with consideration of the number of words in biblical Hebrew.

## The Number of Words in Biblical Hebrew

Another significant way that biblical Hebrew differs from English is that biblical Hebrew has an extremely small number of words. The very small number of words has an important effect upon precision of expression in biblical Hebrew. An understanding of the small number of words can be obtained by considering dictionaries of biblical Hebrew and a dictionary of the English language.

*Strong's Exhaustive Concordance of the Bible* lists 8,674 words in the Hebrew and Chaldee dictionary.[3] Each word is assigned a number. These 8,674 "Strong's numbers" identify almost all the Hebrew words. The 8,674 Strong-numbered words are an overestimate as will be explained later. The actual number of root words in biblical Hebrew is commonly taken to be 2,552 as listed in the *Theological Wordbook of the Old Testament.*[4]

The *Merriam-Webster's Collegiate Dictionary* claims to define 160,000 English words in 1,529 pages.[5] This is an average of 104.6 words per page. If Strong had also defined 104.6 words per page, the 8,674 Strong-numbered Hebrew words would fill 83 pages. The sketch below shows this graphically.

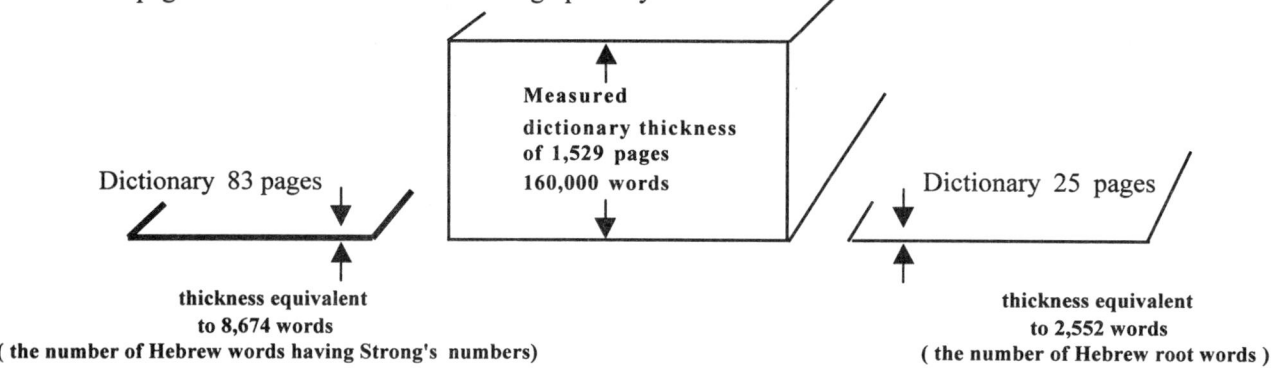

The 160,000 words are represented as the measured thickness of the stack of 1,529 pages of Merriam-Webster's Collegiate Dictionary. The other thicknesses are scaled to closely approximate the actual thicknesses of the indicated number of pages. The visual comparison, while inexact, permits some appreciation of the differences. The difference in the number of words leads to more than one possible English translation of some Hebrew words. How this comes about will be illustrated in following discussions.

## How Words are Written in Biblical Hebrew

Writing is a representation of the sounds of a spoken language. Words in a spoken language consist of a series of sounds generally described as consonants and vowels. The consonants, such as "m," usually involve motion of the lips or the tongue. The vowels generally involve airflow deeper in the throat. In English both the consonants and the vowels are written so that the reader is instructed as to all the sounds needed to pronounce the word. Biblical Hebrew, as originally written, is different.

Hebrew words are usually written using only the consonants. The vowels are omitted except for a few words. Because almost all words in Hebrew are written without vowels, several different spoken words may have the same spelling. As a consequence, many of the written Hebrew words can represent several different meanings. In the current Hebrew texts additional vowel marking has been added which removes much of the ambiguity. There is a different "Strong's number" for each Hebrew word written with the same consonants but having different vowels. As an example of the effect, consider "brd" as representing an English word written using only consonants. In English the words "bread," "board," "bard," and "bird" would all be spelled "brd" when written without vowels.

The Hebrew consonantal word בקר is presented as an example of the multiple meanings of consonantal words. The three forms of this word shown on the facing page are all spelled with the same consonants. In addition to the consonants, the words are vowel marked, below or within the letters, to indicate the missing vowels. These vowel marks, commonly referred to as "pointing," were added to the Hebrew text after 100 A.D. They were not in the original text and do not appear in the manuscripts of the Dead Sea Scrolls.

Three biblical Hebrew consonantal words with vowel markings are shown below. The bracketed English is a phonetic spelling indicating the pronunciation of the vowel-marked Hebrew word. The Hebrew word בקר starts with the ב, i. e., בקר ← **starts here**. Hebrew words and sentences read from right to left. A listing of the Hebrew letters is given on page 154.

Vowel-marked forms and meanings
- בקר    the consonantal word without "pointing" marking the vowels
- בָּקַר   (bāqar)    a verb meaning "seek" or "inquire"
- בָּקָר   (bāqār)    "ox" when singular or "herd" when plural
- בֹּקֶר   (bôqer)    occurs in Genesis One and is translated "morning"

The three words with their associated Strong's numbers and two English forms indicating pronunciations:

#1239 בָּקַר baqar {baw-kar}    #1241 בָּקָר baqar {baw-kawr'}    #1242 בֹּקֶר boqer {bo'-ker}

As stated earlier, the 8,674 Strong's numbered words are an overestimate of the actual number of root words in biblical Hebrew. The *Theological Wordbook of The Old Testament* lists 2,552 consonantal root Hebrew words which are usually composed of three consonants.[4] The 8,674 words listed by the "Strong's numbers" includes the different words spelled with the same consonants but having different vowels, as well as derivative words resulting from the addition of consonants to a root word.

## Vocabulary: The Multiple Meanings of Words

Because the ancient Hebrew was written using only consonants, each of the written words needed to be interpreted by the reader. Each word usually had more than one meaning. As a consequence, a reader or a translator was faced with multiple choices. The following treatment attempts to give a perspective of the process.

The number of vowel-marked Hebrew words which may be associated with a tri-consonantal root word can be estimated by dividing the 8,674 Strong's numbers by 2,552, the number of root words. This yields an expected average of about four recognizable words for each tri-consonantal root word and the words derived from it. There are some consonantal words with only one recognizable form and some with more than four. For some verses the correct choice is easily made by considering the context. For other verses the possible choices lead to honest differences in translation because the context is unclear or insufficient to exclude all but one of the possible choices.

After a translator has recognized the Hebrew word, including the appropriate vowels, there remains an additional problem. Because there are so few words in biblical Hebrew, each Hebrew word is used to cover a much wider range of meaning than does an English word. Each Hebrew word will often have as many as four English words with which the Hebrew word may be correctly translated. The figure below illustrates the potential progression from unmarked consonantal form to the translated English meaning for the Hebrew consonantal word בקר. בקר was used in the example at the top of the page.

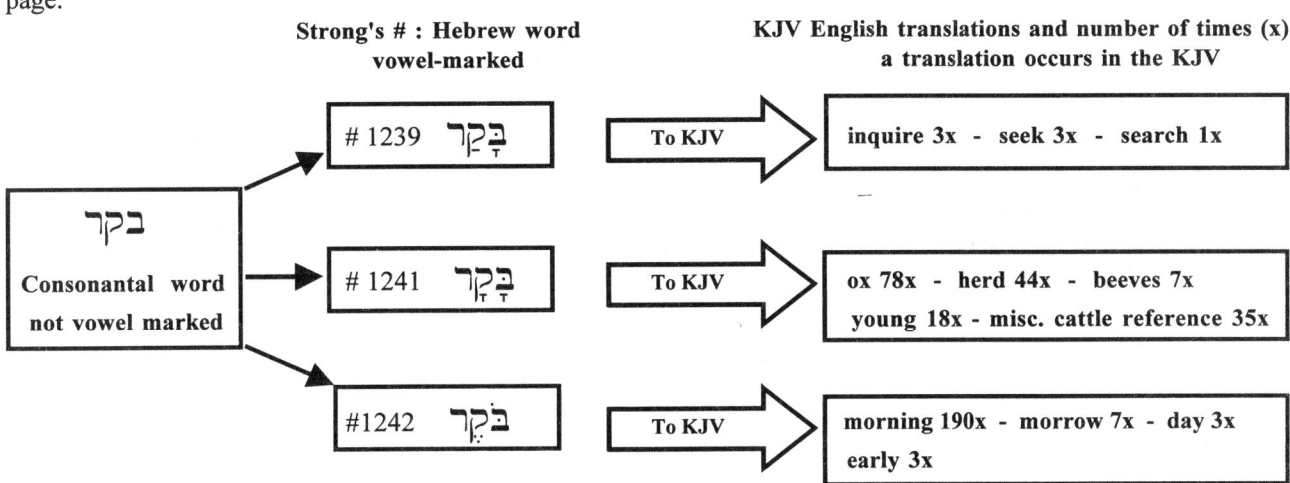

Because there are some vowel-marked words with multiple English meanings, the translator must make a choice. Which English word is chosen depends upon the context and the translator's view of the meaning of the verse. A reader of the Hebrew will ordinarily resolve the choice by using the context of what has gone before and by what follows the verse. This is also done in English for words which have more than one meaning. Consider the common English word "with" which has two often-encountered meanings.

"With" can mean "together with," as in "I went **with** my children to the movie."
"With" can mean "using," as in "He carved the stick **with** his knife."

Other common English words with multiple meanings are "bore," "tie," and "date."

In the Hebrew of the Bible, the occurrence of multiple possible meanings of the consonantal written words is the rule, not the exception. Context is always important for the choice of translation.

The Hebrew word מלך is an interesting example of how ambiguity is removed by vowel marking.

Vowel-marked מֶלֶךְ, the word means king, governor, leader, chieftain, etc.

Vowel-marked מֹלֶךְ, the word means Molech. This use is very rare.

Molech was the pagan deity to which the Cannanites sacrificed their infants.

In the absence of vowel marking, the context of the passage must be considered to determine if some type of leader is indicated or if the subject was Molech. Even when it is obvious that a leader is indicated, the appropriate status level of the leader must be supplied from the context. The meaning of the phrase "King of Kings" might also mean "king of chieftains" or "leader of leaders" if the context of each use of the Hebrew word מלך were clearly known. The consonantal form מלך also represents the verb, usually vowel-marked מָלַךְ, which is the verb often translated "reign."

The word מַלְכֶת is a derivative of מלך to which a feminine suffix ת has been added to the left side of the word. In the KJV מַלְכֶת is translated queen as in "Queen of Sheba."

## Word Meaning and the Translation of Genesis One

For the reader of Genesis One the problem is **not** recognition of the words, but rather the consequence of the very small number of root words. This small number of root words is of great importance with respect to the definition of categories which are used to classify similar things. Categories in biblical Hebrew are both broader and different from categories in English. One important example of this is the Hebrew phrase נֶפֶשׁ חַיָּה, which is phonetically pronounced "nephesh haya." A study of Genesis 1:20 will show that this phrase includes frogs, crocodiles, and cattle in its category. These creatures are presently categorized separately as being amphibian (frog), reptile (crocodile), and mammal (cattle). Considerable care will be given to representing categories correctly from the biblical Hebrew perspective.

Genesis One is written using few Hebrew words from an already small Hebrew vocabulary. It uses less than 100 different Hebrew root words augmented by the prepositional prefixes, and the suffixes representing pronouns. Many of these words are used more than five times. The total number of Hebrew words in the first 31 verses, including the multiple uses, is 426. These few words are used to describe the creation of the universe and portions of the history of planet Earth. The Earth's history starts with the description of an early condition and ends with the creation of mankind. This extreme brevity means that we cannot view Genesis One as a complete and exhaustive description of the preparation of the Earth for the introduction of mankind. We are told very little about the preparation of planet Earth for mankind. We must not infer that what happened is only that which we are told.

This reading of Genesis One will not be based on possible meanings of English words and tenses used by other translators. This reading will proceed by working directly from the preserved Hebrew text.

## Nouns, Prefixes, and Suffixes

Most words in biblical Hebrew are formed using word roots composed of three consonantal letters. Scholars determined these roots primarily by analysis and study of the use of words throughout the Bible. The basic formulation of the present understanding of the three-letter word root system was accomplished between 900 A.D. and 1150 A.D.[6] Since then, the work of many scholars has added to the understanding of these roots. Each word root has an associated meaning or group of meanings. Often the word roots represent actions and are also called "verb stems." From these roots additional associated words, such as nouns and descriptive words, are formed by the addition of more consonants. Because Hebrew reads from right to left, the prefixes are letters added to the right of the root and suffixes are letters added to the left of the root. In many cases where English uses separate words, Hebrew uses prefixes. In Genesis One, three prefixes are encountered in almost every verse. These are the consonantal letters:

    ב (beth)      a prefix most frequently meaning "in," "at," or "by."

    ה (heh)      a prefix meaning "the." Hebrew does not have a separate word "the."

    ו (waw)      a prefix most commonly translated "and." This is also used in verb constructions as will be explained later.

The uses of the prefixes can be exemplified by the single Hebrew word וְהָאָרֶץ meaning "and the Earth." This word occurs as the first word of Genesis 1:2 and is a composite of three elements. The prefixed conjunction ו meaning "and," the article ה meaning "the," and the singular noun אֶרֶץ "erets" meaning land, ground, earth, or Earth (the planet). The additional markings below the letters are markings which indicate the missing vowels. These vowel markings are called "pointing," and often change as prefixes of suffixes are added. The vowel marking will not usually be discussed, but are included because they are found in reference sources.

    וְהָאָרֶץ  =  אֶרֶץ  +  ה  +  ו    ← A Hebrew word starts here.
    and the Earth     Earth     the     and    ← The English is a translation of the Hebrew.

Hebrew also has suffixes which indicate the plurals of nouns, and suffixes which indicate the pronouns of possessive attribution. More clearly, where English would say "her horses," Hebrew would use one word with a plural suffix representing both the plural and the "her." For the reading of Genesis One it is sufficient to recognize that suffixes are used to represent pronouns and plurals. The actual details of the words will be presented to the reader so that no detailed grammatical knowledge will be needed. Hebrew words also have gender. Gender will be familiar to persons knowing Greek, Latin, or another Western European language other than English. Gender is used to identify adjectives and the words which the adjectives describe (modify). The Hebrew nouns and the related adjectives will all have word endings indicating the same gender and number. English uses word order to indicate the connections.

One frequently encountered plural word is the noun הַשָּׁמַיִם , meaning the sky, the skies, or the heavens.

    הַשָּׁמַיִם  =  יִם  +  שָׁמַ  +  הַ     ( The root שמ is unusual in being two letters.)[7]
                  suffix     root    prefix
                  (dual)            "the"

The noun is prefixed by ה (heh) meaning "the" and is suffixed by a two-letter suffix ים. Hebrew prefixes and suffixes may be single letters or several letters. Hebrew has some nouns which exist only in a plural form. The word "heavens" is one of these nouns. The vowel marking of the suffix יִ indicates a restricted type of plural meaning "two," and is called a dual.

In the absence of a vowel marking, the ending ים would be recognized as a plural suffix but not as a dual. The dual is not indicated in the consonantal spelling. Hebrew words which have only a plural form are translated singular or plural depending on the context. The word אלהים (Elohim) is another important word which has a plural form and which is translated singular. אלהים (Elohim) is the plural word translated "God" and is discussed more fully in the translation of Genesis 1:1.

## The "Untranslated" Word אֵת , The Direct Object Marker

The אֵת "direct object marker" is another feature of biblical Hebrew which will often be encountered. אֵת (or אֶת ) is a "word" placed in front of a noun which is the direct object. Words which are between the אֵת and the noun are modifiers describing the noun. The direct object marker is spoken in the Hebrew but is **not** translated into the English. In English translations the direct object is recognized by the position it has in the sentence and is usually preceded by "the" which may or may not exist in the Hebrew text. The direct object marker is also used with suffixes which represent pronouns. When used in this manner, the meaning of the suffix is itself the direct object. An example of this is אֹתָם = ם + אֵת where ם is the suffix meaning "them" and is translated as the direct object; there is no separately written noun representing the direct object.

## More About Verbs

This section discusses the following topics:

> Biblical Hebrew does not have tenses
> The Hebrew perfect
> The Hebrew imperfect
> The "waw-consecutive" verb form
> An example of verb translation.

## The Biblical Hebrew Verb Does Not Have Tense

Verbs in English tell the reader "when" the action occurred, the sequence in which the actions occurred, and often inform about the duration of the action. This information is called "tense."

**Verbs in biblical Hebrew do not tell "when" an action takes place, do not tell the sequence in which the actions take place, and do not tell the duration of the action.**

In biblical Hebrew, an action is regarded only as complete or incomplete. There is an exception. This is the Hebrew participle/infinitive, which approximates the verbal pattern of the English participle formed by adding "ing" to a verb. For the Hebrew verb, the completed action is usually referred to as the "perfect" and the incomplete action is referred to as the "imperfect." This significant difference in tense structure means that the English verb used by the translator is not fully equivalent to the Hebrew verb. **Because the English verb inaccurately represents the Hebrew, subtle inferences of the "when" of actions cannot be extracted based on the verb used by the translator.**

### The Hebrew Perfect (Completed Action)

The Hebrew verb למד, meaning "to learn," or "to study," provides an example of the formation of the Hebrew perfect. The Hebrew למד is the tri-consonantal word root and the verb stem for the Hebrew "Qal" verb form. The Q in "Qal" is pronounced "k" so "Qal" pronounces like the English word "call." The term "Qal" comes from the Hebrew word קַל meaning "simple."[8] The Qal is the simplest verb form, the stem being the three-letter word root. The Qal form of the verb stem is encountered about 80 percent of the time in Genesis One. Generally, the Qal indicates simple direct action such as "learned" in the statement "I learned." The Hebrew form for the completed action (the "perfect") in the first person singular will be used as an example. The first person singular is the form where the person "I" performs the action. In the first person singular, a suffix תי is added to the left of the root למד yielding למדתי. The suffix תי indicates the number (one), the person ( I ), and the gender (masculine). The forming sequence is:

למדתי   =   תי   +   למד    ← Hebrew starts here.
word       suffix       word root    ← English identifies what the Hebrew represents.
           meaning "I"

What is the meaning of the word למדתי ? This verb (Qal perfect, first person (I), singular) has at least five possible tense form translations. In addition to the usual translation "learn," the translation "study" has been suggested.[9] Inclusion of "study" increases the total number of translation possibilities to ten. This also illustrates the potential for a translator's word choice to subtly alter meaning in a translation. The ten possible translations of למדתי are:

**I learned, I have learned, I had learned, I had been learning, or I did learn.**

**I studied, I have studied, I had studied, I had been studying, or I did study.**

There are five different English tense forms and two different English words which can appropriately translate the Hebrew verb למתתי. These depend on the context and the view of the translator as to the meaning of the text. It is important to notice the lack of location in time as to when the action "studied" took place.

The information conveyed is that the action "studied" is completed. English is extremely concerned with specifically stating *when* the action "studied" took place. Biblical Hebrew, and some other languages,[10] do not convey this information in the verb tense structure. English speakers expect to have the *when* provided. Because we expect the *when* to be provided, we are vulnerable to improperly inferring a *when* not in the original text. The use of the completed action (perfect) also does not tell us about the time required to complete the action. The result of the completed action may last a moment, years, or forever.

The problem the translator faces is this: How is the completed action meaning to be translated into English without introducing a "when" not present in the consonantal Hebrew verb form? Use of the simple past tense does not accomplish this. Using the simple past tense can unintentionally introduce an easy misreading which introduces a "when" not found in the text. One possible unintentional "when" comes about by reading the simple past as an action occurring at a point in time, a meaning **not** conveyed by the Hebrew verb which is being translated. This reading is sometimes called the "punctiliar aspect" and is often discussed in grammars of biblical Greek.[11] Because Genesis One is translated in narrative style, the English reader may easily misread the simple past as a "punctiliar" and not as a completed action. The issue of the "punctiliar aspect" also arises in the translation of the New Testament Greek into English.[12]

Examples of a correct completed action understanding contrasted with an incorrect "punctiliar" are illustrated in the following two examples.

A person is first declared to be at a sandy ocean beach, and then a related action occurs.

1. **A person at the beach. That person had walked.**

In this case the action of walking is clearly completed. This meaning is consistent with the meaning of biblical Hebrew completed action verbs. "When" the walking took place is not conveyed and cannot be inferred from the verb in the sentence.

2. **A person at the beach. That person walked.**

In this case the action of walking can be initiated at, or just before, the speaking of the sentence "That person walked." There are three possible inferences as to the "when" of the action "walked."

a. The action may be viewed as starting in the "near past" just a moment ago, and may be continuing, i.e., not completed.

b. The action may be viewed as a present action which takes place at the speaking.

c. The action may also be viewed as being in the past and as being a completed action.

Only the completed action view is consistent with the biblical Hebrew completed action verb meaning. Many secular interpretation errors are rooted in not interpreting the English past verb as the completed action indicated by the translated Hebrew verb.

Understanding Genesis One requires that the completed action meanings of the verbs be correctly translated. A "study translation" will be made and used in the analysis of Genesis One. This "study translation" of Genesis One will uniformly translate the Hebrew completed action verbs using "had." The pluperfect is the English verb form constructed by placing "had" in front of the past tense of a verb; i. e., the "had walked" of the previous example. The pluperfect verb form using "had" conveys the completed action meaning most emphatically and reduces the potential for interpretation in any sense other than completed action. This **tutorial** use of the pluperfect using "had" requires placing one significant restriction upon the "study translation." The simple English past tense verb (e.g. walked) will generally not be used in the study translation for a completed action verb. This is required because biblical Hebrew does not use the verb to convey the time ordering of events. English uses the pluperfect form (e.g. had walked), in combination with ordinary past tense, to convey the order in which past actions have taken place. Because of this restriction (not using any simple past tense forms), the use of the English pluperfect **in the study translation** is **not** equivalent to the English pluperfect as normally encountered.

When the pluperfect form is used uniformly for all completed action verbs, a misleading "when" is not introduced. The narrative style still exists but the completed action verbs cannot easily be read as expressing the "punctiliar aspect." This is done as a **tutorial** assistance as an aid to understanding. Many of the secular objections to Genesis One involve issues of "time" and "when." The purpose of this study is to clarify what Genesis One actually says regarding these issues.

When the study of a verse has been completed and the "whens" of the actions determined, a "Good English" translation will be provided which uses both the past and pluperfect tenses. Completed action verbs will be translated using the simple past tense unless a pluperfect reference is discovered in the verse analysis. As a consequence, the events of the narrative which begins in Genesis 1:3 will progress in time by means of a series of past tense verbs, just as in the KJV. Differences will arise when pluperfect references to actions which had already taken place are found in the text.

The "Good English" translation is the translation which represents the results of this study, and represents the "when" determined for the actions in the creative times.

## The Hebrew Imperfect and the "Waw-consecutive"

Genesis One also uses the Hebrew imperfect verb. Most often it is used prefixed by ו (waw) in the form called the "waw-consecutive." The imperfect verb will be explained first, followed by an explanation of the "waw-consecutive" in the next section. The imperfect form, when not prefixed by ו "waw," represents actions as being "not completed." The imperfect verb form does not convey a "when" for the starting of the action nor does it imply a "when" for the completion of the action. The formation of an imperfect verb, and the possible translations of the imperfect, are illustrated in the example of the Qal verb root שָׁמַר , meaning "to keep."

In Hebrew, imperfect verbs are formed by adding prefixes to the word root. The imperfect for the first person singular, meaning "I," is formed by adding a prefix א. The prefix א indicates the number (one), the person (I), and the gender (male).

אֶשְׁמֹר = שָׁמַר + א ← The Hebrew word starts here.
               word root   prefix

The possible meanings of the word אֶשְׁמֹר imperfect first person singular are:

I shall keep, I will keep, I shall be keeping, or I will be keeping.

In normal conversation the verb might also be translated "I am going to keep." The verb form represents an incomplete action, "keeping." The Hebrew word does **not** specify **when** the action will take place, only that the action will take place sometime in the future. The verb אֶשְׁמֹר can also represent an incomplete action taking place in the present, such as "I am keeping." Genesis One uses the incomplete action (imperfect) for actions which continue to occur in the future, after they have been first commanded. Another related verb form called the "jussive" is also used in Genesis One and will be discussed when it is encountered.

## The "Waw-consecutive" Verb Form

The imperfect verb form used most often in Genesis One is the "waw-consecutive," a construction used in almost every verse. The "waw-consecutive" is formed by adding the prefix ו "waw" to an imperfect Hebrew verb. The "waw-consecutive" is the form used to indicate the continuing story line of a narrative and is the form normally encountered in Genesis One. The effect of the prefix ו "waw" in the "waw-consecutive" is to change the action of an imperfect verb to mean the completed action of the Hebrew perfect. The ו "waw" prefix is usually translated "and" for the "waw-consecutive." The "waw-consecutive" can also be formed using a perfect verb and the action of the perfect verb is then altered to mean the incomplete action of the Hebrew imperfect. Both of these verb constructions are termed the "waw-consecutive." The "conjunctive" use of the ו "waw" prefix also exists and is discussed later on this page.

In summary, the action of the prefix ו (waw) in the "consecutive," on the action of a verb, is as follows:

When an imperfect verb is prefixed by a ו , the imperfect form is read as the **perfect** completed action.

When a perfect verb is prefixed by a ו , the perfect form is read as an **imperfect** incomplete action.

In Hebrew translation, sentences and clauses connected by "and" are very common. English instructors teach that this is not "good" English, but this arrangement is good biblical Hebrew. **Note:** Sentences which begin with "and" in English translation cannot be assumed to begin with the "waw-consecutive." English translators often change the word order, thereby making it impossible to determine if the Hebrew verb was the first word of the sentence. The important consequences of the Hebrew word order will be carefully discussed when considering Genesis 1:2.

### An Example of the "Waw-consecutive"

Genesis One often uses the word יאמר , a form of the verb יאמר meaning "to say." The word יאמר is in the Qal imperfect and is formed by adding a prefix י to the root Qal stem יאמר. The prefix letter י (yod) represents "he" (Qal, third person, singular, masculine). The resulting verb יאמר has the meanings:

he shall say, he will say, he will be saying, he shall be saying, or he is saying.

The translator has the option of using any of these forms depending upon the context or the translator's view of the meaning of the text.

The "waw-consecutive" of יאמר is ו + יאמר = ויאמר which may be translated :

and he said, and he had said, or and he did say.

In Genesis the subject of the sentence, a noun, often follows the verb. This noun gives the name of the "he" to whom the verb refers. In Genesis One this noun is usually אֱלֹהִים "God ." As a consequence, וַיֹּאמֶר is the verb in the phrase

וַיֹּאמֶר    אֱלֹהִים , which is translated in the KJV as "And God said."
God      and had said      ← Start English here.

This phrase can be translated three ways: "And God had said," "And God did say," or "And God said."

The action is **completed,** but the *when* is not specified.

## The conjunctive "waw"

A complication exists because there are two possible interpretations of the function of the prefix ו "waw" when prefixed to a verb. The prefix ו "waw" may be considered to be a "consecutive" or a "conjunctive." The "conjunctive" is equivalent to the English use of the word "and," and the action of the verb is unchanged. The "conjunctive" use of ו "waw" occurs infrequently in Genesis One and will be specifically pointed out in the study where it occurs. The determination of "consecutive" or "conjunctive" is made by the translator considering the context and structure of the Hebrew passage. In the "conjunctive" use, the ו "waw" does not change the action of the verb.

## An Example of Verb Translation

The point has been made that any Hebrew verb form has several possible English tense translations. The translator's choice depends upon the context of the verse and /or his view regarding the meaning of the verse.

Genesis 21:1 provides a good example of translation as it appears in the KJV. This verse has four perfect (completed action) verbs. The KJV translates two verbs using the past tense and two verbs using the pluperfect. One of the perfect meaning verb forms is a "waw-consecutive." The KJV translation of Genesis 21:1 and the alternative translation using "had" with every verb are shown in the example below. The differences between the translations are instructive, as is the comparison to the actual content of the Hebrew text. The Hebrew is shown with each word translated into English underneath the Hebrew. Both the Hebrew words and the English underneath read in sequence from right to left across the page.

Genesis 21:1 (Alt. means "alternative.")

KJV:   And the LORD **visited** Sarah       as he **had said**, and the LORD **did** onto Sarah       as he **had spoken**.

Alt.   And the LORD **had visited** Sarah  as he **had said**, and the LORD **had done** onto Sarah  as he **had spoken.**

| אָמַר | כַּאֲשֶׁר | שָׂרָה | אֶת | פָּקַד | וַיהוָה | ← Hebrew starts here. |
|---|---|---|---|---|---|---|
| he had said | like which | Sara | dir. obj. marker | (he) had visited | and Yahweh | ← English starts here. |
| (Qal perfect) | | | | (Qal perfect) | ("waw" + noun) | |

| דִּבֶּר | כַּאֲשֶׁר | לְשָׂרָה | יְהוָה | וַיַּעַשׂ | ← Hebrew starts here. |
|---|---|---|---|---|---|
| *(he)* had said | like which | for Sara | Yahweh | and had done | ← English starts here. |
| (Piel perfect) | | | | ("waw" + Qal imperfect) (completed action) | |

The KJV has four underlined verb forms which have the biblical Hebrew perfect (completed action) meaning. Two of the Hebrew verbs are translated in the KJV using the simple past, "visited," and "did." The verb which the KJV translates "did" is an example of the Hebrew imperfect prefixed by וַ "waw" having the perfect (completed action) meaning. This Hebrew verb construction is called the "waw-consecutive." Two of the Hebrew verbs are translated by the KJV using the English pluperfect (had said). In Hebrew, the actions are completed but the "when" and the time sequence of the actions are not stated.

The alternative (Alt.) translation does not indicate the "when" of the completed actions. In the KJV, the time sequence is introduced by the use of the pluperfect for two of the completed action verbs and by the use of the simple past for the other two verbs. The first KJV pluperfect "as he had said" tells the English reader that the "had said" is a completed action and that the "had said" was completed before the preceding simple past verb "visited." This time ordering is not knowable directly from the Hebrew completed action verbs. The Hebrew text simply states that both actions are completed; the sequence of completion is not given. The KJV time sequence depends on the knowledge of Genesis 18:10 and Genesis 18:14.

KJV Genesis 18:10   And he said, I will certainly return unto thee according to the time of life; and, lo, Sarah thy wife shall have a son.

KJV Genesis 18:14   Is any thing too hard for the LORD? At the time appointed I will return unto thee, according to the time of life, and Sarah shall have a son.

Knowledge of these preceding verses permitted translators of the KJV to introduce the time ordering of the completed actions. The reader of the Hebrew text is required to supply this information from his own knowledge of the context; it is not in the Hebrew text of the verse. In translation, all the verbs could have been translated in the pluperfect using "had" as has been done in the alternative translation (Alt.) or as simple past without the "had." Such translations would have been faithful to the Hebrew text but would not read as fluent English. The reader would be required to supply the time sequence, based upon context or the word order, just as a Hebrew reader would need to do. As will be discussed later, in connection with Genesis 1:2, the Hebrew word order of the first two words of Genesis 21:1 is also an indicator of the pluperfect. The significance of this word order was not known to the translators of the KJV.

Genesis 21:1 also provides a good example of the errors which can be introduced by uniformly translating the Hebrew perfect completed action by using the simple English past tense. For this illustration the KJV translation is written first, followed by a translation in which the KJV has been modified. The modification consists of writing all the KJV verbs in their simple past tense forms.

| | | | | |
|---|---|---|---|---|
| KJV: | And the LORD **visited** Sarah | as he **had said**, | and the LORD **did** onto Sarah | as he **had spoken**. |
| All past tense: | And the LORD **visited** Sarah | as he **said**, | and the LORD **did** onto Sarah | as he **spoke**. |

In the all past tense version the reader correctly infers that "as he **said**" precedes the "**visited** Sarah." However, the reader can incorrectly infer that "**did** onto Sarah" is simultaneous with "as he **spoke**." This incorrect understanding of the "when" of the actions is the result of the tense choice of a single verb. Again, it is the purpose of this study to find and remove this type of error from the interpretation of Genesis One.

There is one final issue to be mentioned about Hebrew verbs. The examples have illustrated the Hebrew verb using the Qal which is used for about 80 percent of the verbs in Genesis One. The Qal is often called "simple" because it represents simple direct action and uses the word root as the "verb stem." There are also other Hebrew verb forms used in Genesis One. These forms are often used to indicate more about the verb action. Examples are causation (who or what caused the action) or passive action (who or what was a recipient of the action). These verb forms generally modify the word root by adding letters and are recognizable due to these additions. The perfect, imperfect, and "waw-consecutive" are then formed using these "augmented" verb stems. These forms will not be discussed here but will be identified and discussed as appropriate when they appear in the text of Genesis One. Their identification will allow readers interested in greater detail to consult Hebrew grammars.

## *Procedures Followed in the Study of Genesis 1:1 - 2:4*

Having considered some of the characteristics of biblical Hebrew which are important for this study, the next step is a detailed analysis of Genesis 1:1 and Genesis 1:2.

The analysis of these verses is complex and all the issues cannot be treated at one time. As a consequence, Genesis 1:1 and Genesis 1:2 will be analyzed in a series of steps. These steps are outlined below:

1. Genesis 1:1 - A word-by-word analysis will study the word construction and how the words are used in the sentence. This analysis is based upon the historic Christian understanding of the verb translated "create" as being a Qal perfect verb. The Qal perfect verb has completed action meaning. The word "beginning" is analyzed as a noun in the absolute state. The meaning of the word translated "beginning" is studied in detail considering other verses in the Bible which use the same word. This is followed by consideration of the meaning of the verse as an independent sentence.

2. Genesis 1:2 - An analysis will study the word constructions and meanings. The Hebrew words "tohu" and "bohu" are investigated in great detail by considering other verses in the Bible which use these two words. Based on this analysis, Genesis 1:2 is translated and its meaning is discussed.

3. Genesis 1:1 and Genesis 1:2 are discussed as a unit. This is a detailed study of how the two verses relate to each other and to the following verse, Genesis 1:3.

4. Following the analysis of Genesis 1:1-2, there follows an extensive analysis of Genesis 1:3-5. The individual verses are first considered in sequence. The analysis of Genesis 1:5 contains an extensive study of how the word יום "yom" is actually used in the Bible. Based on this analysis the meaning of the word יום "yom" in the phrases which conclude each creative time is determined and a translation is given.

   Following the study of the word יום "yom" a review of the overall models which the Hebrew text permits for the creative times is presented in a careful and extensive manner. This includes a discussion of the creative times considered as long periods of time and a 24-hour day model which the Hebrew text will permit.

5. Then the analysis of the remaining verses of Genesis One are conducted in a manner similar to that followed in the treatment of Genesis 1:3-5.

**A review of translation analysis procedures for the narrative of Genesis 1:3 through Genesis 2:4**

Because the determination of the "when" of each action is important to this study, a review comment about analysis procedures will be repeated here. An analysis to determine the "when" of an action requires that the completed action meaning of the Hebrew perfect be properly expressed. The expression must avoid adding meanings which the Hebrew verb did not convey.

The method which will be generally followed is to present a study translation under the Hebrew words of a verse. As already discussed on page 10, the verbs of the study translation will be translated using only the English pluperfect, the form using "had." English uses both past tense and pluperfect tense forms to convey the time ordering of past actions. An action described in the pluperfect is indicated as being a completed action, and is also indicated to have been completed **before** an action described by a past tense verb. In biblical Hebrew, time ordering is not a function of the verb form. The study translation (written under the Hebrew) presents the completed action meaning of the English pluperfect without introducing time ordering. This is achieved by not using any English past tense verbs in a study translation. When this is done the English pluperfect verbs which are used can accurately represent Hebrew completed action verbs.

**With one exception, no simple past tense forms will be used in the study translations.** The exception is for three repetitions of a phrase which appears for the first time in Genesis 1:7. The subsequent repetitions of this phrase will be translated using the Good English translation determined in the analysis of Genesis 1:7. The study translation is not the final translation. It is a tool.

The reason for avoiding the English past tense in the study translation is twofold. The English past tense can be interpreted as indicating actions which have just happened or as actions which are started and continuing. This was already discussed in the examples (1) and (2) on page 9. The other reason is that the KJV and other English translations use the English past tense for almost every verb. The reader then approaches the analysis with a preprogrammed interpretation which inhibits any clear analysis of the Hebrew.

When the study of a verse has been completed and the "whens" of the actions determined, a Good English translation will be provided which uses both the past and past perfect tenses. Completed action verbs will be translated using the simple past tense unless a pluperfect reference is discovered in the verse analysis. As a consequence, the events of the narrative which begins in Genesis 1:3 will progress in time by means of a series of past tense verbs, just as in the KJV. Differences will arise when pluperfect references to actions which had already taken place are found.

The Good English translation is the translation which represents the results of this study, and represents the "when" determined for the actions in the creative times. A Good English translation will be given at the end of each section and as a complete translation at the end of this book. The Good English translation provides the reader with the expected time ordering of the actions, as normally found in English. The tenses used represent the time ordering found in the analysis of Genesis One when considering the structure and context of each sentence.

The reader may wonder why the simple past tense was accepted as an appropriate verb form for translating the Hebrew completed action. The English translation of Genesis One is primarily the result of a historic chain of translation. The acceptance of ambiguity in the verb representing completed action goes back to the initial translation of the Greek Septuagint. The completed action Hebrew verb has no direct past tense equivalent in Greek. The only Greek past tense which could have the completed action meaning was the aorist. The aorist is called undefined because it can represent either a past action which is completed **or** a past action which is continuing.[13] The tense form does not tell the reader which is intended. The ambiguity introduced into the Septuagint has persisted to the present day in the English translations. A review of the various tense possibilities of the languages in the historic chain of translations of Genesis One is presented in the section "History of the English Genesis One Text" (page 88).

**Hebrew words, their markings, and how they are represented in English transliteration**

The Hebrew word בְּרֵאשִׁית meaning "in beginning" will be presented as an example. The dots which appear with the first letter בּ "beth," and with the other letters, are markings which indicate the missing vowels. These vowel markings were added after 100 A.D. by scholars called the Masorete and were not in the earlier Hebrew text. The markings were added gradually and were mostly complete by about 1000 A.D. The vowel markings also indicate how the Masorete understood the word at the time the marks were added. These marks will be included as they appear in the current biblical Hebrew text, but little use is made of these marks in this book. One mark, the ־ "maqqep" which indicates the joined pronunciation of two words has been omitted.

The first word of Genesis 1:1 will be written: בְּרֵאשִׁית  ← A Hebrew word starts here.
in beginning  ← Start English here.

Because Hebrew is written from right to left, the English translations underneath the Hebrew must also be read in sequence from right to left. The English translation for each word is written normally as the "in beginning" shown above. After the verse has been written in this manner the words will be studied individually and the grammar will be explained. These explanations will allow for the gradual introduction to the limitations on meaning placed by the characteristics of biblical Hebrew. The translated Hebrew word meanings will be verified by reference to other verses in the Bible where the same word is used. These verses will usually be the KJV (King James Version) text or the YLT (Young's Literal Translation) text. The YLT is an 1862 translation by the same Young who compiled *Young's Analytical Concordance*.[14] The YLT will be used when the KJV has excessively modified the word order of the Hebrew. In many cases both versions will be presented so that the differences can be compared. The KJV English spellings date to 1769 and sometimes look to be misspelled, but are not. Importantly, words added by the translators will be indicated in *italics*. When quoting these verses the Hebrew word will often be inserted just before the corresponding English word in the translation. By this procedure the reader can verify that the word in the reference verse is the same as the Hebrew word in the Genesis verse. For example, KJV Genesis 1:1 will be written as:

KJV Genesis 1:1    In *the* beginning אֱלֹהִים God created the heavens and the earth (erets).

The word "God" is the translation of the preceding Hebrew word אֱלֹהִים (Elohim). Elohim is an English phonetic rendering (transliteration) of the Hebrew pronunciation of the word אֱלֹהִים The phonetic rendering of אֱלֹהִים will be indicated either by "Elohim" or by (Elohim), the use of quotation marks or parenthesis being equivalent. This same procedure will be used to indicate the phonetic renderings of other Hebrew words. The phonetic renderings are intended to be pronounced when reading the English sentence.

A phonetic rendering (in parenthesis) following an English word is also used to indicate the root of the Hebrew word translated by that English word. In the above example (erets) is used to indicate that אֶרֶץ is the root of the Hebrew word translated "earth." The (erets) expresses an English phonetic pronunciation of the root Hebrew word אֶרֶץ, and is not the phonetic representation of the actual word in the sentence. The actual word which appears is הָאָרֶץ "the earth," a prefixed form of the word אֶרֶץ (erets). The phonetic pronunciation of הָאָרֶץ would be represented as "ha'erets." The "ha" results from the prefix ה (heh) meaning "the." This procedure will be used throughout the study to identify the root of the actual Hebrew word being translated.

The phonetic representations (transliterations) of the Hebrew root words which are used in this study are listed in a table on page 152. Phonetic representations of the exact form appearing in the Hebrew verse are not often used in the study.

The first verse of Genesis in Hebrew, with a word-by-word English translation, will appear as:

| הָאָרֶץ | וְאֵת | הַשָּׁמַיִם | אֵת | אֱלֹהִים | בָּרָא | בְּרֵאשִׁית | Genesis 1:1 |
|---|---|---|---|---|---|---|---|
| the Earth | and + dir. obj. marker | the heavens (skies) | dir. obj. marker | God (Elohim) | had created (KJV "created") | in beginning ← | Start English here. |

**Chapter Two**  　　　　　　**THE FIRST VERSES: GENESIS 1:1-2**

# THE FIRST VERSE: GENESIS 1:1　　　　　　　　　　　In the Beginning God

The foregoing brief discussion of verbs and other words in biblical Hebrew was preparation for the study of the first verse of the Bible. Genesis 1:1 is eloquent and foundational to all that follows in both the Old and New Testaments. This verse will be examined carefully with regard to what it teaches and how these teachings have been received by the secular world.

Genesis 1:1 consists of seven Hebrew words. The detailed construction of each of these Hebrew words is shown below. This is done to illustrate how words are constructed using prefixes and suffixes. This level of detail will not be shown for the words in the verses following Genesis 1:1.

**Genesis 1:1**

| הָאָרֶץ | וְאֵת | הַשָּׁמַיִם | אֵת | אֱלֹהִים | בָּרָא | בְּרֵאשִׁית | ← Hebrew starts here. |
|---|---|---|---|---|---|---|---|
| the Earth | and + dir. obj. marker | the heavens (skies) | dir. obj. marker | God (Elohim) | had created (KJV "created") | in beginning | ← Start English here. |

The first word is בְּרֵאשִׁית "in beginning," which is constructed as:

| בְּרֵאשִׁית | = | ת | + | י | + | רֵאשׁ | + | בְּ | ← A Hebrew word starts here. |
|---|---|---|---|---|---|---|---|---|---|
|  |  | suffix |  | "vowel" |  | word root |  | prefixed preposition | ← Start English here. |

The first letter on the right, בְּ (beth), is a prepositional prefix. בְּ has a number of translated meanings depending on the context. When used with a noun these meanings are often "in," "at," or "by." The meaning of the Hebrew prepositions are much less specific than the meaning of English prepositions. The following three letters רֵאשׁ are the word root of the noun. The final letter ת (taw) is the noun ending in the feminine gender. The י (yod) preceding the ת is a vowel indicator. Here, in the first word of the Bible, there is an example of the occasional use of the letter י (yod) to indicate a vowel instead of a consonant. The word "in beginning" is a noun in the absolute state which means it acts as a noun does in English. Another example of "beginning" in the absolute state is found in Isaiah 46:10 and will be studied later.

The word "beginning" is singular and of feminine gender. The singular indicates only one beginning. The gender shows that the beginning refers to the direct objects, "the heavens and the Earth," which are of feminine gender. The word order here deviates from the most common Hebrew word order which places the verb first in the sentence. The meaning of this word order will be discussed later.

The second word of Genesis 1:1 is the verb בָּרָא "bara" which means "had created." The verb בָּרָא "bara" is in the Qal perfect (completed action) form, and is third person masculine singular (i.e., there is a "he" who performs or causes the action). This form of the Qal verb has no suffix and is the same as the verb stem. The root of "bara" has more than the basic meaning of "create." "Bara" also carries the concept of making or creating something new. The completed action can be translated

**"created," "had created," or "did create."**

The word "created" is a past completed action, but "had created" presents the **completed** nature of the action more explicitly. "Had created" also conveys more clearly that both the "when" and the amount of time taken to complete the creation are not stated in the Hebrew. Another method which emphasizes the completed nature of the action is to use an augmented translation representing the simple past tense "created." One such augmentation is:

**created** (*a past completed action with the time and duration of action not given*).

The augmentation in parenthesis, in a cumbersome manner, restricts the meaning of the completed action verb to be that which the "had created" expresses succinctly. Translating the verses using both methods yields:

In *the* beginning God
> **had created**
>> the heavens and the earth.

And
> In *the* beginning God
>> **created (*a past completed action with the time and duration of action not given*)**
>>> the heavens and the earth.

There are two things to be noted. First the italicized word "*the*" does not appear in the Hebrew. Second, the use of "had created" does not alter the meaning of Genesis 1:1.

The third Hebrew word of Genesis 1:1 is the word translated God. God is the one who does the creating. The word אֱלֹהִים (Elohim) is a masculine plural noun and is the plural subject of a singular verb. The suffix ים is the ending which makes the noun masculine plural. In this word an additional letter ה occurs before the suffix. The noun is translated by the singular "God" when referring to the God of the Bible. The two-letter form אל "El" is used in the Bible to represent god, God, mighty one, or strength. El is used for gods of all sorts. Elohim is translated "gods" when referring to gods other than the God of the Bible. Many commentators see the plural אֱלֹהִים (Elohim) used with the singular verb as the first indication of the doctrine of the Trinity.[15]

The final four words of Genesis 1:1 are:  הָאָרֶץ   וְאֵת   הַשָּׁמַיִם   אֵת  ← Hebrew starts here.
                                                   the Earth   and + dir. obj.   the heavens   dir. obj.
                                                                 marker                              marker

This phrase will be considered as a unit because "the heavens and the Earth" constitutes a Hebrew phrase known as a merism. These two words have a different meaning when coupled together than when they are used separately. A similar thing is done in English where words are often joined directly. The word "blackboard" is an example of this. A blackboard need not be black and is usually not made of wooden boards. The Hebrew words in sequence are:

אֵת is the direct object marker for the noun הַשָּׁמַיִם which phonetically is "ha' shamayim." The direct object marker is not translated because English uses word position to indicate a direct object. The direct object marker will be encountered in almost every verse.

הַשָּׁמַיִם "ha' shamayim" formed as:   יִם  +  שָׁמַ  +  הַ   ← A Hebrew word starts here.
                                                         dual suffix   word root   prefix "the"

The noun שָׁמַיִם "shamayim" means "heavens" or "heaven." The noun is prefixed by ה meaning "the" and is vowel marked as a dual noun indicating that there are two heavens. The suffix ים indicates a dual. It is a vowel marked form of the plural suffix ים. Hebrew has some nouns which exist only in plural or dual forms. The noun for heavens is translated as a singular or plural depending on the context. The noun is attributed to an assumed three-letter root שמה which has been shortened to שָׁמַ.[16] The final two words are:

וְ + אֵת = וְאֵת   the direct object marker אֵת for the noun "erets," prefixed by וְ meaning "and." The וְ is translated "and" but the direct object marker is not translated into English, and

ה + אֶרֶץ = הָאָרֶץ   the noun אֶרֶץ "erets" meaning land, ground, earth (as in earthenware), or Earth as we now use the word to refer to planet Earth. The noun is prefixed by ה meaning "the."

The phrase הַשָּׁמַיִם the heavens and הָאָרֶץ "the erets" (as a merism) means everything which can be seen and or has physical existence. The phrase translated "the heavens and the Earth" represents the totality of all that an observer can see. Two distinct types of heavens can be seen. One is the "daytime" heavens characterized by the visible blue "dome" with which we are all familiar. The second is the nighttime heavens in which the stars of the Universe are seen. The "erets" referred to in the phrase is composed of the land and the bodies of water.

In terms of present day English the phrase translated "the heavens and the Earth" would mean the entire Universe. אֶרֶץ "erets" usually means land and its use to indicate both land and water is **very** infrequent, mostly appearing in poetic metaphor. This use is verifiable by reference to Psalm 148:7.

KJV Psalm 148:7     Praise the LORD from the הָאָרֶץ earth, ye dragons, and all deeps:

Psalm 148:7 includes the deep in the meaning of "erets" when referring to the surface of planet Earth. Other examples of אֶרֶץ "erets" including the surface waters is discussed in an end note.[17] These verses also show the correlation between the word deep and the waters of the seas.

The Bible's view of the Universe as a composite of two separate parts is evident in Psalm 115:15-16. Two versions are shown for Psalm 115:15 to illustrate the differing word orders and words used in translations. In Psalm 115:15 the phrase " שָׁמַיִם heaven וָאָרֶץ and earth " represents everything.

KJV Psalm 115:15 Ye *are* blessed of the LORD which made שָׁמַיִם heaven and וָאָרֶץ earth.

YLT Psalm 115:15 Blessed {are} ye of Jehovah, maker of שָׁמַיִם heaven and וָאָרֶץ earth,

KJV Psalm 115:16     הַשָּׁמַיִם The heaven, *even* שָׁמַיִם the heavens, *are* the LORD'S:

וְהָאָרֶץ but the earth   hath he given to the children of men.

In KJV Psalm 115:16 the "heavens" are said to belong to the "LORD" (Yahweh). The American Standard Version translates "The heavens are the heavens of Jehovah." Psalm 115:16 assigns the "erets" to mankind. Both of the "heavens" are distinguished from the land and the liquid surface waters.

## The Meaning of Genesis 1:1

The first step in the investigation of the meaning of Genesis 1:1 will be to consider the meaning of the Hebrew word בְּרֵאשִׁית "in beginning." The historic Christian and Hebrew view of Genesis 1:1 is that the first verse is an independent sentence. That is the position taken in this study. This study's translation of Genesis 1:1 is given below. The word "*the*" is italicized to show that "*the*" is not in the Hebrew.

**In *the* beginning God *had* <u>created</u> the heavens and the Earth (i.e., the Universe).**

**What is the "beginning"?** Answering this question requires understanding the concept of the Hebrew word. The word רֵאשִׁית "beginning" in the Hebrew **does not** refer to something which happens in an instant like a bolt of lightening. "Beginning," as will be shown, refers to events which take place over a longer time period of unstated length.

The English word "beginning" can also refer to events which take place over a long time period of unstated length. It is in this sense that the English word "beginning" is to be understood.

The Hebrew word בְּרֵאשִׁית **does not** mean the first of a series. In English the word "prologue" would be an apt translation of the word "beginning" as used in Genesis 1:1. This will be demonstrated in verses which follow.

Consider how the Bible uses the root ראש word in the form בְּרֵאשִׁית "in beginning" in other verses.

In Genesis 1:1 the word translated "beginning" is used with an attached preposition which means "in." The Hebrew prefix ה meaning "the" is not used. The use of the word "beginning" with the preposition "in" also occurs four times in Jeremiah in the first verses of chapters 26, 27, 28 and 49. These chapters tell of events which are said to have happened "in *the* beginning" of the reign of Jehoiakim and the reign of Zedekiah. The events take place over considerable periods of time. In the case of Jeremiah chapter 28, the verse specifically includes events which are said to take place four years after Zedekiah starts to rule. The NIV (New International Version) translation recognizes this and translates בְּרֵאשִׁית ". . . early in the reign of . . . ."

| | |
|---|---|
| KJV Jeremiah 28:1 | And it came to pass the same year, בְּרֵאשִׁית in *the* beginning of the reign of Zedekiah king of Judah, **in the fourth year, *and* in the fifth month**, *that* Hananiah the son of Azur the prophet, which *was* of Gibeon, spake unto me in the house of the LORD, in the presence of the priests and of all the people, . . . . |

The word רֵאשִׁית "beginning" is also used in Genesis 10:10 and refers to the Kingdom of Nimrod. The KJV translation of this verse reads:

| | |
|---|---|
| KJV Genesis 10:10 | And *the* רֵאשִׁית "beginning" of his kingdom was Babel, and Erech, and Accad, and Calneh, in the land of Shinar. |

Clearly the "beginning" refers to a considerable amount of time. Time enough to build, or come to rule, four cities. The situation for which the four cities are said to be the "beginning" is the kingdom of Nimrod. The kingdom amounted to many more cities than the mentioned four. The Bible does not state the length of the life of Nimrod. The lives of those who could be contemporary with Nimrod range from 250 to 450 years. This implies that the "beginning of his kingdom" could easily refer to a time span of 50 to 100 years, or more.

The third time the word רֵאשִׁית "beginning" is used is in Exodus 23:19. Here the passage refers to the "first of" the "first fruits." The first fruits are the early portion of the harvest of any crop. First fruits do not spring into existence suddenly. First fruits are the result of a long time period of growth and development which precedes the yield called "first fruits." In the harvest cycle, seed has been planted or a fruit tree has been planted and has reached maturity sufficient to form fruit. The crop then grows with the fruit of the plant growing and maturing with the passage of time during the growing season. At the time of harvest, either some of the crop ripens first or some of the crop is the first to be harvested. These are the "first fruits." Again, the use of the word "beginning" indicates a considerable period of time. The "beginning" is not an "instant."

| | |
|---|---|
| KJV Exodus 23:19 | The רֵאשִׁית "first of" the first fruits of thy land thou shalt bring into the house of the LORD thy God. Thou shalt not seethe a kid in his mother's milk. |
| YLT Exodus 23:19 | The רֵאשִׁית "beginning of" the first-fruits of thy ground thou dost bring into the house of Jehovah thy God; thou dost not boil a kid in its mother's milk. |

The KJV translates the word רֵאשִׁית as "first of" and the YLT translates it as "beginning of." The Septuagint uses the Greek word ἀπαρχὰς meaning "first portion."

**In Genesis 1:1 the translation "In *the* beginning" is a correct translation of the Hebrew provided that the reader does not interpret the word "beginning" as implying "instantaneous" creation. The Hebrew word בְּרֵאשִׁית does not allow "instantaneous." The word translated "in *the* beginning" includes a period of time of unstated length which precedes the conditions described by Genesis 1:2. Genesis 1:1 places no limits on how old the Universe may be.**

**What had God created?**

Genesis 1:1 states that God *had created* (completed action) the הַשָּׁמַיִם (heavens) and the הָאָרֶץ (land, earth). He had created all the material things which we can see in the Universe. Genesis 1:1 answers a theological question concerning the appearance of life on Earth.

**In the beginning "God"?   or   In the beginning "the physical matter of the Universe?"**

The theological importance of the traditional Christian and Hebrew view of the first verse of the Bible cannot be overemphasized. The first verse tells us that:

**God was already in existence, before the beginning of the Universe.**
**The Universe was created, it did not always exist.**
**The God of the Bible was the Creator of this Universe.**

In other passages, the Bible gives additional information about God, the Universe and creation.

We will consider the meaning of Genesis 1:1 again following the analysis of Genesis 1:2. This will be done because the two verses need to be considered together with regard to the Christian doctrine of absolute creation, a doctrine often referred to by the Latin words "ex nihilo." This doctrine interprets Genesis 1:1 as referring to an absolute beginning. This means that the matter which is now seen was created, and did not exist before the "beginning." This was also the view of the Septuagint. The Septuagint translated the first Hebrew word בְּרֵאשִׁית using ἐν ἀρχῇ which means "at the first" in relation to time. The same two Greek words are used as the first two words of John 1:1 in the New Testament.

KJV John 1:1    In the beginning (ἐν ἀρχῇ) was the Word, and the Word was with God, and the Word was God.

Because the word order in Hebrew differs from the word order in English, there are some stylistic details which are not apparent in the English translation. In Hebrew, Genesis 1:1 consists of seven words. In the ancient world great significance was attached to certain numbers. Seven was considered a number conveying the sense of a completed cycle or an accomplished task, hence the first sentence implies a sense of task completion. In Hebrew, the second word is not God (Elohim) but rather create (bara). The first word בְּרֵאשִׁית (in *the* beginning) and the second word בָּרָא (had created) have the same first three consonants. This gives a remarkable cadence to the opening words of the Bible as they are spoken. In the ancient world, reading typically meant reading aloud. This ancient practice is recorded in Acts 8:30 where Phillip hears the Ethiopian reading the prophet Isaiah. In the present time this seems odd because our schools teach silent reading.

Genesis 1:1, being the first sentence of Genesis, provides past completed background information which is necessary for understanding the narrative which follows. The Hebrew word sequence is "noun followed by verb"; a sequence which is used to insert pluperfect background information into biblical Hebrew text at the beginning of a narrative. This type of Hebrew word sequence will be extensively discussed when Genesis 1:2 is considered. Genesis 1:2 also uses a "noun followed by verb" word sequence. The example of Job 1:1 is presented here in advance of the more extensive treatment to illustrate the pattern which provides the background information necessary to understand a following narrative. As shown below, the Hebrew word sequence of Job 1:1 is "noun followed by verb," the sequence which appears in Genesis 1:1.

KJV Job 1:1    There was a man in the land of Uz, whose name *was* Job; and that man was perfect and upright, and one that feared God, and eschewed evil.

YLT Job 1:1    A man there hath been in the land of Uz -- Job his name -- and that man hath been perfect and upright -- both fearing God, and turning aside from evil.

| תָּם | הַהוּא | הָאִישׁ | וְהָיָה | שְׁמוֹ | אִיּוֹב | עוּץ | בְּאֶרֶץ | הָיָה | אִישׁ | Job 1:1 |
|---|---|---|---|---|---|---|---|---|---|---|
| perfect | the same | the man | and had been (and + Qal perfect) | name of | Job | Uz | in land of | had existed (Qal perfect) | *A* man (noun) | |

| מֵרָע | וְסָר | אֱלֹהִים | יְרֵא | וְיָשָׁר |
|---|---|---|---|---|
| evil | and turning from | God | fearing | and upright |

Job is described as "perfect and upright," conditions which take a considerable time to establish as the character and behavior of a person. Job's existence in this state is described in the translation under the Hebrew as "had existed" to convey that the completed action verb represents a considerable amount of time, not a condition arrived at in an instant. The YLT of Job 1:1 recognized this completed action meaning in the translation "hath been." The past completed nature of the character of Job is also recognizable by readers of the KJV in its translation "was."

The narrative of the story of Job begins in Job 1:2, a verse which starts with a "waw-consecutive" verb. Sentences in Hebrew narrative usually start with a "waw-consecutive" verb.

# THE SECOND VERSE: GENESIS 1:2          Before the Start of the Story

The analysis of Genesis 1:2 will:
1. Determine the meaning of the two words תֹהוּ וָבֹהוּ "tohu and bohu."
2. Show that the events of Genesis 1:1 and Genesis 1:2 are completed before the start of Genesis 1:3.
3. Show that Genesis 1:3 is the start of the first of the six creative periods of time.

Genesis 1:2 describes the state of the Earth after the **completed** creation of the Universe and before the events which are described in Genesis 1:3. Genesis 1:2 consists of three clauses numbered in the KJV shown below. The KJV has been modified by inserting two untranslated Hebrew words followed by a phonetic equivalent.

**KJV Genesis 1:2 - as modified:**    (1) And the earth was תֹהוּ "tohu" וָבֹהוּ "and bohu,"
                                      (2) and darkness (*was*) over the surface of the deep;
                                      (3) and the Spirit of God moved over the surface of the waters.

The Hebrew words represented by "tohu" and "bohu" are translated "without form and void" in the KJV and "formless and void" in other current English translations. The phrase "tohu and bohu" has presented a great amount of difficulty to translators. Correctly understanding the meaning of these two words is very important. The KJV inserts the verb "*was*" into Genesis 1:2, a verb which does not appear in the Hebrew. The verb which the KJV translated "moved" is a participle better translated "moving." The verbs will be discussed later during the discussion of the three clauses. The verb "*was*" will be omitted in the final translation of Genesis 1:2.

## (1) The Meaning of תֹהוּ וָבֹהוּ "Tohu and Bohu"

What do the words תֹהוּ "tohu" and וָבֹהוּ "and bohu" mean? Both words are nouns. The word וָבֹהוּ "and bohu" of this verse is formed as וָבֹהוּ = בֹהוּ (bohu) + וָ , where וָ "waw" is the prefix meaning "and."

The word בֹהוּ "bohu" is only used three times in the Bible and is used with "tohu" each time. The usage indicates that the words are a phrase or some sort of figure of speech. The two other passages where these words are used together will be considered in great detail. These two other passages are **all** that is available to determine the meaning when the words are used together. After examining these two verses, other verses where "tohu" is used alone will also be considered.

The first passage, Jeremiah 4:23-28, is a prophetic reference to the judgement of the Babylonian captivity. Verse 23 uses the phrase תֹהוּ וָבֹהוּ "tohu and bohu." The meaning of "tohu and bohu" will be determined considering the total context of the passage. Remember, the words in *italics* do not appear in the Hebrew.

**KJV Jeremiah 4:23-28**
23. I beheld the earth (erets), and, lo, *it was* תֹהוּ וָבֹהוּ "**tohu and bohu**";
    and the heavens, and they *had* no light.
24. I beheld the mountains, and, lo, they trembled, and all the hills moved lightly.
25. I beheld, and, lo, *there was* no man, and all the birds of the heavens were fled.
26. I beheld, and, lo, the fruitful place *was* a wilderness, and all the cities thereof were
    broken down at the presence of the LORD, *and* by his fierce anger.
27. For thus hath the LORD said, The whole land (erets) shall be desolate; yet will I not make a full end.
28. For this shall the earth (erets) mourn, and the heavens above be black: because I have spoken *it*,
    I have purposed *it*, and will not repent, neither will I turn back from it.

Notice that:
1. Mountains exist and can be seen. Hills exist and can be seen.
2. The "fruitful place" can be seen. Presumably the ruins of the cities can be seen.
3. There are no people in the land. The land (erets) was desolate.

In this passage the same word הָאָרֶץ (the "erets") is translated as "land" once and as "earth" twice. Here "land" is preferred in all the verses because the entire planet Earth is not in view. The "land," mountains, and hills are seen, but the sea is not mentioned. Recall that "earth" appears in earthenware, fuller's earth, diatomaceous earth, earth tones, earthworm, earthworks and other similar usages. Early readers of the Hebrew would have considered "erets" to primarily mean "land" or "ground," and historically "earth" had the same meaning. Now the English word "earth" is used almost exclusively to indicate the planet Earth. This use is a significant barrier to correctly understanding Genesis One.

For historical perspective, recall that the voyage of Columbus, which established the planetary view, occurred in 1492. Galileo's astronomical observations became known in 1610, one year before the KJV 1611 translation. The KJV follows the 1390 Wycliffe translation which translated אֶרֶץ (erets) as "erthe." The present, nearly exclusive planetary meaning of the word "earth" would not have been primary in the minds of the KJV 1611 translators. The other meanings were well-established and had historical precedence in translation, even before Wycliffe.

As already stated, the KJV translation of "tohu and bohu" is "without form and void." Other English translations use "formless and void." Now here is the point.

**There is no hint of "formless" or "without form" in Jeremiah 4:23-28.** Mountains, hills, and ruins have form. Whatever the term "without form" meant to the translators of the KJV, Jeremiah 4:23-28 does not support that translation in the English language of today.

It is important to observe the emphasis on the absence of people; there is no human life. The land is called a wilderness.

Isaiah 34:8-12 also uses "tohu" and "bohu" in the same line, but the words are not joined as "tohu and bohu." This is a prophecy of judgement on the nation of Edom. The Bible does not prophesy that the nation of Edom will be totally destroyed; the Bible does prophesy that the land Edom, initially occupied, will become uninhabited. The subject of this verse is the prophecy against the land.

**KJV Isaiah 34:8-12**

8   For *it is* the יוֹם day of the LORD'S vengeance, *and* the year of recompences for the controversy of Zion.
9   And the streams thereof shall be turned into pitch, and the dust thereof into brimstone, and the land thereof shall become burning pitch.
10  It shall not be quenched night nor day; the smoke thereof shall go up for ever: from generation to generation it shall lie waste; none shall pass through it for ever and ever.
11  But the cormorant and the bittern shall possess it; the owl also and the raven shall dwell in it: and he shall stretch out upon it the line of "tohu," and the stones of "bohu."
12  They shall call the nobles thereof to the kingdom, but none *shall be* there, and all her princes shall be nothing.
13  And thorns shall come up in her palaces, nettles and brambles in the fortresses thereof: and it shall be an habitation of dragons, *and* a court for owls.
14  The wild beasts of the desert shall also meet with the wild beasts of the island, and the satyr shall cry to his fellow; the screech owl also shall rest there, and find for herself a place of rest.

The KJV translates "tohu" here as "desolation" which is different from "without form." The word "bohu" is translated "emptiness." The word "line" in front of "tohu" is an equivalent of a "tape measure."

Notice, just as with Jeremiah 4:23-28:

1. The mountains still exist and can be seen. The dry streambeds still exist and can be seen.
2. There **is** life in the land (the cormorant, the bittern, owls, wild beasts).
3. There is no human life in the land. The land is not suitable for human habitation.

**There is no hint of "formless" or "without form" in Isaiah 34:8-12.** Mountains, hills, and ruins have form.

Whatever the term "without form" meant to the translators in the KJV, Isaiah 34:8-12 does not support that translation in the English language of today. It is important to observe the absence of people. There is no human life, but not the absence of all life. This is consistent with Deuteronomy 32:10 where "tohu" is translated "waste" by the KJV and "wasteland" by the NAS. This is also consistent with Isaiah 45:18 discussed in the section "More About 'Tohu' and 'Bohu' " (page 43).

The conclusion is that "tohu and bohu" as a phrase refers to a condition of being **"unsuitable for human habitation (desolate) and empty of human habitation."** With this reevaluation of the meaning of "tohu and bohu," Genesis 1:2 can be translated as:

(1)    **And the Earth** (land, water, and atmosphere)
           **had existed** (completed action)
               **unsuitable for human life (desolate)**     **and empty of human life**
                    "tohu"                                              and "bohu"

(2)    **and darkness on the surface of the deep**
          **and the Spirit of God moving over the surface of the waters.**


**How did the translation "tohu and bohu" as "formless and void" come about?**

The answer is that it developed through the historical chain of translation starting with the Septuagint. Translators have a choice of two different styles. Broadly categorized, these styles are a word-for-word translation, or a meaning-for-meaning translation. In fact, translations are often a mixture of both.[18] In the Septuagint the words "tohu and bohu" are translated by the words "unseen and unformed." The question is "why unseen?"

In Genesis 1:2 (line (1) above) the word "erets" has been translated Earth in accordance with the present planetary view. This is permitted as a translation of meaning even if "erets" is considered to mean land. So considered, the "erets" (land) and the "deep" representing surface waters provide the two components of the planetary surface. The meaning intended for "erets" may have been "land." The evidence of the Septuagint translation and the Aramaic Targum paraphrases is that "erets" was understood as meaning land. The Septuagint translated the Hebrew "erets" by the Greek word γη (pronounced "ge") which has the meanings of ground, land, and earth. An answer to the question "why unseen?" can be found by reading the words "erets" and the word γη as "land" or "ground." The next step is to consider Genesis 1:9 where הַיַּבָּשָׁה "the dry" becomes seen.

In Genesis 1:9 הַיַּבָּשָׁה "the dry" is commanded to appear. The word הַיַּבָּשָׁה is translated "dry *land*" by the KJV because it is subsequently called "erets" (land) in Genesis 1:10. Before the "dry *land*" appears all that can be seen is water, no land. The word יַבָּשָׁה "dry" is used in 14 verses, seven of which refer to the "dry" on which the sea was crossed during the Exodus or the crossing of the Jordan. As a consequence, "dry" is considered to refer to land which has been under water and which has become dry.[19] Therefore the land is unseen, an inference derivable from its later appearance in Genesis 1:9. It is not actually stated that there is no land. Prior to Genesis 1:9, the land (erets) is described as "unformed," not because it does not exist, but because it is covered by water. This understanding translates אֶרֶץ "erets" as "land" or "ground" and not the planetary meaning assigned to it in this passage. The ancient world at the time of Moses did not have a planetary view. The concept of the Earth hanging in space and circling the sun was unknown to them.

A series of translations leads to the influential translation of Calvin. Calvin translated "tohu and bohu" into Latin as "informis et inanis." In English, this is "unformed and empty." Calvin's "informis," which translates into "unformed," is consistent with the "unseen" of the Septuagint because the dry land "erets" does not appear until Genesis 1:9. Being covered by water, the land "erets" has not yet been formed. The next significant step in the chain of translation was the KJV in 1611 where "without form" replaced the "unformed" of Calvin.

**KJV (1611)   Genesis 1:2**        And the earth was **without form, and void;**

From this translation, it was but a short step to "formless and void." Notice that the translations "without form" and "formless" are **not** equivalent to "unformed." These words cannot represent the view that the "dry land" cannot be seen because it has not yet emerged above the water covering the surface of the planet.

This brief summary of the sequence of the translations of "tohu and bohu" is repeated with greater detail in the section "More about 'Tohu' and 'Bohu' " (pages 43-46). That section also examines and lists the translations of "tohu" in other verses of the Bible.

**Genesis 1:1-2 as an introduction**

With the translation of "tohu and bohu" as "unsuitable for human life and empty of human life," Genesis 1:1-2 functions as an introduction. It introduces important elements which will be central to the narrative which follows.

These important elements are:

**God, the heavens and the Earth, and the habitability of the Earth and human life.**

This sequence indicates that Genesis One is about preparing for the introduction of "Adam," male and female.
With this translation the first two verses do two things. They provide needed background information about the condition of the Earth before the start of the narrative, and they introduce the theme of the narrative which follows. The translations "without form and void" and "formless and void" obscure this theme at the beginning of the story. When the translation is "formless and void" secularists can easily consider the story line to be about the physical sequence of the development of planet Earth. Once accepted, this secularist view colors the interpretation of all of the remaining verses.

The surface of planet Earth is described as being without visible light, and as being a waterscape and not a landscape. The word תְהוֹם "tehom" translated "deep" appears five times in reference to water in descriptions of the crossing of the Red Sea during the Exodus and refers to water many other times in the Bible. It is not stated that the water is of a uniform depth but that deep water is present. It is not stated that there are no shallow water areas or that there are no minor outcroppings of rock which may penetrate the surface of the water somewhere. The statement is that the surface of the deep can be "seen" and that it is in darkness. Planet Earth, and whatever land which does exist, are said to be unsuitable for human habitation and empty of human habitation. The usually assumed absence of land is an inference based on the "dry" which is commanded to appear in Genesis 1:9. In Genesis 1:10 the "dry" is called "erets" (land) upon which plants then grow. It is this land, the "dry," which is later suitable for human occupation. The "erets" of Genesis 1:2 is unsuitable for human life and empty of human life, either as unsuitable land or as land which is covered by water. The composition of the atmosphere is not given and may not be the same as that which presently exists. Knowing that the story is about suitability for human life, the reader is properly prepared to view the actions of God as the unsuitability is removed. Most of the subsequent actions inform the reader of preparations for the introduction for "Adam," male and female. The communicated actions are not a complete description of the natural history of the surface of planet Earth or of the introduction of life on planet Earth.

## (2) Genesis 1:1-2 Completed Before the "And God said" of Genesis 1:3

It will now be shown that Genesis 1:1-2 are completed before the "And God said" of Genesis 1:3. The three clauses of Genesis 1:2 will be considered as a unit. The Hebrew of the verse, arranged by numbered clauses, is:

| | | | | | |
|---|---|---|---|---|---|
| וָבֹהוּ | תֹהוּ | הָיְתָה | וְהָאָרֶץ | (1) | ← Hebrew starts here. |
| and "bohu" | "tohu" | had existed (Qal perfect) | and the Earth ("waw" + noun) | | ← Start English here. |

| | | | | | |
|---|---|---|---|---|---|
| תְהוֹם | פְּנֵי | עַל | וְחֹשֶׁךְ | (2) | ← Hebrew starts here. |
| deep | face of | over | and darkness | | |

| | | | | | | |
|---|---|---|---|---|---|---|
| הַמָּיִם | פְּנֵי | עַל | מְרַחֶפֶת | אֱלֹהִים | וְרוּחַ | (3) | ← Hebrew starts here. |
| the waters | face of | over | moving (participle) | God (Elohim) | and spirit of | | |

The first word in line (1) is וְהָאָרֶץ = אֶרֶץ "earth" + הָ "the" + וְ "and" or "now." The word is a noun of feminine gender. In Genesis 1:2 אֶרֶץ "erets" is translated as "Earth" referring to the entire planet Earth. This includes the land, the bodies of water, and the atmosphere. The other meanings of dry ground, land, and earth as in the word earthenware are excluded. The reason for this exclusion is that the word אֶרֶץ "erets" is specifically assigned the meaning of dry ground or land in Genesis 1:10 when the "dry" appears.

The second word of the verse is a verb הָיְתָה (haya). Phonetically הָיְתָה is pronounced "hay'eta." The root הָיָה (haya) of the verb means "to be," "to exist," "to become," or "to happen." The verb is in the Qal perfect form, third person feminine singular. The Qal perfect verb הָיְתָה represents a completed action. The completed action can be translated "had existed," "had been," "existed," or "was." The suffix ה of הָיְתָה makes the verb third person feminine gender. This suffix indicates that the subject of the verb is the word אֶרֶץ (erets) which has the same gender.

The verb הָיְתָה will be translated "had existed." The "had" indicates the completed nature of the action and avoids the introduction of a simple past tense. The traditional translation in the KJV is "**was**." Both "had existed" and "was" express the same meaning. The state of the Earth which is being described is a condition which had already been achieved at some time in the past. How long ago this state was achieved we do not know; we are not told. How long the Earth had existed in the described condition is not stated and remains unknown. Grammatically, the important issue of clause (1) is the word order.

| וָבֹהוּ | תֹהוּ | הָיְתָה | וְהָאָרֶץ (1) | ← Hebrew starts here. |
|---|---|---|---|---|
| and "bohu" | "tohu" | had existed (Qal perfect) | and the Earth ("waw + noun") | ← Start English here. |

The word order is "waw + noun" followed by a "perfect verb," and will be referred to as a "waw + noun--perfect verb" construction in subsequent discussion.[86] "Waw + noun" is used to denote a ו "waw" prefixed noun as a word preceding the perfect verb. The "waw + noun--perfect verb" is a construction which has not been considered before. In Genesis 1:2 the "waw + noun" is the word וְהָאָרֶץ "and the Earth" and the "perfect verb" is the word הָיְתָה "had existed" (KJV "was"). Sentences and clauses that begin with a "waw + noun--perfect verb" have the function of providing background information at the start of a narrative. This background information is about events or conditions which have been completed before the start of the narrative which follows. The pluperfect translation "had existed" clearly represents the existence of the Earth as completed before Genesis 1:3, the start of the "waw-consecutive" narrative which follows.

**Genesis 3:1: An example of the "waw + noun--perfect verb" construction**

To illustrate the function of the "waw + noun--perfect verb" construction Genesis 3:1 will be studied. Genesis 3:1 is a verse which introduces a new story and provides background information before the narrative about Eve and the serpent begins. The narrative starts with the "waw-consecutive" verb translated "and he said." The KJV translation printed below starts with Genesis 2:24 so that the context and the change in subject may be seen. The first two Hebrew words of Genesis 3:1 are in the "waw + noun--perfect verb" sequence just discussed.

**KJV Genesis 2:24-25**

    2:24    Therefore shall a man leave his father and his mother,
            and shall cleave unto his wife: and they shall be one flesh.
    2:25    And they were both naked, the man and his wife, and were not ashamed.

**KJV Genesis 3:1**    **(1)    Now the serpent was more subtil than any beast of the field**    } Past Background
                 **(2)    which the LORD God had made.**    Information

(A new narrative starts with "and he said.")
        **(3)**    And he said unto the woman, Yea, hath God said,
                Ye shall not eat of every tree of the garden?

**KJV Genesis 3:2**    And the woman said unto the serpent, We may eat of the fruit of the trees of the garden:

The verb translated "was" in Genesis 3:1 is the same verb used in Genesis 1:2. It is in a different gender and therefore is spelled differently. The gender difference is to make reference to the serpent. "Now the serpent" is the "waw + noun" of the "waw + noun--perfect verb" construction.

| הַשָּׂדֶה | חַיַּת | מִכֹּל | עָרוּם | הָיָה | וְהַנָּחָשׁ | Genesis 3:1 |
|---|---|---|---|---|---|---|
| the field | life of | out of all | subtil | had existed (Qal perfect) (KJV "was") | Now the serpent ("waw + noun") | ← Start English here. |

The "waw" prefixed noun--perfect verb which the KJV translated "Now the serpent was" starts a clause (1) which provides background information for the new narrative. It also signals that the previous narrative has ended. The second clause (2) "which the Lord God had made" also provides the information that the serpent had been made by God. In the KJV translation of Genesis 3:1 both "was" and "had made" are translations of Qal perfect completed action verbs. They represent actions completed before the start of the narrative. The new narrative starts with "And he said unto the woman." The KJV verb "and he said" is a "waw" consecutive imperfect verb, the type which is normally used to tell past narrative. A "waw" consecutive imperfect verb expresses the perfect completed action meaning.

When Genesis 3:1 is read in context, it is easy to see that the first two clauses tell of actions or conditions which were completed in the past, **before** the "And he said onto the woman." It is this "completed **before** the start of the narrative" which is important to understanding Genesis 1:2.

### Genesis 1:2 Places No Restriction on the Age of Planet Earth

In Genesis 1:3 the KJV "And God said" is a "waw-consecutive" imperfect verb. The verb in "And he said onto the woman" of the KJV Genesis 3:2 is also a "waw-consecutive" imperfect verb. The parallels of the verb use in the two passages demonstrate the following:

> In the KJV the "And the Earth was" of Genesis 1:2 must describe a condition of the Earth which was **completed before** the "And God said" of Genesis 1:3. The "when" of this completed condition is the same as the "when" that is described by the translation "had existed."

> Genesis 1:2 states that the Earth was in existence **before** the start of the first creative period. The nature of the Hebrew perfect completed action verb does not indicate when this completed state had been achieved or how long the Earth had been in this state. How long the Earth continues in this state before the commands of Genesis 1:3 is also unstated and unknown.

## As a consequence, Genesis 1:2 places no restriction on the age of the Earth or on the age of the Universe.

The function of the "waw + noun--perfect verb" is not new knowledge. That Genesis 1:2 places no restriction on the age of the Earth is well-known to those of the Christian community who hold an Old Earth view of Genesis One. Arguments used to ignore the completed action meaning of Genesis 1:2 are usually based upon arguments made using quotes from Hebrew grammars in an incorrect manner. An extensive discussion of the grammatical issues and the errors made is given in the section **More About "waw + noun--prefect verb," a Pluperfect Indicator**, starting on page 37. The topics are:

(1) Additional examples of "waw + noun--perfect verb" which refer to completed past events.
(2) A grammatical analysis of Genesis 1:2 describing errors typically made by Young Earth advocates.
(3) More grammatical information about nominal clauses containing a verb such as occurs in Genesis 1:2.

### Another analysis relating to Genesis 1:2

In order to provide a coherent exposition of the meaning of Genesis 1:2 as it relates to the age of the Earth, this study will now present another analysis which shows that Genesis 1:2 is completed before the start of the first creative period. In Hebrew, each of the creative periods is described by the Hebrew word יוֹם "yom." Because this study has not yet investigated the meaning of יוֹם "yom," the "yom" will be used in referring to the creative periods. The phonetic pronunciation of "yom" is (yome) which rhymes with "dome"; the "o" is long. The meaning of יוֹם "yom" when referring to the creative periods (creative "yom") will be extensively investigated later when Genesis 1:5 is considered. The result of the analysis here does not depend on the length of time attributed to the creative "yom."

The method is to follow the pattern of the ending and starting of the six creative periods, working backward from the completion of the sixth period. The completion of the sixth period is recorded in Genesis 2:1 given below.

KJV Genesis 2:1    Thus the heavens and the earth were finished, and all the host of them.

The method then uses two recurring patterns of Genesis 1:1-35. In the KJV these are:

1. Each of the six creative periods (creative "yom") ends with a phrase which starts with:

   KJV  " **And the evening and the morning were** "

2. Each of the six creative periods (creative "yom") begins with a sentence which starts with:

   KJV  "And God said "

## (3) Analysis Showing Genesis 1:3 is the Start of the First Creative יוֹם "Yom"

Genesis 2:1 indicates that the six "creative yom" have been completed and that Genesis 1:31
is the final verse of "creative yom" six.

**KJV Genesis 2:1    Thus the heavens and the earth were finished, and all the host of them.**

*step 1*        *the end of the sixth "creative yom" is Genesis 1:31*

end      1:31     And the evening and the morning were . . . KJV
start    1:24     And God said . . .

*step 2*        *the end of the fifth "creative yom" is Genesis 1:23*

end      1:23     And the evening and the morning were . . . KJV
start    1:20     And God said . . .

*step 3*        *the end of the fourth "creative yom" is Genesis 1:19*

end      1:19     And the evening and the morning were . . . KJV
start    1:14     And God said . . .

*step 4*        *the end of the third "creative yom" is Genesis 1:13*

end      1:13     And the evening and the morning were . . . KJV
start    1:9      And God said . . .

*step 5*        *the end of the second "creative yom" is Genesis 1:8*

end      1:8      And the evening and the morning were . . . KJV
start    1:6      And God said . . .

*step 6*        *the end of the initial "creative yom" is Genesis 1:5*

end      1:5      And the evening and the morning were . . . KJV

start    1:3      And God said . . . ←**This command in Genesis 1:3 starts the initial creative "yom."**

**Genesis 1:1 and Genesis 1:2 take place and are completed before the start of the first creative "yom."**
**The translation of Genesis 1:1-2 below is that found in the study just completed. It is not the KJV.**

    **1:2    And the earth had existed "tohu and bohu";**
        **and darkness over the surface of the deep**
        **and the Spirit of God moving over the surface of the waters.**

    **1:1    In the beginning God had created the heavens and the earth.**

The translations "had created" and "had existed" emphasize the completed nature of the actions in Genesis 1:1-2 and indicate to the reader that these verbs meaningfully differ from the past tense verbs following in Genesis 1:3. The uniform past tense KJV translation does not reveal this meaningful difference in the Hebrew being translated.

Whenever the forgoing analysis has been presented, questions have been asked about other verses of the Bible.
A question often asked is, "How is Exodus 20:11 to be understood in relation to Genesis 1:2?"

That question will be addressed in the next section.

## Analysis of Exodus 20:11

In the previous sections it has been shown that the events of Genesis 1:1-2 take place and are completed before the "And God said" of Genesis 1:3. It was also shown that Genesis 1:1-2 places no limit on the age of the Earth or on the age of the Universe. Nevertheless, there are people who contest the issue and assert that the Bible says that the Earth and Universe are about 6,000 years old. Exodus 20:11 is one of the verses which is typically used to support this claim, and as a consequence deserves careful analysis to show it does **not** support this claim. Two issues which will be addressed carefully are:

1. The word *"in"* which appears in Exodus 20:11 and Exodus 31:17 does not appear in the Hebrew text of either verse. The insertion of the word *"in"* into the translation of Exodus 20:11 significantly distorts the meaning of the verse. The *"in"* appears italicized in the KJV, but is not italicized in most other English translations or in some recent printings of the KJV. Typically, the reader of Exodus 20:11 is unaware that the *"in"* is not in the Hebrew text.

2. The Hebrew words בָּרָא "bara" (create) and עָשָׂה "asah" (made) have different meanings and are **not** equivalent as some claim. The difference between these words will be shown by reference to Genesis 2:3 and other verses. This will contradict the arguments of the 6,000 year old Earth advocates regarding Exodus 20:11 because their arguments critically depend upon asserting that בָּרָא "bara" (create) and עָשָׂה "asah" (made) have the same meaning.

Exodus 20:11 in the YLT and KJV translations are shown below with the Hebrew of the verse.

YLT Exodus 20:11     **for six days** (yoms) hath Jehovah made (asah) the heavens and the earth, the sea, and all that {is} in them, . . .

KJV Exodus 20:11     **For *in* six days** (yoms) the LORD made (asah) heaven and earth, the sea, and all that in them *is*, and rested the seventh day: wherefore the LORD blessed the sabbath day, and hallowed it.

| הָאָרֶץ | וְאֵת | הַשָּׁמַיִם | אֵת | יְהוָה | עָשָׂה | יָמִים | שֵׁשֶׁת | כִּי | Exodus 20:11 |
|---|---|---|---|---|---|---|---|---|---|
| the earth | and + dir. obj. marker | the heavens | dir. obj. marker | Yahweh | had made (Qal perfect) | "yoms" | six of | For | |

| בָּם | אֲשֶׁר | כָּל | וְאֵת | הַיָּם | אֵת |
|---|---|---|---|---|---|
| in them | which | all | and + dir. obj. marker | the sea | dir. obj. marker |

Step one of the analysis is to consider the italicized word *"in."* The KJV of Exodus 20:11 writes the second word *"in"* in italics indicating the this word does not exist in the Hebrew text. The YLT for this verse omits the word *"in"* and translates the Qal perfect verb עָשָׂה "asah" as a completed action by inserting the word "hath" before Jehovah. The accuracy of the YLT for this verse is verified by the Hebrew, shown with its literal translation for the portion of the verse in question. The meaning of the YLT and the translation of this study is quite different from that which is often incorrectly ascribed to this verse based on the KJV. Regarding Exodus 20:11 there are two issues relevant to Genesis 1:1-2.

1. Exodus 20:11 **does not** refer to any of the creative action (bara) of God referenced in Genesis 1:1 or to any creative action בָּרָא "bara" of God which preceded Genesis 1:3. It cannot make this reference because עָשָׂה "asah" (made) is different from "bara" (create). Exodus 20:11 does not indicate that the creative actions (bara) of Genesis 1:1 are included in the events referred to by this verse. Exodus 20:11 **does** refer to actions taken by God to modify, or further perfect, those things which He had already created (bara).

2. Exodus 20:11 and Exodus 31:17 cannot include the creative actions of God in Genesis 1:1-2 because the correct translation in the KJV style is, "For six days (yoms) . . . . " Assertions of such inclusion which depend on "For *in* six days . . . ." are wrong because "*in*" does not appear in the Hebrew.[20] This is independent of the time length assigned to the creative day (yom), and applies equally to long creative times or to an assumed 24-hour day.

Step two in the analysis will be to consider Genesis 2:3 which uses בָּרָא "bara" (create) and עָשָׂה "asah" (made) which have different meanings. Genesis 2:3 shows that the writer of Genesis considered "bara" (create) and "asah" (made) to have different meanings. The difference in meaning is clear but requires careful explanation of the KJV translation of the Hebrew infinitive לַעֲשׂוֹת "to make" and the KJV margin note. In Genesis 2:3 below, the YLT translation "for making" is a correct translation.

KJV Genesis 2:3      And God blessed the seventh day, and sanctified it:
because that in it he had rested from all his work which God created (bara) and made†.
†*Heb. created to make.* (*This is a margin note in the 1611 KJV.*)

YLT Genesis 2:3      And God blesseth the seventh day, and sanctifieth it,
for in it He hath ceased from all His work which God had prepared (bara) **for making**.

| אֹתוֹ | וַיְקַדֵּשׁ | הַשְּׁבִיעִי | יוֹם | אֵת | אֱלֹהִים | וַיְבָרֶךְ | (1) | Genesis 2:3 |
|---|---|---|---|---|---|---|---|---|
| it + dir. obj. marker | and had sanctified | the seventh | "yom" | dir. obj. marker | Elohim | and had blessed | | ← Start English here. |

| לַעֲשׂוֹת | אֱלֹהִים | בָּרָא | אֲשֶׁר | מְלַאכְתּוֹ | מִכָּל | שָׁבַת | בּוֹ | כִּי | (2) |
|---|---|---|---|---|---|---|---|---|---|
| for making (asah) (Qal infinitive) | Elohim | had created (bara) (Qal perfect) | which | work (business) | from all | he had ceased (Qal perfect) | in it | for | |

Line (2) of the Hebrew uses בָּרָא "bara" which is followed by לַעֲשׂוֹת "asah" in an infinitive form translated "for making." The infinitive form also means "to make" as indicated by the KJV margin note. The Hebrew verbs שָׁבַת translated "had ceased" and בָּרָא translated "had created" are both in the Qal perfect form indicating completed action. The "making" indicated by the word לַעֲשׂוֹת "asah" takes place after the completed action "had created." Not only does the text indicate that "bara" and "asah" have different meanings, but it indicates that the subsequent "makings" were intended to follow the "creating." The ordering does not depend upon the translation "had created." This ordering is also apparent in the translation **"for making"** given below the Hebrew text.

The translation of לַעֲשׂוֹת (asah) as "for making" or as the "to make" of the KJV margin note is correct for the following reasons: לַעֲשׂוֹת = ל + עֲשׂוֹת is the infinitive עֲשׂוֹת prefixed by the preposition ל which means "for" or "to" and expresses purpose. The preposition ל is not the preposition ו "waw" meaning "and" as it is translated in the KJV, excluding the 1611 KJV margin note. The margin note indicates the KJV translators were aware that the Hebrew differed from the English "and made" which they had translated in the main text.[21] "For making" is an equivalent of the English infinitive "to make."

Only in Genesis 2:3 does the KJV translate לַעֲשׂוֹת "and made." Elsewhere the KJV translates the לַעֲשׂוֹת differently, examples being "to do" (91 times) and "to make" (21 times).

Genesis 2:3 shows that the word "asah" is used to refer to actions taken by God to additionally modify or perfect things which God had already "created." By its use here it shows that the writer of Genesis considered the words בָּרָא "bara" (create) and עָשָׂה "asah" (made) to have different meanings. The "making" is a subsequent action and is **not** equivalent to the creating indicated by the word "bara." Additional examples of verses indicating the difference and nonequivalence of בָּרָא "bara" and עָשָׂה "asah" will be given after consideration of the "*in*" added by the KJV in Exodus 20:11.

Isaiah 45:7 provides another example where (bara) and (asah) are used in a contrasting pattern. The KJV and YLT translations and the Hebrew are given on the next page. Isaiah 45:7 is written in poetic progression. The second line is not an exact repeat of the first line, but expands upon the first line. "Bara" in line (1) is used in parallel to "bara" in line (2). The word אֲנִי "I" inserted at the beginning of the KJV parallel lines is not present in the Hebrew. All the verbs are participles translatable by the English verb form ending in "ing" as shown in the YLT. Isaiah 45:7 should be read in the context of the entire chapter.

KJV Isaiah 45:7     (1)     I form (yatsar) the light, and create (bara) darkness:
                      (2)     I make (asah) peace,    and create (bara) evil:
                                   I the LORD do (asah) all these *things*.

YLT Isaiah 45:7     (1)     Forming (yatsar) light, and preparing (bara) darkness,
                       (2)     Making (asah) peace, and preparing (bara) evil,
                                   I {am} Jehovah, doing (asah) all these things.

Isaiah 45:7

| יוֹצֵר | אוֹר | וּבוֹרֵא | חֹשֶׁךְ | עֹשֶׂה | שָׁלוֹם | וּבוֹרֵא | רָע |
|---|---|---|---|---|---|---|---|
| forming (yatsar) | light | and creating | darkness | making (asah) | peace | and creating (bara) | evil |

| אֲנִי | יְהוָה | עֹשֶׂה | כָל | אֵלֶּה |
|---|---|---|---|---|
| I | Yahweh | making (asah) | all | these |

This verse is sometimes used to argue that the words "bara," "asah," and "yatsar" are equivalent. However, this verse actually employs the distinctions between the words in a poetic form. In the poetic parallelism, "yatsar" is used parallel to "asah" and "bara" is used parallel to "bara." "Asah" is used for the summing up, "doing all these things," because the meaning of "bara" does not include "asah." The argument for equivalence asserts parallelism between the words in the same line, something which is not shown by the pattern of the verse.

The use of differences in words to expand the meaning of sequential parallel lines can be illustrated by considering Psalm 1:1. Again, there are three parallel statements expressing the total description of "Blessed *is* the man . . . ."

KJV Psalm 1:1    Blessed *is* the man    (1)   that walketh not    in the counsel    of the ungodly,
                                                 (2)   nor standeth       in the way        of sinners,
                                                 (3)   nor sitteth          in the seat       of the scornful.

There is a sequence of physical action in the three lines: walketh, standeth, sitteth. The use of these words in parallel statements of similar poetic meaning does not indicate that these words are equivalent. They are not equivalent. This same conclusion is true for the other two sequences of three words: counsel, way, seat and ungodly, sinners, scornful. The difference in the meaning of the words is used to expand the meaning of the three parallel statements when considered in their entirety.

An expanded explanation of the meaning of the word "bara" is given in the section **More About "Bara," "Asah," and "Yatsar"** on page 32. This section includes analysis of more verses which show that "bara" is not equivalent to "asah." Exodus 34:10 and Isaiah 43:7 are analyzed on pages 34-35 and show that "bara" is not equivalent to "asah." This is in contradiction to claims sometimes made for these verses.

## "Young Earth" and Other Translation Issues

It has been shown that the first two verses of Genesis do not place any limit on the age of the Earth or on the age of the Universe. The reader may well wonder how others reading the same verses can come to the conclusion that the Earth is only 6,000 to 10,000 years old. Understanding the Young Earth interpretation of Genesis necessitates an understanding of its origin. The issue is fossils.

The Young Earth interpretation which will be discussed is that advocated by Henry Morris.[22] Morris considers the events of Genesis 1:1 to instantaneously take place as the first act of the events of the first creative time. His interpretation would explain the fossils as a result of the flood of Noah. The time interval between Genesis 1:1 and Genesis 1:2 represented a difficulty.

As has been shown by the analysis of this study, Genesis 1:1 and Genesis 1:2 are actions completed before the start of Genesis 1:3. By the grammar of the Hebrew there exists between these verses an interval of time of unstated length. This interval had been noted and interpreted by other Christian interpreters as providing for the existence of geologic ages before the start of Genesis 1:3. The 1909 and the 1917 Scofield Reference Bibles contained a footnote for Genesis 1:1 which read in part, "The first creative act refers to the dateless past, and gives scope for all the geologic ages." Exodus 20:11 is used to justify eliminating the troublesome time interval between Genesis 1:1 and Genesis 1:2.

In quoting Exodus 20:11 emphasis is placed on the word "in," because the "in" places the referenced events within the six creative times. The "in" is not sufficient by itself because Exodus 20:11 uses "asah" and Genesis 1:1 uses "bara." Asserting that "bara" is equivalent to "asah" is the procedure used to apply Exodus 20:11 as the instrument which removes the troublesome time interval between Genesis 1:1 and Genesis 1:2. This study has shown that "bara" is not equivalent to "asah," and that the "*in*" is an added word not in the Hebrew. As a consequence, the attempt to place the events of Genesis 1:1 within the first creative time fails. The figure below indicates the differences in time sequence in an easily understood format.

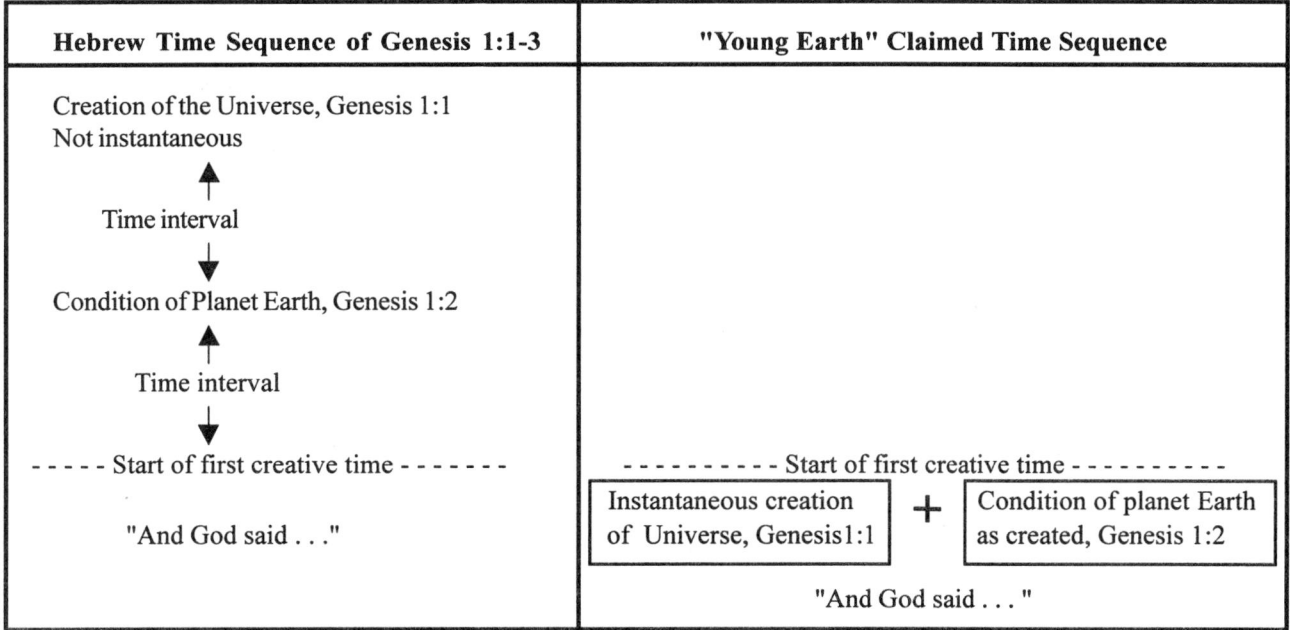

For Genesis 1:1 to be contained within the assumed 24 hour first creative time period, the word translated "beginning" is taken as representing an extremely short period of time. The planet Earth and the Universe are assumed to appear in less than a 12-hour "daytime." This assumption of an "instantaneous" appearance of planet Earth and the Universe is not supported by the actual uses of the Hebrew word "beginning" in the Bible.

The events of Genesis 1:2 also describe a condition completed before Genesis 1:3. The amount of time that the Earth had been in the described condition and the time interval until the "And God said . . ." of Genesis 1:3 is also not stated. Those advocating the Young Earth view wish Genesis 1:2 to be included within the first creative time following the creation of Genesis 1:1. This is argued for by a difficult (and incorrect) grammatical analysis of Genesis 1:2 which ignores the "waw + noun -- perfect verb" construction. The descriptions of the Earth are then considered to be conditions included within the time interval of Genesis 1:3. The reader will recall that this assertion is contradicted by the example of Genesis 3:1 which has been considered in detail. The argument which the Young Earth view uses is explained, and shown to be in error, in the section **More About "waw + noun -- prefect verb," a Pluperfect Indicator.** This section starts on page 37. The section includes three additional examples of the "waw + noun -- perfect verb" construction. The explanation of why the Young Earth view is not valid is given in the subsection entitled "A grammatical analysis of Genesis 1:2" (pages 40- 42).

In Genesis 1:2, this study translated הָיְתָה (haya) as "had existed." The KJV translated הָיְתָה (haya) as "was."
Many people hold the view that the correct translation of this word should be "became" or "had become." A survey of the KJV translations of "haya" shows that the KJV does translate this word as "became." It is further noted that "haya" is the verb often translated by the familiar phrase "and it came to pass." "And it came to pass" is a translation that also conveys the meaning of "became." Those opposed to the translation "became" have generally assumed that if "became" was excluded, then the first two verses would not be completed before the KJV "And God said" of Genesis 1:3. It has been shown that this assumption is **not true. This study does not advocate the translation "became" but provides a review of the translation issues in the section "More About 'Haya' Translated 'Became' " (page 47).**

An additional issue for some is the implied assertion of Young Earth advocates that accepting an Old Earth is equivalent to accepting Darwinian Evolution. **This is not so.** Today many Christians hold an Old Earth view of Genesis and are vigorous and effective opponents of Darwinism. This has been true historically as well.

In the years 1909-1917 a set of booklets entitled *The Fundamentals* were published which set forth the Christian faith. These booklets, or articles, were edited and published in four volumes which are still available today.[78] Those who wrote in *The Fundamentals* defended evangelical Christianity and presented the Gospel of Jesus Christ. With respect to Darwinism, they did not view the old Earth as the issue; they recognized that the essence of Darwinism was a denial of design and thereby a denial of a creator God.

Genesis 1:1-2 has been shown to be consistent with an old Earth and an old Universe. This result does not depend on the length of the creative "yom" or on any interpretation of events and effects resulting from the flood of Noah. This conclusion is entirely based upon the text of the Bible, using the Bible itself as the determiner of the meaning of the Hebrew words, and has been found without any reference to scientific evidences. The Bible says there was a beginning; science now agrees that there was a beginning. What the Bible says about the more recent creation events on planet Earth starts with the analysis of Genesis 1:3 on page 54.

For completeness, a section "More About Ex Nihilo" has been included. This section refutes the assertion by some that Genesis 1:1 is not an independent statement. The advocates of this view alter the vowel markings of the words in Genesis 1:1. This makes Genesis 1:1 a verbless nominal clause and makes the "when" of Genesis 1:1 the same as the "when" of Genesis 1:2. Because Genesis 1:2 is completed before the start of the first creative period, this modification does not alter the conclusions of this study about the age of the Earth and the Universe. The theological difficulty with the asserted modification is that Genesis 1:1 is no longer consistent with the creation of matter (i.e., creation ex nihilo). See "More About Ex Nihilo" (page 50).

**Choices:** Fast forward to the study of Genesis 1:3 or read additional material regarding Genesis 1:1-2

The next six sections (pages 32-53) continue to expand the study regarding various aspects of the translation of Genesis 1:1 and Genesis 1:2. They provide a basis for the defense of the Christian interpretation of Genesis 1:1-2 made in this study. These sections also explain specific errors of analysis made by those advocating a Young Earth view. These sections are valuable for attaining an improved understanding of Genesis One and the Bible.

Those who are satisfied that Genesis 1:1 and Genesis 1:2 place no limit on the age of planet Earth or the Universe may wish to temporarily bypass these sections and fast forward to the section on Genesis 1:3 which begins on page 54. The study of Genesis 1:3-5 deals with the questions regarding the length of the six creative time periods. The meaning of the Hebrew word "yom," translated "day" by the KJV, is studied extensively in the section on Genesis 1:5.

The six sections dealing with Genesis 1:1 and Genesis 1:2 are:

More About "Bara," "Asah," and "Yatsar".................................... page 32
More About "Waw + Noun--Perfect Verb," a Pluperfect Indicator.. page 37
More About "Tohu" and "Bohu"................................................ page 43
More About "Haya" Translated "Became"...................................page 47
More About Ex Nihilo ................................................................page 50
The section, THE FIRST CREATIVE "YOM":GENESIS 1:3, begins on page 54.

## More About "Bara," "Asah," and "Yatsar"

This section provides additional evidence that the words בָּרָא "bara," עָשָׂה "asah," and יָצַר "yatsar" do not have the same or equivalent meanings.

This issue is important because some interpreters of Genesis One attempt to position the events of Genesis 1:1-2 with the events of Genesis 1:3 and thereby obtain a "young" age of the Earth and the Universe. Typically, an age of 6,000 to 10,000 years is then asserted. As part of these arguments, the words בָּרָא "bara," עָשָׂה "asah," and יָצַר "yatsar" are claimed to have the same or equivalent meanings. Verse analyses which follow will show conclusively that the words are different. Some preparation will be given before considering the verses. Two short paragraphs will repeat information which has already appeared, then new material will be presented.

The difference between "bara" and "asah" was discussed earlier in the analysis of Exodus 20:11 on pages 28-30. It was shown there that the word "bara" (create) is not equivalent to the word "asah" (make). It was also shown that the author of Genesis had illustrated the difference in Genesis 2:3 where the word "asah" was used in the infinitive ("ing" form) with the prefix ל meaning "for" or "to" when indicating purpose. The KJV acknowledged the Hebrew infinitive in a margin note "Heb. created to make." This study translated לַעֲשׂוֹת "for making."

As a point of departure for this additional section, a modified KJV of Genesis 2:3 will be printed below where the prefixed infinitive of "asah" is translated as ***"for making."*** Note: translating לַעֲשׂוֹת "to make," as done in the KJV margin note, or translating לַעֲשׂוֹת as "to do" leads to the same meaning.

**KJV Genesis 2:3** And God blessed the seventh day, and sanctified it: because that in it
**(modified)** he had rested from all his work which God בָּרָא created לַעֲשׂוֹת ***"for making."***

As shown above, the word עָשָׂה "asah" is used to refer to actions taken by God to modify or perfect things which God had already created (bara). The "making" (asah) is a subsequent action and is **not** equivalent to the creating indicated by the word בָּרָא "bara."

**An example illustrating the meaning of "bara"**

Suppose a child was making birdhouses for sale. After much design, thought, and effort a **new** design was developed and the first birdhouse was constructed. After building the first one, another nine birdhouses were constructed from the same design as the first.

A buyer comes and the child proudly says, "I made (asah) all of these birdhouses." Then the child selects the first birdhouse and says, "I created (bara) this. I made this birdhouse first, as a new design."

The statement that the child "made" (asah) all the birdhouses is true. The statement that the child "created" (bara) the first birdhouse, as a new design, is also true. Nine of the birdhouses were copies of an already-existing design. The first birdhouse was "made" (asah), but also, because it was the first of a new design, it was "created" (bara). The aspect of newness which we have ascribed to the word "create" (bara) is applicable to only one of the birdhouses.

Additional verses will now be presented showing that the word "bara" includes the connotation of a "new thing." Also, verses in which בָּרָא "bara" is used with עָשָׂה "asah" and יָצַר "yatsar" will be reviewed to show that these verses **do not** indicate an equivalence of "asah" or "yatsar" to the word "bara." The word "bara" is used 54 times in the Bible of which 49 times are in the Qal. Each of these 49 times the word בָּרָא "bara" refers to the actions of God. "Bara" is not used in the Qal for the actions of any other agent.

**More verse examples**

Numbers 16:30 uses the verb יִבְרָא "bara" preceded by a noun בְּרִיאָה derived from the Hebrew word "bara."

KJV Numbers 16:30   But if the LORD make (bara) a new thing (בְּרִיאָה), and the earth open her mouth,
and swallow them up, with all that *appertain* unto them, and they go down quick into
the pit; then ye shall understand that these men have provoked the LORD.

| פִּיהָ | אֶת | הָאֲדָמָה | וּפָצְתָה | יְהוָה | יִבְרָא | בְּרִיאָה | וְאִם | **Numbers 16:30** |
|---|---|---|---|---|---|---|---|---|
| mouth | dir. obj. marker | the ground | and shall open "waw-consecutive" (ו + Qal perfect) | Yahweh | shall create (Qal imperfect) | a new thing | and if | |

The noun בְּרִיאָה, which the KJV translates as "a new thing," recognizes the connotation of "newness" of the Hebrew root word "bara." The following Hebrew word יִבְרָא is the verb "bara." In this verse the KJV fails to translate "bara" as "create." The translation "make" in this verse conceals the use of "bara" from the English reader and thereby adds confusion about the difference in meaning between "bara" and "asah." This verb יִבְרָא is a Qal imperfect form indicating incomplete action which this study translates "shall create." The prefix י of יִבְרָא refers to "Yahweh" as the one creating. The association of the verb "bara" with "new thing" is clear from the KJV translation of the Hebrew once the reader knows that the verb used is "bara." The KJV translates "bara" as "create" 42 times and as "make" two times.

Isaiah 65:17 is another verse which uses "bara" to refer to new things. Isaiah 65:17 uses a participle (translatable by the "ing" form) to speak of the "creating" of new things. The YLT translates the participle as "creating"; the KJV uses the present tense "create." This verse indicates "bara" includes the connotation of "something new."

KJV Isaiah 65:17  For, behold, I create new heavens and a new earth:
and the former shall not be remembered, nor come into mind.
YLT Isaiah 65:17  For, lo, I **am creating** new heavens, and a new earth, . . . .

| חֲדָשָׁה | וָאָרֶץ | חֲדָשִׁים | שָׁמַיִם | בוֹרֵא | הִנְנִי | כִּי | Isaiah 65:17 |
|---|---|---|---|---|---|---|---|
| new | and earth | new | heavens | I am creating (Qal participle) | behold | For | |

| לֵב | עַל | תַעֲלֶינָה | וְלֹא | הָרִאשֹׁנוֹת | תִזָּכַרְנָה | וְלֹא | |
|---|---|---|---|---|---|---|---|
| heart | above | shall ascend | and not | the beginning time | shall be remembered | and not | |

Exodus 34:10 will now be considered and the differentiation which it makes between "bara" and "asah" explained. The word "asah" is used first and then the newness of the "marvels" is explained using the word "bara." The word "bara" is the word the KJV translates "have not been done." The negated verb "bara" indicates a meaning which the verb "asah" did not convey. Only line (2) of Exodus 34:10 below is given in the Hebrew.

KJV Exodus 34:10
(1) And he said, Behold, I make a covenant: (literally "I am cutting a covenant")
(2) before all thy people I will do (asah) marvels, such as have not been done (bara) in all the earth, nor in any nation: and all the people among which thou *art* shall see the work of the LORD: it *is* a terrible thing that I will do with thee.

| הָאָרֶץ | בְּכָל | נִבְרְאוּ | לֹא | אֲשֶׁר | נִפְלָאֹת | אֶעֱשֶׂה | עַמְּךָ | כָּל | נֶגֶד | (2) |
|---|---|---|---|---|---|---|---|---|---|---|
| the earth | in all | been created (bara) (Niphal perfect) | not | which | marvels | I shall do (asah) (Qal imperfect) | people | all of | before | |

The two words לֹא נִבְרְאוּ, which the KJV translated "have not been done," are the verb בָּרָא "bara" in the Niphal perfect following the negation לֹא "not." The Niphal is formed by adding the letter נ "nun" as a prefix, and expresses passive action. The "marvels" are produced by the actions of God. The "bara" indicates newness. The unspecified "marvels" are things which have not been done before. The use of the word "bara" in this passage is in contrast to the word "asah." This contrast indicates that "asah" does not include the new thing meaning of "bara." "Asah" does not convey the new thing uniqueness of some of the coming events. The uniqueness is conveyed by the use of "bara." The KJV translation also does not fully express the content of the verse. By using the verb "bara" this verse not only indicates the newness of the marvels but also indicates that they are things which only God (Yahweh) could do. They are more than new; they are marvels which others cannot do.

The Greek Septuagint text for Exodus 34:10 is shown below with one line translated into English.

Exodus 34:10
καὶ εἶπεν κύριος πρὸς Μωυσῆν ἰδοὺ ἐγὼ τίθημί σοι διαθήκην ἐνώπιον παντὸς τοῦ λαοῦ

σου ποιήσω ἔνδοξα ἃ οὐ γέγονεν ἐν πάσῃ τῇ γῇ καὶ ἐν παντὶ ἔθνει
    I will do  glories  which  not  been created  in  all  the  earth (land)

καὶ ὄψεται πᾶς ὁ λαὸς ἐν οἷς εἶ σύ τὰ ἔργα κυρίου ὅτι θαυμαστά ἐστιν ἃ ἐγὼ ποιήσω σοι
                                                                                                                                                            I will do

The verb ποιήσω (a form of ποιέω) translates "asah" and appears twice. The verb γέγονεν (a form of γίνομαι) translates "bara" and appears once. The use of different words indicates that the translators of the Septuagint considered "asah" and "bara" to not be equivalent. These same two Greek words appear in the Septuagint's translation of Genesis 2:4. The correspondence of these Greek words is shown by insertion into the KJV before the English words with which they correspond.

KJV Genesis 2:4

These *are* the generations of the heavens and of the earth when they were **created** (ἐγένετο a form of γίνομαι),
in the day that the LORD God **made** (ἐποίησεν a form of ποιέω) the earth and the heavens,

The Vulgate similarly considered "bara" and "asah" not equivalent and translated the words differently. In Exodus 34:10 below, the appropriate English translation has been inserted in brackets following the Latin verbs which are indicated in bold.

VUL Exodus 34:10   respondit Dominus ego inibo pactum videntibus cunctis signa **faciam** (do)

quae numquam **sunt visa** (were seen) super terram nec in ullis gentibus ut cernat populus

in cuius es medio opus Domini terribile quod **facturus sum** (will do).

Not all English translations follow the KJV in translating all three of these verbs using a form of the word "do." The table below summarizes the translations which are made, thereby indicating that the words are not considered equivalent. The KJV translation is acceptable as long as it is not used to assert that "asah" and "bara" are equivalent and interchangeable. That "asah" and "bara" are not equivalent has already been shown in other examples.

| Bible Version | Word translating the the first "asah" | Word translating the word "bara" | Word translating the second "asah" |
|---|---|---|---|
| Septuagint | A form of ποιέω Translates "asah" in Genesis 2:4 | A form of γίνομαι Translates "bara" in Genesis 2:4 | A form of ποιέω Translates "asah" in Genesis 2:4 |
| Vulgate | faciam (do) | sunt visa (were seen) | factors sum (will do) |
| ASV<br>NAS<br>RSV | do<br>perform<br>do | wrought<br>produced<br>wrought | do<br>perform<br>do |

In Isaiah 43:7, the words "bara," "asah," and "yatsar" are used in the same passage. The words are **not** used interchangeably. The words are used in a poetic progression. Isaiah 43:6 is included to provide context.

KJV Isaiah 43:6   I will say to the north, Give up; and to the south, Keep not back:
bring my sons from far, and my daughters from the ends of the earth;

KJV Isaiah 43:7   *Even* every one that is called by my name:
   (1)   for I have created (bara) him for my glory,
   (2)   I have formed (yatsar) him; yea,
   (3)   I have made (asah) him.

In Isaiah 43:7 there are three sequential statements referring to Israel. Within the sequence there is a progression in meaning. Statement (1) refers to the creation of Israel by the action of God. This statement uses the word "bara" which, in the Qal, is only used for actions of God. It emphasizes that Israel is a new thing and that Israel did not come into existence by natural means. The Exodus is the defining event in the creation of Israel, an event which was due to the action of God. Subsequently, there were forty years in the wilderness, a forming of the nation. Then there was the time in the land after crossing the Jordan, a making of the nation under David.

The progression in the sequential statements of the Hebrew poetic form indicates that "bara," "asah," and "yatsar" are not equivalent. The differences are exploited to expand the meaning. The net result of the three statements is to assert that all the events which had "formed," "made," and "created" Israel up to the time of Isaiah were under the sovereign control of God.

The sequential use of differences in words to expand the meaning of parallel lines can be illustrated by considering Psalm 1:1. There are three statements expressing the total description of "Blessed *is* the man..."

| KJV Psalm 1:1 | Blessed *is* the man | (1) | that walketh not | in the counsel | of the ungodly, |
|---|---|---|---|---|---|
| | | (2) | nor standeth | in the way | of sinners, |
| | | (3) | nor sitteth | in the seat | of the scornful. |

There is a sequence of physical action in the three numbered statements: walketh, standeth, sitteth. The use of these words in parallel sequential statements of similar poetic meaning does not indicate that these words are equivalent. They are not equivalent. This same conclusion is true for the other two sequences of three words: counsel, way, seat and ungodly, sinners, scornful. The difference in the meaning of the words is used to expand the meaning of the three parallel statements when considered in their entirety.

Another verse which uses "bara," "asah," and "yatsar" is Isaiah 45:7. Isaiah 45 is a prophetic passage where God speaks to, and of, Cyrus. The KJV verses Isaiah 45:4-7 are given below to show the pattern of the verse parallelism of successive statements. There is a repeated parallelism of the final statements of successive verses which have been italicized for clarity. Verse seven contains a parallelism where "yatsar" and "asah" are in parallel. "Bara" is used in contrast to both "yatsar" and "asah."

4   For Jacob my servant's sake, and Israel mine elect, I have even called thee by thy name:
    I have surnamed thee, *though thou hast not known me.*
5   I *am* the LORD, and *there is* none else, there is no God beside me:
    I girded thee, *though thou hast not known me:*
6   That they may know from the rising of the sun, and from the west, that *there is* none beside me.
    *I am the LORD, and there is none else.*
7   I form (yatsar) the light, and create (bara) darkness:
    I make (asah) peace,    and create (bara) evil:
    *I the LORD do* (asah) *all these things.*

Isaiah 45:7 is again shown below in the KJV, YLT and in the Hebrew. The information below was presented earlier and is repeated here as a convenience in completion of the treatment of Psalm 1:1 and Isaiah 45:7. The verbs in this passage are all participles ("ing" form) indicating continuing actions.

**KJV Isaiah 45:7**   I form (yatsar) the light, and create (bara) darkness:
                      I make (asah) peace,    and create (bara) evil:
                      I the LORD do (asah) all these *things*.

**YLT Isaiah 45:7**   Forming (yatsar) light, and preparing (bara) darkness,
                      Making (asah) peace, and preparing (bara) evil,
                      I {am} Jehovah, doing (asah) all these things.

| רָע | וּבוֹרֵא | שָׁלוֹם | עֹשֶׂה | חֹשֶׁךְ | וּבוֹרֵא | אוֹר | יוֹצֵר | Isaiah 45:7 |
|---|---|---|---|---|---|---|---|---|
| evil | and creating (bara) | peace | making (asah) | darkness | and creating | light | forming (yatsar) | |

| אֵלֶּה | כָּל | עֹשֶׂה | יְהוָה | אֲנִי |
|---|---|---|---|---|
| these | all | making (asah) | Yahweh | I |

In Isaiah 45:7 the parallelism of successive lines is:   (yatsar) "forming" parallel to (asah) "making"
                                                    and (bara) "creating" parallel to (bara) "creating."

Verse seven does not, in any way, indicate that "bara" is equivalent to "asah" or "yatsar." "Bara" has the connotation of a new thing. The summary of the final line does not use "bara." "Asah" is used for summarizing all the preceding actions because two of the actions ("asah" and "yatsar") do not include the connotation of a new thing. The restriction of the parallelism of "bara" to "bara" indicates that words "bara," "asah," and "yatsar" are not equivalent. The word אֲנִי "I" inserted at the beginning of the KJV parallel lines is not present in the Hebrew.

# More About "waw + noun--perfect verb," a Pluperfect Indicator

This section continues the study of Genesis 1:2 and supplements the analysis of Genesis 3:1-2 which was given on page 25. This section provides additional examples of "waw + noun--perfect verb" clauses. The topics are:

(1) Additional examples of "waw + noun--perfect verb" which refer to completed past events. These examples give a more complete illustration of the use of the "waw + noun--perfect verb." They also illustrate the use of the pluperfect to represent actions completed before the start of the narrative. The narratives use past tense verbs in the sequence of actions which they describe.

(2) A grammatical analysis of Genesis 1:2. This section will point out errors which are typically made in attempts to make the events of Genesis 1:2 concurrent with the events of Genesis 1:3.

(3) More about nominal clauses containing verbs. References are made to recent books analyzing the use, translation, and grammar of the "waw + noun--perfect verb" construction.

## (1) Additional examples of "waw + noun--perfect verb"

This section will present three additional examples of the use of a clause or sentence to provide background information and to introduce a narrative about a new subject. The discussion of Genesis 4:1 prepares for the discussion of Genesis 16:1-3 which follows.

The story of Eve and the serpent begins in Genesis 3:1 and concludes in Genesis 3:24 with God expelling Adam and Eve from the garden. Genesis 4:1 shifts to some time after the expulsion. The time interval is not stated. Genesis 4:1 provides the background information that Adam and Eve had had sexual relations. The introductory clause is of the form "waw + noun--perfect verb." The KJV of Genesis 4:1 is shown below with the Hebrew of the first part of the verse. The introductory clause is the first five Hebrew words.

KJV Genesis 4:1    And Adam knew Eve his wife; *(introductory "waw + noun--perfect verb" clause)*
and she conceived, and bare Cain, and said, I have gotten a man from the LORD.

| וַתֵּלֶד | וַתַּהַר | אִשְׁתּוֹ | חַוָּה | אֶת | יָדַע | וְהָאָדָם | Genesis 4:1 |
|---|---|---|---|---|---|---|---|
| and she bore | and she conceived | his wife | Eve | dir. obj. marker | had known (Qal perfect) | and Adam ("waw" + noun) | ← Translation |
| "waw" + imperfect verb | "waw" + imperfect verb | | | | | | |

The introductory clause places the prefixed noun "Adam" first in the sentence. The prefix is וְ meaning "and" or "now." After the introductory clause, the normal narrative sequence of "waw-consecutive" Hebrew verbs resumes with the verbs translated "and she conceived" and "and she bore." The amount of time which transpired between the initiation of sexual relations and the conception is not stated and cannot be inferred from the information in the text. It may have been months or years. The pluperfect translation "had known" (under the Hebrew) reflects the past background meaning of the "waw + noun--perfect verb." The translation "had known" is also made for this verse by Zevit in his book *The Anterior Construction In Classical Hebrew*.[23] This book describes the pluperfect meaning of the "waw + noun--perfect verb" construction and lists more than 100 examples.

A "Good English" translation of Genesis 4:1-2 would be:

"Good English" Genesis 4:1    And Adam had known his wife; and she conceived, and bore Cain
and said, I have gotten a man from the Lord.
"Good English" Genesis 4:2    And she again bore his brother Abel. And Able was . . . .

In the "Good English" translation the narrative begins with the וַתַּהַר which is a waw-consecutive of an imperfect verb. This construction has completed action meaning. The first part of Genesis 4:2 is given below to show that the first word of the next sentence is also a waw-consecutive of an imperfect verb, the usual beginning of sentences in a continuing past narrative.

KJV Genesis 4:2    And she again bare his brother Abel. And Abel was . . .

| הֶבֶל | וַיְהִי | הֶבֶל | אֶת | אָחִיו | אֶת | לָלֶדֶת | וַתֹּסֶף | Genesis 4:2 |
|---|---|---|---|---|---|---|---|---|
| Abel | and was | Abel | dir. obj. marker | his brother | dir. obj. marker | to bearing of | And she added (KJV "again bare") (waw-consecutive, a "waw" + Qal imperfect verb) | |

Another example is Genesis 16:1. Genesis 16:1-2 will be analyzed in detail starting with Genesis 16:1 to illustrate the function of the "waw + noun--perfect verb" structure to provide background information in Hebrew passages. The information provided is about conditions completed before the start of the following narrative. In this case, they are of long duration.

KJV Genesis 16:1　　　(1)　Now Sarai Abram's wife bare him no children:
　　　　　　　　　　　(2)　and she had an handmaid, an Egyptian, whose name *was* Hagar.

YLT Genesis 16:1　　　(1)　And Sarai, Abram's wife, hath not borne to him,
　　　　　　　　　　　(2)　and she hath an handmaid, an Egyptian, and her name {is} Hagar;

|  | לוֹ | יָלְדָה | לֹא | אַבְרָם | אֵשֶׁת | וְשָׂרַי | (1) | Genesis 16:1 |
|---|---|---|---|---|---|---|---|---|
|  | to him | had born (Qal perfect) | not | Abraham | wife of | And Sarai ("waw + noun") | | |

Genesis 16:1 is of the form "waw + noun--perfect verb," but is a little more complicated because the verb does not immediately follow as the second word. The sentence begins with "And Sarai," which is of the form "waw + noun." This is followed by a construct chain of two words which modify Sarai telling us who Sarai is. The verb יָלְדָה "had born" is a Qal perfect completed action verb that completes the "waw + noun--perfect verb" structure. The negation לֹא "not" precedes the verb.

The remainder of Genesis 16:1, line (2), consists of two verbless clauses which add information about Hagar. The verbless clauses completing Genesis 16:1 line (2) are shown below:

KJV Genesis 16:1　　　(2)　and she had an handmaid, an Egyptian, whose name *was* Hagar.
(verbless clauses)

| הָגָר | וּשְׁמָהּ | מִצְרִית | שִׁפְחָה | וְלָהּ | (2) | Genesis 16:1 |
|---|---|---|---|---|---|---|
| Hagar | and name of | Egyptian | a maid servant | and to her (KJV "and she had ") | | |

The "had" in "she had a handmaid" is a verb added in the KJV because a verb is expected in the English. Genesis 16:1 is similar to Genesis 1:2 where the initial "waw + noun--perfect verb" clause is followed by a verbless clause. In Genesis 1:2 the Hebrew verbless clause is literally "and darkness on face of deep." Notice that the Hebrew "not had born" in Genesis 16:1 is a condition which had been true for a long period of time. The KJV uses "bare" to translate the perfect verb, but the YLT uses "hath not borne." The KJV past tense "bare" does not correctly convey the long period of time for which "not had born" had been true.

A "Good English" translation of Genesis 16:1-2 would use the pluperfect to indicate the past-completed state of "having not born a child." Sara also possessed Hagar as a handmaid before the start of the narrative in Genesis 16:2. The verbless clauses are part of the background information of the conditions before the start of the narrative. The pluperfect "had not born" also indicates that this condition was in existence before the first past tense verb "said" of the narrative in "And Sarai said." The "waw + noun--perfect verb," which yields the translation "had not born" does not limit the time for which this condition had existed before the "And Sarai said." This is similarly true for Genesis 1:2. The "waw + noun--perfect verb" translated "And had existed" does not limit the amount of past time for which "And had existed" had been true.

"Good English" Genesis 16:1　　And Sarai Abram's wife had not born *a child* to him;
　　　　　　　　　　　　　　　　and she had a handmaid, an Egyptian, whose name *was* Hagar.
"Good English" Genesis 16:2　　And Sarai said to Abram, . . . .

The Hebrew for the first clause of Genesis 16:2 is now presented to show that the word order of this sentence starts with the "waw + imperfect verb" used in Hebrew narrative. This is difficult to illustrate from the English translations because the English changes the word order. The KJV places the subject noun before the verb for verses Genesis 16:1-3. In Hebrew the verb ("waw + imperfect verb") is the first word in Genesis 16:2.

KJV Genesis 16:2　　And Sarai said unto Abram, . . .

| אַבְרָם | אֶל | שָׂרַי | וַתֹּאמֶר | Genesis 16:2 |
|---|---|---|---|---|
| Abraham | onto | Sarai | And had said (KJV "And said") "waw" + Qal imperfect verb | |

This section will present one final example of the use of the "waw + noun--perfect verb" beginning a clause which provides background information and introduces a narrative about a new subject. Recall that Genesis 1:1-2 performs this function for the narrative which starts in Genesis 1:3. This example is the final preparation for a detailed study of the three clauses of Genesis 1:2.

The final example is Genesis 21:1. This verse was previously considered as an example of translation as done by the KJV (page 12). The KJV translators did not recognize the pluperfect meaning of the "waw + noun--perfect verb" sequence. The verse preceding Genesis 21:1 had concluded the story of Sarah, Abraham, and Abimelech. Genesis 21:1 shifts the point of view and provides the background information that the things that were promised in Genesis 18:14 have taken place. The Hebrew of Genesis 21:1 is correlated with the KJV translation below the Hebrew so as to correspond with the earlier example using this verse on page 12.

KJV Genesis 21:1    And the LORD visited Sarah as he had said, and the LORD did unto Sarah as he had spoken.

| | אָמַר | כַּאֲשֶׁר | שָׂרָה | אֵת | פָּקַד | וַיהוָה | (1) | **Genesis 21:1** |
|---|---|---|---|---|---|---|---|---|
| | he had said (Qal perfect) | as | Sarah | dir. obj. marker | visited (Qal perfect) | and the LORD ("waw"+ noun) | ← | KJV translation words |

| | דִּבֶּר | כַּאֲשֶׁר | לְשָׂרָה | יְהוָה | וַיַּעַשׂ | (2) | |
|---|---|---|---|---|---|---|---|
| | he had spoken (Piel perfect) | as | unto Sara | the Lord | and did "waw"+ Qal imperfect | ← | KJV translation words |

The introductory clause places the noun יְהוָה (Yahweh) first in the sentence prefixed by וְ "and." The perfect verb (visited) which follows the noun completes the "waw + noun--perfect verb" structure. The second verb of the clause (he had said) continues the background information and is not the start of a new narrative.

The normal narrative sequence of "waw-consecutive" Hebrew verbs resumes with the verb translated "and the LORD did" in the second line. The "waw-consecutive" verb is וַיַּעַשׂ = יַעַשׂ + וַ . The יַעַשׂ is a Qal imperfect verb which is prefixed by וַ "waw."

A "Good English" translation of Genesis 21:1-2 would use the pluperfect to indicate the reference to the completed past action "had visited." The pluperfect "had visited" represented the visiting as having been completed before the actions which are described using past tense verbs in the narrative which follows.

"Good English" Genesis 21:1    And the Lord (Yahweh) had visited Sarah as he had said,
                                and the LORD did unto Sarah as he had spoken.
"Good English" Genesis 21:2    And Sarah conceived, and bore Abraham . . . .

The Hebrew of the first clause of Genesis 21:2 is also presented. The purpose is to show that the word order of this verse also starts with the "waw" + imperfect verb used in Hebrew narrative. Again, this is difficult to illustrate from the KJV translation because the word order is changed. The KJV places the subject noun before the verb in the translation of Genesis 21:2. In Hebrew the first word is the "waw" + imperfect verb.

KJV Genesis 21:2    For Sarah conceived, and bare Abraham . . . .

| | לְאַבְרָהָם | שָׂרָה | וַתֵּלֶד | וַתַּהַר | **Genesis 21:2** |
|---|---|---|---|---|---|
| | to Abraham | Sarai | and bare "waw" + Qal imperfect | and had conceived "waw" + Qal imperfect verb | |

The next two verses similarly start with a "waw-consecutive" Qal imperfect verb.

KJV Genesis 21:3    And Abraham called . . . .      Literally in the Hebrew "And had called Abraham . . . ."
KJV Genesis 21:4    And Abraham circumcised . . . .  Literally in the Hebrew "And had circumcised . . . ."

Now, Genesis 1:2 can be analyzed in greater detail because of the preparation just completed.

## (2) A grammatical analysis of Genesis 1:2

**This is a difficult section, but is sufficient for pointing out errors in similarly difficult grammatical analyses which are offered to justify a Young Earth.** For Genesis 1:2 shown below, each of the three clauses have their sequence of word types shown below the translation:

|  | (1) **And the earth** / | **had existed** / | **"tohu"** / | **and "bohu"** |
|---|---|---|---|---|
| A complex nominal clause: | "waw + noun" / | perfect verb / | noun / | "waw + noun" |
|  | (2) **and darkness** / | **on** / | **the surface of** / | **the deep** |
| A verbless nominal clause: | "waw + noun" / | prep. / | noun / | noun |
|  | (3) **the Spirit of** / | **God / moving** / | **over / the surface of** / | **the water(s).** |
| A verbless nominal clause: | "waw + noun" / | noun / participle / | prep./ noun / | noun |

Clause (1) is the only clause which contains a perfect completed action verb. All three clauses start with a noun or with a "waw + noun." A "waw + noun" (a "waw" prefixed to a noun) is one word in the Hebrew. For clause (1) the translation "had existed" conveys that the Earth has existed before the start of the narrative in Genesis 1:3. As with the example of Genesis 16:1 (page 38) the "waw + noun--perfect verb" construction places no limit on how long the Earth had existed in the state described as "tohu and bohu." In the example of Genesis 3:1 (page 25) the "waw + noun--perfect verb" construction placed no limit on how long the serpent had existed or how long the serpent had been "more subtil" before the "and he said . . ." which started the narrative.

Clauses (2) and (3) describe conditions which exist at the same time as the condition described by clause (1). This is because (2) does not have a verb and (3) has a verb in the "ing" participle form. Hebrew clauses like these are governed in their "when" by the verb of the clause or the sentence to which they refer. In this case the governing verb is the "had existed" in clause (1). The "had existed" is an action which is completed before the KJV "And God said . . ." of Genesis 1:3. A "waw" prefixed noun followed by a perfect verb is a construction used to provide background information and to start a narrative.

Having just studied three examples, the reader may be surprised to learn that advocates of a Young Earth often try to deny the demonstrated function of the "waw + noun--perfect verb." This is often done by arguing in the following sequence: [24]

(A) The first clause of Genesis 1:2 is a nominal clause. Then *Gesenius' Hebrew Grammar* [25] says that a nominal clause represents a time contemporaneous with the sentence to which it refers.

(B) The first clause of Genesis 1:2 refers to Genesis 1:1, so it is contemporaneous with Genesis 1:1.

(C) Then, after Genesis 1:2 and Genesis 1:1 are asserted to be contemporaneous, Exodus 20:11 is used to bring the events of both verses within the first creative time.

Item (A) and (B) of the foregoing argument were directed at removing the time interval between Genesis 1:1 and Genesis 1:2. This was in opposition to the view which accounted for the fossils as having appeared in the time interval. A view exemplified by the 1917 Scofield Reference Bible which contained a footnote for Genesis 1:1 which read in part: "The first creative act refers to the dateless past, and gives scope for all the geologic ages."

Even if Genesis 1:1 and Genesis 1:2 are considered contemporaneous, the failure of argument (C) results in an old Earth and an old Universe. Recall that Exodus 20:11 has already been shown to not be appropriate for this use because the word "*in*" does not appear in the Hebrew and because "bara" and "asah" are not equivalent. (See page 28.)

This study does not hold that Genesis 1:2 is contemporaneous with Genesis 1:1. The action of the "waw + noun--perfect verb" of Genesis 1:2 is considered to represent a disjunctive initial statement relating the background conditions necessary for understanding the events of Genesis 1:3 which starts with "And God said . . .." The term "disjunctive" generally means that either the scene and participants have changed, or the action being described has changed, or a parenthetical explanatory clause has been inserted. Argument (A) above requires that Genesis 1:2 be considered an explanatory sentence relating to Genesis 1:1.

Argument (A) fails to differentiate between nominal clauses having a perfect verb and those which do not. The *Gesenius' Hebrew Grammar*, dating from 1909, does not clearly distinguish between nominal clauses containing a perfect completed action verb and those which do not. The definition used for a nominal clause was any clause which did not begin with a verb. A good understanding of the "waw + noun--perfect verb" construction and its uses has only been achieved within the last forty years.

*Gesenius' Hebrew Grammar*, in section 141c, footnote 2, acknowledges that Genesis 1:2 is not a pure noun clause. Section 141i states that " הָיְתָה is used here really only for the purpose of referring to past time . . ." and then refers the reader to Genesis 3:1 as an example.

Genesis 3:1 is the example about Eve and the serpent which was considered in detail on page 25. It was shown there that the "waw + noun--perfect verb" clause referred to events completed before the start of the following narrative. The "waw + noun--perfect verb" of Genesis 3:1 is cited by Thomas O. Lambdin as an example of the use of a disjunctive "waw," which is "*Terminative or Initial*, indicating the completion of one episode or the beginning of another."[26] The examples cited are Genesis 3:1, 4:1, 16:1 and 21:1, the same verses which have been studied in this section, all of which use the "waw + noun--perfect verb" construction.

Genesis 1:2 is both terminal and initial. The creation of Genesis 1:1 is completed. In Genesis 1:2 both the scene and the participants change. The scene has been changed from the entire Universe to "the face of the deep." The participant has changed from God (Elohim) to "the spirit of God (Elohim)." The action also changes from creation (bara) to "moving over face of waters." Genesis 1:2 is also initial. It is a statement relating the background conditions necessary for understanding the events of Genesis 1:3.

Now the pluperfect translation of Genesis 1:2 will be discussed with reference to both older grammars and the more recent improved understanding of the Hebrew verb and its use.

### (3) More about nominal clauses containing verbs

This study has translated Genesis 1:2 as "And the Earth had existed . . . ." The pluperfect indicates that the earth "had existed" before the "And God said" of Genesis 1:3. The quote below, from *A Treatise on the Use of the Tenses in Hebrew and Some Other Syntactical Questions*, relates to the pluperfect translation of the Hebrew "waw + imperfect verb" form. In this quote "imperf." indicates "imperfect," "Plupf." indicates "pluperfect," "pf." indicates "perfect" and ו is the Hebrew "waw".

> ". . . the imperf. with ו is, in the first place, certainly not the usual idiom chosen by Hebrew writers for the purpose of expressing a Plupf.,: their usual habit, when they wish to do this, is to interpose the subject between the conjunction and the verb, which then lapses into the perfect, a form which we know, §16, allows scope for a plupf. signification, if context requires it[2]."

Footnote two ([2]) of the above quote is:
> "[2] It will be understood that the pf. in this position does not always bear a plupf. significaton: it is often so placed simply for the purpose of giving emphasis to the subject (see further App.I).

S. R. Driver, *Treatise on the Use of the Tenses in Hebrew and Some Other Syntactical Questions*, Oxford At the Clarendon Press, England, 1881, page 102. This is currently available as a reprint.[27]

Driver's footnote two ([2]) is considered to be very seldom, if at all, applicable by Niccacci and Zevit in their writings about the "waw + noun--perfect verb." They do not consider the "waw + noun--perfect verb" construction to be a "nominal clause" which refers to another clause to determine its time of action. Niccacci has introduced the term "complex nominal clause" to distinguish these clauses from the verbless nominal clauses. These writings will be referenced below. Both authors indicate Genesis 1:2 to be a reference to past action completed before the start of Genesis 1:3.

Genesis 1:2 and the examples we have presented are of the structure:

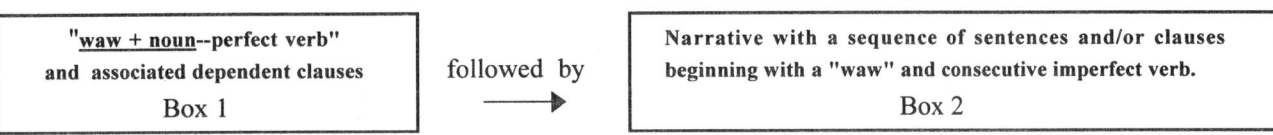

The examples have shown that the conditions referred to by the words and clauses in Box 1 are conditions completed before the start of the narrative in Box 2. These conditions are also the conditions which exist at the start of the narrative of Box 2. In the jargon of the grammars, these conditions at the start of the narrative are contemporaneous with the first sentence of the following narrative. What is generally overlooked, or studiously ignored, is that these same conditions may have existed for a long time before the start of the narrative.

The Hebrew verb form does not limit the time of the existence of these conditions. In the examples, the conditions clearly had existed for a long time before the start of the narratives which followed. Because the conditions are still in existence when the narrative starts, they also describe the conditions at the start of the narrative.

The function of the "waw + noun--perfect verb" to relate conditions existing before the start of a biblical narrative has been the subject of an number of studies which have solidly established the meaning and use. Several of these studies will now be identified for reader reference. The "waw + noun--perfect verb" construction is referred to by different nomenclatures in these studies.

Alveriero Niccacci has presented an extensive discussion of the "waw + noun--perfect verb" construction in his book *The Syntax of the Verb in Classical Hebrew Prose.*[28] In this book Niccacci describes the "waw + noun--perfect verb" construction as "WAW-x-QATAL," and the clause which contains this construction a "complex nominal clause." The QATAL represents the "perfect verb." In other publications he has also described the "waw + noun--perfect verb" as a "finite verb in second position." An example of this latter nomenclature is shown below.

" . . . the sentence with the finite verb in the second position is of a completely different kind from the one with the finite verb in the first position. "

> Alveriero Niccacci, " On the Hebrew Verbal System," page 121, In *Biblical Hebrew and Discourse Linguistics*, Robert D. Bergen Ed., Summer Institute of Linguistics, Eisenbrauns, Winona Lake, IN, 1994.

The phrase, "the one with the finite verb in the first position," refers to the normal verb first construction of the sentences of a continuing narrative. The existence of a real grammatical difference in the two structures is being emphasized. The above statement has real relevance for the interpretation of Genesis 1:2. The Young Earth interpretation of Genesis 1:2 assigns no significance to the presence of the "finite verb." Niccacci provides analysis showing that Genesis 1:1-2 describe conditions existing before the Genesis 1:3 in both the referenced book and in the *Biblical Hebrew and Discourse Linguistics* proceedings.[29] The *Biblical Hebrew and Discourse Linguistics* proceedings provide an interesting overview of translation and the still-to-be-resolved issues of Hebrew syntax, and is highly recommended.

Ziony Zevit in *The Anterior Construction In Classical Hebrew* refers to the "waw + noun--perfect verb" construction as the "anterior construction."*[23]* The "anterior" refers to the function of this construction to provide pluperfect reference. More than 100 examples are listed. Zevit lists Genesis 1:1-2 as indicating actions and conditions existing before the start of Genesis 1:3.

> Ziony Zevit, *The Anterior Construction In Classical Hebrew* (The Society of Biblical Literature, 1998).

There is another pluperfect indicator of significance which appears in Genesis One. This is the pattern of:

(1) First telling of the beginning and the completed result of a series of actions.
(2) Then returning to a time before the result adding informative detail. This informative detail is a pluperfect reference to events which have taken place before the already stated completed result.

The pluperfect meaning of this pattern is discussed on page 98 in the analysis of the translation and time sequence of the actions of Genesis 1:11-12. A quote from Driver's *A Treatise on the Use of the Tenses in Hebrew and Some Other Syntactical Questions* is made and explained there to establish the correctness of the pluperfect translation. The above described pattern of pluperfect indication also occurs in Genesis 1:16-18, and is discussed on pages 106-107 in the analysis and translation of these verses.

This same pattern is discussed by Zevit in *The Anterior Construction In Classical Hebrew* on page 69. Zevit describes the Hebrew sequence as being of the form: " and he-fell   John    and he-pushed him  Max."
　　　　　　　　　　　　　　　　　　　　　　　　　　　　**Hebrew verb    noun    Hebrew verb    noun**

The above word sequence example includes two Hebrew verbs. The "and he-pushed him Max" is a pluperfect reference to the antecedent cause of John falling. In the examples which Zevit presents, the Hebrew verbs are the "waw-consecutive" imperfect verbs of ordinary narrative discourse.

## More About "Tohu" and "Bohu"

Earlier in this study verses were reviewed which contained both "tohu" and "bohu." The oldest known translation of these words is that of the Septuagint, a translation of the five Books of Moses into Greek. For Genesis, this translation is dated by some to about 300 B.C. The Hebrew "erets" is translated by the Greek word γη pronounced "ge." The first clause of the Greek of Genesis 1:2 is shown below.[30]

**Genesis 1:2** ἡ δὲ γῆ ἦν ἀόρατος καὶ ἀκατασκεύαστος . . . .
The but, now land was unseen and unformed
(KJV "earth")

"γη" has meanings of ground, land, and earth and is the source of the "ge" in the English word "geology." The Greek words translating "tohu and bohu" are ἀόρατος καὶ ἀκατασκεύαστος.
unseen and unformed
The question is, "Why unseen?"

The answer can be found in correctly reading the word "erets" and the word "γη" as land or ground. In Genesis 1:9 God commands "the dry" to appear. This indicates that "the dry" had not been in view before the command. The word יַבָּשָׁה "dry" is used in 14 verses, seven of which refer to the "dry" on which the sea was crossed during the Exodus or the crossing of the Jordan. As a consequence, "dry" is considered to refer to land which has been under water and which has become dry.[19] "The dry" is then specifically given the name "erets" which the KJV translates "dry land." The meaning of "erets" must be "dry land" because inclusion of water is excluded by the context of the passage. "Erets" is thus restricted to its meaning of "land," and the planet Earth meaning of the word "erets" is excluded.

Before the "dry land" appears only water is seen, no land. Because the "dry land" is not seen until Genesis 1:9, the Septuagint translates ἀόρατος "unseen." ἀόρατος is the Greek word which translates "tohu." This translation is directly derivable from the later appearance of dry land in Genesis 1:9.

The Greek word translating "bohu" is ἀκατασκεύαστος which means "unformed." Prior to Genesis 1:9 the land is "unformed" because it was covered with water. This is consistent with the later appearance of dry land in Genesis 1:9. The meaning of the word "erets" is land or ground and not the planet Earth. The ancient world at the time of Moses and the time of the Septuagint translation did not have a planetary view; the concept of the Earth hanging in space and circling the sun was unknown to them.

Support for this understanding of Genesis 1:2 is found in *Antiquities of the Jews* by Josephus, written about 100 A.D.[31] This requires a careful translation of the relevant part of *Antiquities of the Jews*. In explaining Genesis 1:2, the Greek text describing and interpreting Genesis 1:1 easily translates to:

In the beginning God created the heaven and the earth,

The Greek words which follow and by which Josephus interpreted Genesis 1:2 are:

ταμτες δε υπο οψιςν ομκ ερχομενες αλλα βαθελ μεν κρυπτομεμες σκοτει
this but from under sight not appearing but rather deep on the being covered by darkness
other hand

The first word ταμτες is a pronoun of feminine gender meaning "this" and referring to the prior word of feminine gender translated Earth in the first verse. In the Greek "this" does not refer to the "heaven" because "heaven" is of masculine gender. The literal translation of the Greek by this author (Whitefield), including the first verse, is:

In the beginning God created the heaven and the earth,
but this (i.e., the land) not coming into sight from under, but rather darkness covering the deep, . . . .

The "from under" would appear to refer to the "deep," normally taken to be the world ocean.

Note: The translation of the Greek shown above does not agree with the translation of Whiston shown on the next page.

Whiston omits the words translated "deep" and "from under." The verbs are not translated as participles and the word "when" is inserted which is not in the Greek. His translation of these words appears to be a rendering of his view of the text rather than a direct word-for-word translation.

Whiston:[32] "But when the earth did not come into sight, but was covered with thick darkness, . . ."

Another translation of *Antiquities of the Jews* is that of Thackery in the *Loeb Classical Library*, 1930, page 15. This translation reads:

"The earth had not come into sight, but was hidden in the thick darkness, . . .."

Another explanation is that of Targum Onkelos (300-400 A.D. or earlier). The Targums are explanatory paraphrases of the Hebrew in the Aramaic language, analogous to our Living Bible. The Targum Onkelos as translated by Etheridge[33] in 1862 paraphrases Genesis 1:2 as:

"And the earth was waste and empty, and darkness on the face of the deep . . .."

A more recent translation replaces "waste" with the word "desolate."[34]

The next major translation to consider is the Latin Vulgate. The first part of Genesis 1:2 translates, "However the Earth was empty and unoccupied."

**VUL Genesis 1:2**   . . . terra   autem   erat   inanis   et   vacua ,   et tenebrae super faciem abyssi . . .
   Earth   however   was   empty   and   unoccupied, . . .

The words translating "tohu and bohu" are:   **inanis**   **et**   **vacua**
   empty or void   and   empty, unoccupied or without something

The words "inanis" and "vacua" are nearly synonymous. If the land is "empty" or "without something," the question which arises is, "What is missing?" An answer to the "what" in this question can be found in the Jerusalem Targum.[35] The translated Jerusalem Targum reads:

In wisdom (be-hukema) the Lord created.
And the earth was vacancy and desolation,
and solitary of the sons of men, and void of every animal;
and the Spirit of mercies from before the Lord breathed upon the face of the waters.

The next major translation to consider is that of John Calvin.[36] Calvin's Latin version is thought to have been based upon the prior version of Leo Juda printed in Zurich in 1543. The second verse of both versions are printed below.

Leo Juda:

Terra autem erat **desolate et inanis,**
tenebraeque erant in superficie voraginis: et Spiritus Dei agitabat sese in superficie aquarum.

John Calvin:

Terra autem erat **informis et inanis,**
tenebraeque erant in superficie voraginis: et Spiritus Dei agitabat se in superficie aquarum.

These translations differ in that the word "tohu" is translated "desolate" by Leo Juda and "informis" by Calvin. Both translations differ from the "inanis" the Vulgate used for "tohu." "Desolate" agrees with the Jerusalem Targum quoted above and with the general meaning of "tohu" found earlier in the study of Jeremiah 4:23-28 and Isaiah 34:8-12. Calvin's "informis" which translates "unformed" is consistent with the "unseen" of the Septuagint because the dry land "erets" does not appear until Genesis 1:9. Being covered by water, the visible land "erets" has not yet been formed.

The relevant portion of Calvin's commentary on "tohu and bohu" is given below. The first six words have been purposely inserted in Latin from Calvin's translation. The Latin words are the words which Calvin used in his translation and in the commentary. Calvin wrote the commentary in Latin. John King, in translating the commentary, inserts the KJV "And the earth was without form and void" as a translation of "Terra autem erat informis et inanis." This could lead the English reader to think that Calvin endorsed the "formless" of the later versions and not understand the remainder of the comment about "tohu" and "bohu." The actual Hebrew words have also been reinserted because the translation represented them as whwt, (tohu), and whwb (bohu)." The English is from the commentary translation of John King.[37]

> Terra autem erat informis et inanis, "I shall not be very solicitous about the exposition of these two epithets, תהו ,"tohu," and בהו ,"bohu." The Hebrews use them when they designate anything empty and confused, or vain, and nothing worth. Undoubtedly Moses placed them both in opposition to all those created objects which pertain to the form, the ornament and the perfection of the world. Were we now to take away, I say, from the earth all that God added after the time here alluded to, then we should have this rude and unpolished, or rather shapeless chaos."

Calvin alludes to the difficulty of translating "tohu and bohu" but skillfully sidesteps the issue. Controversy over the meaning of "tohu and bohu" was not of central importance to the Reformation. Calvin considers the "tohu" to describe the condition of the Earth before the subsequent additions described by later verses. Consequently, it is clear that in his view the land has not yet appeared and is as yet "unformed." There is nothing unreasonable about this meaning conceptually when the consideration of Genesis 1:9 is included, except that it **does not correctly translate "tohu."** The passages defining "tohu and bohu" do not use the words in a description of not being formed. They use the words to describe a condition of being uninhabited and not well-suited for human habitation. The uses of "tohu" without "bohu" also do not describe the condition of not being formed. The uses of "tohu" describe a lack of value or utility to human life. "Tohu and bohu" also do not refer to "chaos" as we understand the word.

With Calvin, in 1543, the planetary view of the Earth has come into general acceptance. This view was given acceptance after the voyages of Columbus. Later in his commentary on Genesis, Calvin admits to holding a planetary view as is indicated by the sentence quoted below:

> "We indeed are not ignorant, that the circuit of the heavens is finite,
> and that the earth, like a little globe, is placed in the centre."

With the acceptance of the planetary view, the interpretation of "erets" in Genesis 1:2 as meaning "land," "ground," or "country" declined. The translation of "erets" as earth is present in the Wycliffe translation of 1390. Present day understanding of the Old Testament is hampered by the present, almost exclusive, use of the word "earth" to refer to the entire planet as a whole.

A sequence of English translations is presented below. The subject of interest is the transition from "unformed" to "formless" for the translation of "tohu." The sequence of translations is:

**(1) Wycliffe (1390) before the planetary view following Columbus in 1492.**

> "Forsothe the erthe was **idel and voide,** and derkness weren on the face of depthe:
> And the Spiryte of the Lord was borun on the watris."

**(2) Tyndale (1530)**

> "The earth was **void and empty,** and darkness was on the deep,
> And the spirit of God moved upon the water."

**(3) KJV (1611) where "without form" replaces Calvin's "unformed."**

> "And the earth was **without form, and void;** and darkness *was* upon the face of the deep.
> And the Spirit of God moved upon the face of the waters."

**And the present translations:**

NIV Genesis 1:2 Now the earth was **formless and empty**.
NAS Genesis 1:2 And the earth was **formless and void,**
RSV Genesis 1:2 The earth was **without form and void,**
NKJ Genesis 1:2 The earth was **without form, and void;**
NLT Genesis 1:2 The earth was **empty, a formless mass** cloaked in darkness.
YLT Genesis 1:2 The earth hath existed **waste and void,**

Notice that the translations "without form" and "formless" are **not** equivalent to "unformed." Neither of these words can represent the view that the "dry land" cannot be seen because it has not yet emerged above the water covering the surface of planet Earth.

The difficulty in translating the word "tohu" is illustrated in the table below which shows translations from six different English versions of the Bible.

## Translations of תֹהוּ "tohu"   Strong's # 8414 תֹהוּ tohuw (to'-hoo)

| VERSES | KJV | NIV | NAS | NKJV | YLT | NLT |
|---|---|---|---|---|---|---|
| Gen. 1:2 | without form | formless | formless | without form | waste | empty |
| Deut. 32:10 | waste | waste | waste | wasteland | void | empty |
| 1Sam.12:21 | vain things | useless idols | futile things | empty things | vain things | worthless idols |
| Job 6:18 | nothing | wasteland | nothing | nowhere | emptiness | nothing |
| Job 12:24 | wilderness | waste (*land*) | waste (*land*) | wilderness | vacancy | wasteland |
| Job 26:7 | empty place | empty space | empty space | empty space | desolation | empty space |
| Ps. 107:40 | wilderness | trackless waste (*land*) | pathless waste (*land*) | wilderness | vacancy | wastelands |
| Isa. 24:10 | confusion | ruined (*city*) | chaos (*city of*) | confusion | emptiness | chaos |
| Isa. 29:21 | naught | false testimony | meaningless arguments | empty (*words*) | emptiness | lies |
| Isa. 34:11 | confusion | chaos | desolation | confusion | vacancy | chaos |
| Isa. 40:17 | vanity | worthless | meaningless | worthless | emptiness | emptiness |
| Isa. 40:23 | vanity | nothing | meaningless | useless | emptiness | nothing |
| Isa. 41:29 | confusion | confusion | emptiness | confusion | emptiness | empty |
| Isa. 44:9 | vanity | worthless | futile | useless | emptiness | foolish |
| Isa. 45:18 | vain | empty | waste place | vain | empty | empty chaos |
| Isa. 45:19 | vain | vain | waste place | vain | vain | for something I did not plan to give |
| Isa. 49:4 | nought | in vain | nothing | nothing | emptiness | - - - - |
| Isa. 59:4 | vanity | empty (*arguments*) | confusion | empty (*words*) | emptiness | lies |
| Jer. 4:23 | without form | formless | formless | without form | waste | empty |

# More About "Haya" Translated "Became"

The verb הָיָה "haya" appears in Genesis 1:2 as הָיְתָה "hay'eta" which is a Qal perfect completed action form. Before considering the translation of הָיְתָה "hay'eta" as "became," three verses will be reviewed to provide a basis for the study. This study will not advocate the translation "became" and will not consider any of the non-grammatical reasons which have been advanced to support such a translation.

First, it is important to know that the KJV does translate forms of the root verb הָיָה "haya" as "became" 36 times and as "become" another 36 times. The KJV translates הָיְתָה "hay'eta," the form of "haya" used in Genesis 1:2, as "became" in four verses. The KJV also translates הָיְתָה as "it came to pass" in two verses and translates using the word "become" in seven verses. Therefore, the translation of the verb הָיְתָה as "became" in Genesis 1:2 cannot be conclusively excluded. One example of the translation of "haya" as "became" is seen in Genesis 19:26, in the story of Lot.

KJV Genesis 19:26  But his wife looked back from behind him, and she **became** a pillar of salt.

**Genesis 19:26** וַתַּבֵּט אִשְׁתּוֹ מֵאַחֲרָיו וַתְּהִי נְצִיב מֶלַח

but had looked | his wife | from behind | and she became | pillar of | salt

The verb וַתְּהִי is a waw-consecutive imperfect form of the verb הָיָה (haya). This form has the meaning of the perfect completed action. The words "pillar" and "salt" are two nouns in the construct sequence. The construct sequence acts like the word "of" which does not exist in Hebrew. This verse is one of more than 15 verses where "haya" is translated "became" and where it is not followed by a phrase or word prefixed with a preposition. This fact will be important later.

Exodus 9:24 is an example of הָיְתָה "hay'eta" translated "became." Exodus 9:24 provides a good example because it uses three forms of "haya" in the same verse. The first form is וַיְהִי translated in the KJV as "so there was." The word וַיְהִי is most often translated by the KJV as "and it came to pass." In alternative translations given below the Hebrew of Exodus 9:24, וַיְהִי is twice translated "and it came to pass" with no change in the meaning of the verse. Exodus 9:23 is included to provide context for the alternative translations of Exodus 9:24 shown below.

KJV Exodus 9:23  And Moses stretched forth his rod toward heaven: and the LORD sent thunder and hail, and the fire ran along upon the ground; and the LORD rained hail upon the land of Egypt.

KJV Exodus 9:24  So there was hail, and fire mingled with the hail, very grievous, such as there was none like it in all the land of Egypt since it **became** a nation.

**Exodus 9:24** וַיְהִי בָרָד וְאֵשׁ מִתְלַקַּחַת בְּתוֹךְ הַבָּרָד כָּבֵד מְאֹד

so there was ( KJV ) | hail | and fire | mingled | in midst | the hail | grievous | much
and there came to pass — Alternative 1
and there came to be — Alternative 2

אֲשֶׁר לֹא הָיָה כָמֹהוּ בְּכָל אֶרֶץ מִצְרַיִם מֵאָז הָיְתָה לְגוֹי

such as | not | had existed (KJV "was") | like it | in all | land of | Egypt | since | had become or KJV "became" | to nation

The second הָיָה "haya" in Exodus 9:24 is translated "had existed" (KJV "was"). The KJV translates this same form of "haya" as "is become" in Genesis 3:22: "And the LORD God said, Behold, the man הָיָה **is become** as one of us, to know good and evil: . . ."

The הָיָה is a Qal perfect completed action form. "Is become" actually expresses completed action even though it uses the present tense "is." The translation "become" would not be appropriate in Genesis 3:22, but "has come to pass" is appropriate. The third "haya" in Exodus 9:24 is the word הָיְתָה "hay'eta," translated "became" by the KJV. The word הָיְתָה is the same Qal perfect feminine singular verb used in Genesis 1:2.

In Exodus 9:24 the KJV translates הָיְתָה "became," and this study translates הָיְתָה "had become." The "had become" more explicitly represents the completed action meaning of the verb. The word לְגוֹי ( לְגוֹי = לְ + גוֹי ) which follows "became" must also be considered. The word גוֹי "nation" is prefixed by the preposition לְ "le" meaning "to," "for," and other meanings. The opponents of the translation of הָיְתָה as "became" often admit the word can mean "became" because KJV translates הָיְתָה as "became" four times and "become" seven times. They then assert that this translation is reasonable only if a following word is prefixed by לְ as in Exodus 9:24. This asserted restriction is contradicted by the first example of Genesis 19:26 where the KJV translates a form of "haya" as "became" when not followed by לְ. There are more than 15 examples of a form of "haya" translated "became" when not followed by לְ or by any other preposition.

There is now sufficient background for discussing the translation of הָיְתָה "hay'eta" as "became" in Genesis 1:2. The examples have established that the KJV does translate "haya" as "became." The question, which must still be answered, is "Should הָיְתָה "hay'eta" be translated "became" in Genesis 1:2?"

The view that "haya" should be translated "became" in Genesis 1:2 is based on the observation that the word "haya" is often translated "become" or "became" throughout the Old Testament. This leads to the assertion that it is reasonable, and in fact desirable, to translate the word "haya" as "became" in Genesis 1:2. The previous examples have established that this is grammatically reasonable. The 36 times that "haya" is translated "became" by the KJV provide additional evidence for the reasonableness of the "became" translation. What is often not noted is that the translation "it came to pass" is also reasonable and leads to the same result. An argument against the translation "became" is not sufficient. "It came to pass" or equivalent must also be shown to be not reasonable or not possible.

As referenced earlier, the KJV translates the verb in Genesis 1:2 as "it came to pass" in two verses. The verses are Jeremiah 52:3 and 2 Kings 24:20. The verb also occurs in Exodus 16:13. It could have been translated "and it came to pass" there as well and correctly express the meaning of the verse. The KJV translates "haya," in the verb form וַיְהִי, as "and it came to pass" 320 times. Understanding the frequency of this use is hampered because there is no specific Strong's number for this form. The verb וַיְהִי is vowel marked as a "waw-consecutive Qal imperfect" which translates as the completed action. In many cases וַיְהִי appears at the beginning of a sentence and is translated "and it came to pass." The "and it came to pass" indicates that there has been an interval of time. Often the information conveyed is:

1. There has been a time interval of unstated length.
2. Events have occurred which may or may not be stated.
3. A new situation exists differing from that existing before this sentence.

In other words, a previously existing situation or set of conditions have "become" different. "And it came to pass" clearly conveys the sense of "become" or "became." The meaning "become" is found in the lexicons for "haya." What is often not stressed is the great number of times the word has this sense of meaning.

Jeremiah 52:3 and Exodus 16:13 provide information regarding the translation of הָיְתָה as "it came to pass." For Jeremiah 52:3 only the first line of the Hebrew is shown below.

KJV Jeremiah 52:3   For through the anger of the LORD it came to pass in Jerusalem and Judah, till he had cast them out from his presence, that Zedekiah rebelled against the king of Babylon.

| Jeremiah 52:3 | כִּי | עַל | אַף | יְהוָה | הָיְתָה | בִּירוּשָׁלַם | וִיהוּדָה |
|---|---|---|---|---|---|---|---|
| | For | through | anger of | Yahweh | it came to pass | in Jerusalem | and Judah |

This shows הָיְתָה translated "it came to pass" when the verb is not the first word of the sentence. Exodus 16:13 is instructive regarding the limits of the deductions which can be made from the KJV about the translation of הָיְתָה. The KJV does not translate הָיְתָה as "it came to pass" but this translation is clearly reasonable and possible. Exodus 16:12 is included to provide context.

KJV Exodus 16:12    I have heard the murmurings of the children of Israel: speak unto them, saying,
At even ye shall eat flesh, and in the morning ye shall be filled with bread;
and ye shall know that I *am* the LORD your God.

KJV Exodus 16:13

(1)    And it came to pass, that at even the quails came up, and covered the camp:

Three translations of Exodus 16:13 line (2) are shown below for comparison.

| | | |
|---|---|---|
| KJV (2) | and . . . . . . . . . . . | in the morning the dew lay round about the host (*camp*). |
| Alternative (2) | and it came to pass | in the morning a coating of the dew around the camp |
| YLT (2) | and . . . . . . . . . . . | in the morning there hath been the lying of dew round about the camp, |

Exodus 16:13 (1) וַיְהִי בָעֶרֶב וַתַּעַל הַשְּׂלָו וַתְּכַס אֶת הַמַּחֲנֶה

And it came to pass,  in evening  that came up  the quail  and covered  dir. obj. marker  the camp (KJV "camp")

(2) וּבַבֹּקֶר הָיְתָה שִׁכְבַת הַטַּל סָבִיב לַמַּחֲנֶה

and in morning  it came to pass  a coating of (KJV "lay")  the dew  around  the camp (KJV "host")

In Exodus 16:12 the events of the evening and the morning of the next day are foretold. Events which had not been the normal experience take place. An alternative translation of line (2) is included which translates הָיְתָה as "it came to pass." This alternative translation (2) expresses the same meaning as the KJV and repeats the style of the line (1). The KJV inexplicably translates the word מַחֲנֶה (prefixed by הַ ) as "camp" in the first line and as "host" in the second line. In the second line מַחֲנֶה is prefixed by לְ. The KJV does not translate the verb הָיְתָה. The YLT translates הָיְתָה as "hath been" which is a completed action equivalent to "had been" or "had existed."

The study of Exodus 16:13 has applicability to the possible translation of הָיְתָה as "became" in Genesis 1:2. If הָיְתָה was translated as "came to pass" in Genesis 1:2, the verse would read:

"And the Earth came to pass tohu and bohu . . ."

or, in better English:

"And the Earth came to be tohu and bohu . . ."

The inclusion of "it came to pass" which indicates a sense of becoming as a possible translation of "haya" shows the meaning "became" is more common than generally acknowledged by those opposed to the "became" translation.

This study does not advocate the translation "became."

# More About Ex Nihilo

The traditional Christian and Hebrew view is that Genesis 1:1 is an independent sentence. Christianity has additional scriptural evidences for this view in the Gospels and the other books of the New Testament. These additional evidences refer to the Creation and to the existence of God before the Creation. In this study's analysis of Genesis 1:1, the words have been interpreted as in the traditional Christian and Hebrew interpretations. The word "in beginning" is considered a noun in the absolute state. A noun in the absolute state functions like an English noun. "Bara," the following verb, is considered a Qal perfect completed action verb. This was the traditional view of these Hebrew words as determined and vowel marked by the Masorete. The Christian view that Genesis 1:1 is an independent sentence results in the verse having the meaning of an absolute beginning which is consistent with the doctrine of creation "ex nihilo."

The doctrine of creation "ex nihilo" holds that the initial creation of Genesis 1:1 includes the creation of matter. The Greek world before and after Christ held the view that matter was eternal. The Christian and Hebrew view that there was an absolute beginning placed them in conflict with Greek science and thought. This conflict with the secular scientific view about the beginning of matter continued until after 1900 A.D. This is mentioned because, at the present time, the secular scientific world now accepts that there was a beginning, and that matter as we know it came into being after this beginning. This beginning is generally referred to as "The Big Bang" and is the subject of many television programs about physics and astronomy.

There are some "modern" translators of Genesis who do not follow the traditional Christian and Hebrew view of Genesis 1:1 as being an independent sentence. These translators advocate considering the first word as a "construct" meaning "in the beginning of . . .." They then generally alter the vowel marking of the next word "bara" to be that of an "infinitive construct" meaning "creating of." The result of these changes is that Genesis 1:1 can then be translated as not indicating a creation of matter. This section is intended to provide the reader with a ready defense of the traditional Christian position when confronted with questions about these proposals.

Before commenting on the historical origin of the proposed changes, three verses affirming the traditional interpretation of Genesis 1:1 will be reviewed. Then, after this preparation, the proposal that the Hebrew word "in beginning" be translated as a "construct" will be reviewed. John 1:1-3 will be considered first, using the NAS, because the verbs of the third verse more closely follow the Greek word order.

**Verses supporting the traditional translation and Ex Nihilo**

ASV John 1:1-3

1. In the beginning was the Word, and the Word was with God, and the Word was God.
2. The same was in the beginning with God.
3. All things were made through Him; and apart from Him nothing came into being that has come into being.

John 1:1 emphasizes the equivalence between the Word (Christ) and God. John 1:3 emphasizes that the Word (Christ) caused all things to come into being. These verses, in conjunction with Genesis 1:1, indicate an absolute beginning to matter. These verses say "matter was created."

Another important verse is Hebrews 11:3. The KJV, YLT and the Greek text are shown below. The KJV uses "worlds," a word which could represent planets and stars hanging in space. "Worlds" is a translation of the Greek word αἰῶνας which means "ages," and is translated "ages" by the YLT. This word refers to the vast ages of time extending back to the "beginning."

KJV Hebrews 11:3  Through faith we understand that the worlds were framed by the word of God, so that things which are seen were not made of things which do appear.

YLT Hebrews 11:3  by faith we understand the ages to have been prepared by a saying of God, in regard to the things seen not having come out of things appearing;

Hebrews 11:3 (Greek)

| Πίστει | νοοῦμεν | κατηρτίσθαι | τοὺς | αἰῶνας | ῥήματι | θεοῦ, |
|---|---|---|---|---|---|---|
| By faith (we) | are understanding | have been prepared | these | ages | by a word of | God |

| εἰς τὸ | μὴ | ἐκ | φαινομένων | τὸ | βλεπόμενον | γεγονέναι. |
|---|---|---|---|---|---|---|
| so that | not | out of (things) | being visible | the (things) | being seen | being made |

The words relevant to the creation of matter are in the second lines of the preceding verses. Things which can be seen are made of matter. Hebrews 11:3 emphasizes that the things which are seen were made from that which cannot be seen. The word "things" does not appear explicitly in the Greek text. The translations are correct, since "things" is included in the Greek by implication. The Greek has been included so that the reader can see how emphatic the Bible is about the visible being made from that which was not visible. Since that which can be seen is made of matter, the conclusion is that matter was created.

The next verse to be considered is 2 Maccabees 7:28. This verse is included in the Apocrypha of the Vulgate, the KJV (1611), and the Roman Catholic Douay-Rheims (DRA) version. The English translation used is the Douay-Rheims version. The translation of the Greek into the Latin Vulgate uses the phrase "ex nihilo" which translates "out of nothing" in English. "Ex nihilo" is a translation of the three Greek words οὐκ ἐξ ὄντων . These words, in a crude word-by-word translation, are literally "not out of existing." A better translation would be "not out of that which existed."

DRA 2 Maccabees 7:28    I beseech thee, my son, look upon heaven and earth, and all that is in them,
and consider that God made them out of nothing, and mankind also:

VUL 2 Maccabees 7:28    peto nate aspicias in caelum et terram et ad omnia quae in eis sunt
et intellegas quia ex nihilo fecit illa Deus et hominum genus

Greek Text of 2 Maccabees 7:28

| ἀξιῶ | σε | τέκνον | ἀναβλέψαντα | εἰς | τὸν | οὐρανὸν | καὶ | τὴν | γῆν |
|---|---|---|---|---|---|---|---|---|---|
| I beseech | you | my son | look | upon | the | heavens | and | the | earth |

| καὶ | τὰ | ἐν αὐτοῖς | πάντα | ἰδόντα | γνῶναι | ὅτι | οὐκ | ἐξ | ὄντων | ἐποίησεν | αὐτὰ | ὁ | θεός |
|---|---|---|---|---|---|---|---|---|---|---|---|---|---|
| and | the | in them | all | seen | understanding | that | not | out of | existing | made | the same | the | God |

| καὶ | τὸ | τῶν | ἀνθρώπων | γένος | οὕτω | γίνεται |
|---|---|---|---|---|---|---|
| and | the | of the | man | kind | in this way | came to be |

2 Maccabees relates a story about events during the revolt against Antiochious IV in about 170-165 B.C. In this passage a mother is urging her youngest son to die rather than eat pig as demanded by Antiochious. The passage is intended to represent a powerfully convincing argument to choose death. It is unlikely that the author would choose to present such an argument unless it represented a widely held view of scripture and as a consequence would be viewed as convincing by the readers. The current dating of the book places the writing of 2 Maccabees between 77-63 B.C.[38] The revolt of the Maccabees is known from the historical record to have taken place at about 166-167 B.C. The success of this revolt is celebrated in the Jewish festival of Hanukkah.

In addition to the vowel markings which are printed in this book, the Hebrew word "in beginning" is marked with an accent sign (a disjunctive Tiphcha). This mark appears as a curved line to the left of the dot under the שׁ of the Hebrew word. This word is shown following: בְּרֵאשִׁית (Typically the first word is printed with a larger first letter.)

The accent sign indicates the there was to be a pause after the first word. The presence of the disjunctive Tiphcha has meaning for how the word was considered. Edward J. Young, in *Studies In Genesis One*, page 5, concludes
that the accent indicates that the Masorete who marked the pronunciation of the Hebrew text considered בְּרֵאשִׁית "in beginning" to be an absolute noun. A Hebrew noun in the absolute functions as a noun, and does not indicate the "of" of the Hebrew construct.[39]

The accent marking of the Hebrew Masoretic text of Genesis 1:1, the Greek Septuagint translation, and the story of 2 Maccabees 7:28 all indicate the traditional Hebrew view. This view was that Creation included the creation of matter.

The phrase "ex nihilo," as applied to this creation of matter, seems to be derived from the Latin words "ex nihilo" used to translate this passage in 2 Maccabees. "Ex nihilo" appears only three times in the Vulgate, and only in 2 Maccabees does it refer to the Creation of Genesis 1:1.

Now consideration will be given to the origin of the proposed changes in the vowel marking of the words in Genesis 1:1. These changes result in a translation not in accord with the doctrine of "Ex Nihilo."

**Why Genesis 1:1 is not to be translated "In beginning of"**

The earliest documented source of the suggested changes in the vowel marking is by a Jewish commentator, Rashi, in about 1105 A.D. This is more than 1,000 years after the writing of the Christian Bible and more than 1,200 years after the translation of the Septuagint. The assertion is that the first word "In beginning" appears elsewhere in the Bible in the "construct state." The "construct" is a form which would translate "In beginning of." In biblical Hebrew, nouns are generally absolute or construct. This change would not require a change in the written letters, but it is not consistent with the historical understanding and it is not consistent with the translation of the Septuagint. After considering the first word to be a construct, advocates then often alter the vowel marking of the second word "bara" to be an infinitive construct. With these changes, Genesis 1:1 then begins "In the beginning of the creating by God of . . .." There has been much opposition to this proposed translation because it is clearly not in accord with the historical understanding of the verses. The result is not in agreement with other verses which indicate a beginning to the heavens and the Earth as a new thing.

The argument usually starts with the word בְּרֵאשִׁית "in beginning." It is asserted that the absence of הַ "the" in the word following the preposition בְ indicates this word must be considered to be in the "construct" indicating the word "of." The argument made for the construct is a general argument. It requires that all nouns having a preposition and not including הַ "the" must be in the construct. The argument fails by the example of Isaiah 46:10 where the word מֵרֵאשִׁית is used. The word מֵרֵאשִׁית is the word רֵאשִׁית "beginning" prefixed by the preposition מֵ "from," and does not include the article הַ "the." The Hebrew of the first line is shown below. The meaning is clearly **not** "from the beginning of the end." The YLT follows the Hebrew here more closely than does the KJV.

KJV Isaiah 46:10    Declaring the end from the beginning (bara), and from ancient times *the things* that are not *yet* done, saying, My counsel shall stand, and I will do all my pleasure:

YLT Isaiah 46:10    Declaring from the beginning the latter end, And from of old that which hath not been done, Saying, 'My counsel doth stand, And all My delight I do.'

| נַעֲשׂוּ | לֹא | אֲשֶׁר | וּמִקֶּדֶם | אַחֲרִית | מֵרֵאשִׁית | מַגִּיד | Isaiah 46:10 |
|---|---|---|---|---|---|---|---|
| done (niphal perfect) negation of the completed action results in the "yet" of the KJV | not | that | and from eternity | end (after part) | from beginning | declaring (Hiphil participle) | |

The foregoing argument for the construct "of" is further contradicted by examples of the word רֹאשׁ (**rosh**).[40] Rosh is used in adverbial expressions, without the article הַ, meaning "the." The verses shown below are examples of the word מֵרֹאשׁ = רֹאשׁ + מֵ translated "from the beginning." מֵ is the preposition "from" and רֹאשׁ (**rosh**) is the word "beginning." The meaning of מֵרֹאשׁ in the verses below is clearly **not** "from the beginning of."

KJV Isaiah 40:21    Have ye not known? have ye not heard? hath it not been told you מֵרֹאשׁ from the beginning? have ye not understood from the foundations of the earth?

KJV Proverbs 8:23   I was set up from everlasting, מֵרֹאשׁ from the beginning, or ever the earth was.

KJV Isaiah 41:4     Who hath wrought and done *it*, calling the generations מֵרֹאשׁ from the beginning? I the LORD, the first, and with the last; I *am* he.

KJV Ecc. 3:11       He hath made every *thing* beautiful in his time: also he hath set the world in their heart, so that no man can find out the work that God maketh מֵרֹאשׁ from the beginning to the end.

**NEXT:**

       **THE**

              **FIRST**

                      **CREATIVE "YOM"**

## Chapter Three  THE FIRST CREATIVE "YOM": GENESIS 1:3-5

## VERSE THREE: GENESIS 1:3    The Start of the "Daytime"

Genesis 1:3 presents an opportunity to apply what was learned earlier about biblical Hebrew verbs. This verse has six Hebrew words and contains the first use of וַיֹּאמֶר אֱלֹהִים "and said God." This phrase is usually translated "and God said," a translation which will also be adopted by this study. The analysis which follows will be used to determine the appropriate English words to use in the translation and to determine if any pluperfect reference is made in this verse. Completed action verbs will be translated using the simple past tense unless a pluperfect reference is discovered in the analysis. As a consequence, the events of the narrative will progress in time by means of a series of past tense verbs, just as in the KJV. Differences will arise when pluperfect references are found. Genesis 1:3 in the KJV and the Hebrew with the study translation is shown below and will be analyzed in detail.

KJV Genesis 1:3    And God said, Let there be light: and there was light.

**Genesis 1:3**

| אוֹר | וַיְהִי | אוֹר | יְהִי | אֱלֹהִים | וַיֹּאמֶר | ← Hebrew starts here. |
|---|---|---|---|---|---|---|
| light | and had existed | light | shall exist | God (Elohim) | and had said | ← Start English here. |
| | ( waw + imperfect ) | | (Qal imperfect "jussive") | | (waw + imperfect) | |
| | (KJV "and there was") | | (KJV "let there be) | | (KJV "and said") | |

The first word וַיֹּאמֶר is usually translated "said." This word, וַיֹּאמֶר = אָמַר + יִ + וַ , is formed using the verb stem אָמַר, the prefix יִ, and the prefix וַ. The prefix יִ (yod) forms the imperfect second person (he). This produces agreement with the subject noun, "Elohim." "Elohim" is plural but has the singular meaning. The verb is in the Qal imperfect singular, but the action of the prefix וַ is to transform the meaning of the verb form to be that of the perfect. As discussed earlier, the perfect means that the action is **completed**. The verb form conveys no information about how long ago the action "said" took place. It only tells us that the action has been completed. The verb can be translated as "said," "had said," "did say," "commanded," or "had commanded." The traditional translation "said" conveys completion and is appropriate for introducing the following commands and events.

The word אֱלֹהִים "God" (Elohim) appears in each of the first three verses of Genesis. In biblical Hebrew, when the verb is the first word of a sentence, the subject is usually the second word. This is the case in Genesis 1:3. English word order expects the subject to be first. As a consequence, the typical English translation alters the word order to read "And God said" instead of the Hebrew word order "And said God."

The third word יְהִי is the verb meaning "to be" or "to exist." The verb can be translated "be," "shall be," "will be," "exist," "shall exist," or "will exist."

This verb is in a Qal imperfect form called the jussive. For most verbs the imperfect form and the jussive form are the same. For the verb "to be," the jussive is a shortened form of the imperfect. The imperfect form יִהְיֶה is shortened by dropping the final ה. The jussive form represents the command "shall be," "shall exist," or "shall occur." The verb יְהִי retains the imperfect (incomplete action) meaning. The action which is commanded takes place at some time in the future, and is an incomplete action at the time of the command. The future timing of the completion is not indicated; the action has been commanded but not completed. The incomplete nature of the action will be of significance.

In most English translations of the Bible the words "let there" are inserted to make the translation read smoothly. These two words do not appear in the Hebrew. The "let there" is derived from the Latin Vulgate which uses a verb in the subjunctive. The subjunctive in Latin is the form for command, hence "Let there be." The verb is just as correctly translated "shall exist." "Shall exist," or "shall be" are preferred here because after the light appears, the light continues to exist. The "shall exist" or "shall be" express the ongoing existence of the light and also express the command.

The fourth word אוֹר (ore) is the usual noun for light, or light giver, and is a singular noun.

The fifth word is וַיְהִי, and is again the verb "to be." The verb form is the Qal imperfect. This is not the verb form יְהִי used as word three of this verse, prefixed by וֹ. This time the imperfect form יִהְיֶה is prefixed by ו meaning "and." In this case, the ו causes the final consonant ה to be dropped from the imperfect form יִהְיֶה. The prefix ו also has the effect of changing the meaning of the verb to be that of the perfect (completed) action. Another verb, the Qal imperfect verb for "shall see," also drops the final ה when prefixed by ו to form the completed action meaning "had seen" or "saw." Both of these verb forms are used repeatedly in Genesis One.

The completed action can be translated "was," "existed," or "did exist." "Had existed" is excluded because there is no indication of pluperfect reference in this verse. These multiple options lead to a number of possible translations of the entire verse, including:

| | | | |
|---|---|---|---|
| And God said, | light shall exist | and light existed. | ⎫ |
| And God said, | light shall exist | and light did exist. | ⎬ Three preferred readings due to the continuing existence of light. |
| And God said, | light shall exist | and light was. | ⎭ |
| And God said, | let there be light | and light was. | KJV |

The last option, the KJV, may result in a possible misreading. The Hebrew text only conveys the completed nature of the action. "Was," "existed," and "had existed" are all past completed actions. A problem of understanding can arise because English has what is sometimes called a punctiliar aspect. The punctiliar aspect means that the reader views the action as taking place at a single point in time.[41] This point in time is usually assumed to be just a moment before the speaking. This can lead to an incorrect interpretation. In this case, because of the command, the punctiliar view would be that the action (was) occurred immediately after the command "Let there be." The Hebrew only tells us that the command (had said) is a completed action and that the result also is a completed action (had existed or was). The time separation between the command and the result is not specified in the Hebrew. The Hebrew also does not tell us that the final intensity of the light was produced instantaneously. The intensity of the light may have increased gradually from a dim light to a brighter light. The "Let there be" is also not a preferred translation because it does not convey the continuing nature of the command.

The translation of choice is: **And God said, light shall exist and light existed**.

The light which was commanded to exist is illumination from the sun in the daytime. This illumination (light) from the sun in the daytime continues to exist. This fact is specifically stated in Genesis 1:5 and will be discussed again during the study of that verse.

Genesis 1:2 had represented planet Earth as having been in a state of darkness. The present understanding of the natural history of planet Earth asserts that early in its history there would have been a dense, permanent, cloud cover. This is not merely a secular model. The Bible, in Job 38:9, indicates that the first ocean was wrapped (swaddled) in a darkness due to clouds.

KJV Job 38:9     When I made the cloud the garment thereof, and thick darkness a swaddlingband for it,

YLT Job 38:9     In My making a cloud its clothing, And thick darkness its swaddling band,

| חֲתֻלָּתוֹ | וַעֲרָפֶל | לְבֻשׁוֹ | עָנָן | בְּשׂוּמִי | Job 38:9 |
|---|---|---|---|---|---|
| swaddling band of it | thick darkness | its garment | cloud | In my making of | |
| | | | | ( an infinitive prefixed by בְּ "in") | |

# VERSE FOUR: GENESIS 1: 4 — About the Separating

Genesis 1:4 introduces the first "and God saw," a phrase which is repeated seven times. Genesis 1:4 has twelve Hebrew words including one direct object marker and three separable prepositions. The sentence in Hebrew is:

| | | | | | | | |
|---|---|---|---|---|---|---|---|
| טוֹב | כִּי | הָאוֹר | אֵת | אֱלֹהִים | וַיַּרְא | (1) | **Genesis 1:4** |
| good | as (KJV "that") | the light | dir. obj. marker | God (Elohim) | and had seen (KJV "saw") | ← | Start English here. |

| | | | | | | |
|---|---|---|---|---|---|---|
| הַחֹשֶׁךְ | וּבֵין | הָאוֹר | בֵּין | אֱלֹהִים | וַיַּבְדֵּל | (2) |
| the dark | and between | the light | between | God (Elohim) | and had separated (KJV "divided") | |

KJV Genesis 1:4     And God saw the light, that *it was* good: and God divided the light from the darkness.

The first word is וַיַּרְא which means "to see," "look at," or "inspect." The verb is in the Qal imperfect form but is prefixed by וַ meaning "and." The effect of the prefix וַ is to cause the verb to act as a Qal perfect and to represent a completed action. As a completed action the verb could be translated as "saw," "had seen," "observed," or "had observed." Translators have usually chosen "saw" which seemingly conveys the completed nature of the action.

The second word is אֱלֹהִים (Elohim) which means "God" and is the plural subject of the singular verb as previously explained. אֱלֹהִים (Elohim) also appears as the second word of line (2) of the Hebrew.

The third word אֵת, the direct object marker, precedes the fourth word הָאוֹר "the light" indicating it is the direct object. The word אוֹר (ore) means "light" and is, in this case, prefixed by the letter ה (heh) which means "the."

The fifth word כִּי is a conjunction which has many meanings. Possibilities are "as though," "as," "because that," "but," "certainly," "except," "for," "surely," "since," "that," "then," "when," etc. Translating the conjunction as "that" requires the insertion of "*it was*" in the KJV. These words do not appear in the Hebrew. Translating the conjunction as "as" does not require additional words.

The sixth word טוֹב (tob) is a masculine singular adjective meaning "good." This consonantal word form can be an adjective, a noun, or a verb. The KJV translates טוֹב (tob) as: good (361 times), better (72 times), well (20 times), goodness (16 times), and more than 35 other ways depending upon the context of what is being described as "good."

The seventh word וַיַּבְדֵּל, the first word on line (2), is a form of the consonantal word בדל (badal). בדל (badal) has the meanings "to divide," "separate," "distinguish," "set apart," "to make a distinction," "difference," and "to divide into parts." This word will be translated using the word "separated." Separated and divided are the words usually used in English translation of this verse. וַיַּבְדֵּל is a verb in the Hiphil imperfect form prefixed by וַ meaning "and." The verb is in the third person masculine singular. The subject of the verb is the word אֱלֹהִים (Elohim) which follows. The Hiphil is a form used to indicate that the subject is the cause of the action. The prefix וַ causes the verb, which is in the imperfect, to have the meaning of the perfect (completed action).

The final four words of line (2) are two nouns each of which is preceded by the preposition בֵּין meaning "between." The second of these prepositions is prefixed by the conjunction וַ meaning "and." The nouns הָאוֹר and הַחֹשֶׁךְ are prefixed by ה which means "the." The word אוֹר (ore) is the word "light" discussed as word four of line (1). The word חֹשֶׁךְ (hoeshek) is the word meaning "darkness" which first appeared in Genesis 1:2. The typical translation of these two words and the prepositions omits the first "between" and translates the second "between" as "from."

A comparison between the study translation under the Hebrew and the KJV is given on the next page. Phrases in the translations have been re-spaced to enhance the ease of comparison.

Study Translation
        And God had seen the light, . . . . . . . .as good . . . . and God had separated between the light and between the dark.
KJV    And God saw the light, . . . that *it was* good . . . and God divided the light from the darkness.

The difference between these two translations lies in the implied time sequence of the actions. The Hebrew does not say that the "separating" had taken place after the "seeing," only that both actions are completed. The KJV implies, because of the possible punctiliar aspect of the English, that the separating followed the seeing. Superficially, in this example, no apparent harm has been done. When the "separating" occurred relative to the "seeing" does not ordinarily seem to have significance. If the time sequence of the actions is significant, the event ordering of the KJV would need to be altered.

**Here the sequence is significant**

It is often assumed that the order in which the actions are related is the order in which the actions take place. This assumption is never stated to be valid in Genesis One and leads to significant misunderstandings of the meaning of some verses. Based on the forgoing assumption, the expectation would be that the "separating" by God followed the command for the existence of the light. Actually, this is not to be expected from the Hebrew but rather is an expectation generated by the assumption.

For planet Earth, the solar illumination of the "day" side of the planet requires the simultaneous existence of night on the backside of the planet. This is a general requirement and applies to all physical models of the Earth having a directional (sun-like) light source. This means that the light and the dark were separated when light appeared at the surface of planet Earth in Genesis 1:3. The separation was simultaneous with the appearance of the light. The Hebrew completed action and the translation "and had separated" are fully consistent with this requirement. The KJV translation is not. This illustrates the care which must be taken to clearly translate the completed action verbs as completed actions. The result of this study is also consistent with the naming of the light as יוֹם "yom" in Genesis 1:5. יוֹם "yom" is the Hebrew word which refers to the daytime. In Genesis 1:5 the dark is named לַיְלָה (layil) meaning night or nighttime.

The darkness, which already existed, becomes night only in contrast to the daytime which has now appeared.
Genesis 1:3-5 is about the start of an observable daytime-nighttime cycle at the surface of planet Earth where mankind will live. The text does not say that the atmosphere has become clear at this time. Genesis 1:4 is consistent with the model of an initial darkening opaque cloud layer which then thins sufficiently that discernable solar illumination becomes evident at the surface of planet Earth. This model is consistent with Job 38:9 (quoted on page 55) and will be discussed again in connection with Genesis 1:16-18. The wonderful habitability of planet Earth depends on adequate sunlight and on the daytime-nighttime cycle which results from the Earth's rotation.

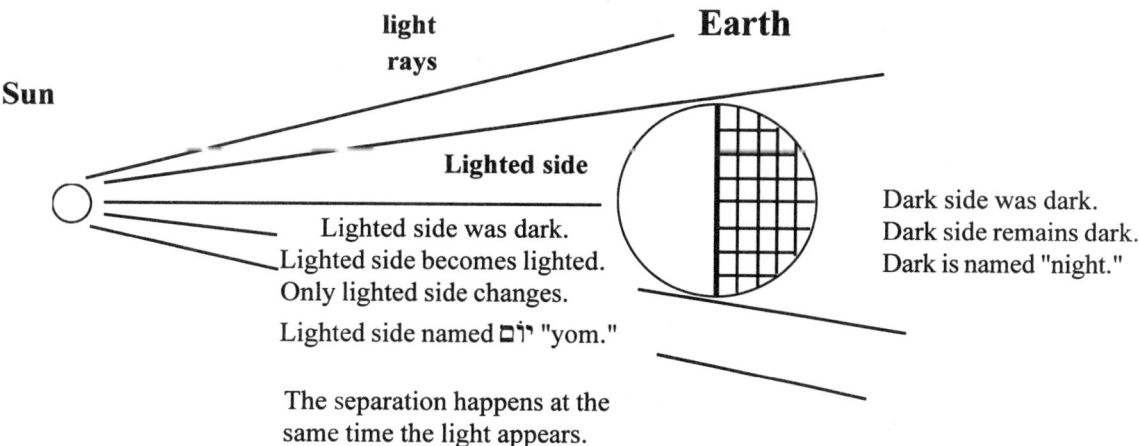

In accordance with the analysis of this section, the translation adopted for Genesis 1:5 will adopt the pluperfect for both verbs. "As good," a more direct rendering of the Hebrew, replaces the "that *it was* good" of the KJV.

The translation is: And God had seen the light as good, and had separated between the light and between the dark. The meaning of the word יוֹם "yom" will be extensively studied in the next section.

# VERSE FIVE: GENESIS 1:5        The Naming and The Concluding Phrases

The first seven Hebrew words of Genesis 1:5 will be considered as a unit before considering the remainder of the verse. The concluding words will subsequently be studied in great detail.

The English below the Hebrew of Genesis 1:5 will translate יוֹם as "yom." The word יוֹם "yom" requires an extensive analysis which will subsequently be conducted in an unbiased manner. The translation "yom" is used to avoid the confusing use of the word "day" during this analysis. Questions about the English translation of the word יוֹם "yom" as it is used in the concluding phrase of Genesis 1:5 will be resolved later. Biblical Hebrew uses יוֹם "yom" for meaning "daytime," for meaning "time," and for representing 24 hours. It will be shown that יוֹם "yom" should be translated "time" in the concluding phrase of Genesis 1:5.

**Genesis 1:5 line (1)**

| (1) | לַיְלָה | קָרָא | וְלַחֹשֶׁךְ | יוֹם | לָאוֹר | אֱלֹהִים | וַיִּקְרָא | ← Hebrew starts here. |
|---|---|---|---|---|---|---|---|---|
| | night | he had called (KJV "called") | and the darkness | "yom" | the light | God (Elohim) | and had called (KJV "called") | ←Start English here. |

The Hebrew word order is the same as in the previous two verses. The verb is the first word of the sentence. The subject of the sentence "God" (Elohim) is the second word of the sentence. The verb קרא is prefixed by a ו (and). The prefixed verb יִקְרָא is in the Qal imperfect third person singular. Because of the presence of the ו , the verb is translated as the perfect and denotes a completed action. The KJV translated the verb as "called."

In this part of Genesis 1:5, God names the two separated (or distinguished) states. The states are described as "the light" and "the darkness." The light state is named (KJV "called") יוֹם "yom" and the dark state is named לַיְלָה (layil) "night." Based on the use of both "yom" and "night" in the sentence, the יוֹם "yom" refers to the duration of the solar illumination at a location on the surface of the Earth (i.e., daytime). This is not a constant amount of time. The amount of time depends upon both the latitude of observation and the time of year. The duration of the daytime portion of the day-night cycle is about 12 hours when averaged over an entire year.

**It is important to notice that the first use of "yom" in Genesis does not refer to 24 hours.**

Here יוֹם "yom" is specifically defined to refer to the time of illumination by the sun. This is the period of time which we normally refer to as daytime, a time which does not include the night.

The Hebrew word יוֹם "yom" is used 241 times in the Bible. יוֹם "yom" is also used with prefixes more than another 1,000 times. "Yom" is most often used to refer to activities which take place, or can be expected to take place, during the time of illumination by the sun (i.e., the daytime). The second most common use of the word "yom" is to refer to long periods of time. This use occurs more than 200 times. Verses will be studied in detail to illustrate the actual uses of the word יוֹם "yom." This study will also show that the association of the word יוֹם "yom" with a time period of 24 hours is **very infrequent**. Examples of these associations will be considered. The assertion that יוֹם "yom" commonly had a 24 hour meaning is not supported by the use of the word "yom" in the Bible.

The naming of "the light" in Genesis 1:5 has theological significance. Naming, in the ancient world, often implied that the person doing the naming had an understanding of the nature of the thing named and had power over the thing named. By naming "the light" and "the darkness" the text, by implication, asserts that God is in sovereign control of the light-dark sequence, and that this sequence exists because God so commands. This statement was of theological significance at the time of Moses because the sun and the moon were viewed as gods by the other peoples of that time; the sun and the moon were objects of worship. The reality of this worship at the time of Moses is verified in Deuteronomy 17:3 in a section where such worship is condemned.

    KJV Deuteronomy 17:3    And hath gone and served other gods, and worshipped them, either the sun, or moon, or any of the host of heaven, which I have not commanded;

The remaining six words of Genesis 1:5 constitute a phrase which will be studied in considerable detail.

The phrase being studied is:

**Genesis 1:5 line (2)**

| (2) | אֶחָד | יוֹם | בֹּקֶר | וַיְהִי | עֶרֶב | וַיְהִי | ← Hebrew starts here. |
|---|---|---|---|---|---|---|---|
| | one | "yom" | morning | and had been ("and *there* was") | evening | and had been ("and *there* was") in NAS, NIV and RSV | ← Start English here. |

This phrase is repeated six times in Genesis One. The six-word phrase differs in each case by the numerical word used. The numerical word in this case is אֶחָד (one). The careful repetition of the first five words of this phrase after each creative יוֹם "yom" indicates that we **cannot** ignore the phrase as a whole unit and simply read "yom one." The study which follows will show that this phrase means a long period of time. The following study will also illustrate the many times יוֹם "yom" is used to mean long periods of time.

Excluding the six concluding phrases, Genesis 1:1-31 uses the singular יוֹם "yom" (or a singular form of "yom") four times and the plural form יָמִים "yoms" one time. The four verses using singular forms of יוֹם "yom" all refer to the time period of solar illumination between sunrise and sunset. The verses do **not** refer to 24 hours. The singular יוֹם "yom" is used in three forms:

        יוֹם     "yom"

        בְּיוֹם     "in yom," where the prefix בְּ meaning "in" is prefixed to the "yom"

and    הַיּוֹם     "the yom," where הַ "the" is prefixed to יוֹם "yom."

The verse segments where "yom" is used are:

KJV Genesis 1:5     And God called the light יוֹם "**yom**," and the darkness He called night.

KJV Genesis 1:14     Then God said, "Let there be lights in the expanse of the heavens to separate הַיּוֹם "**the yom**" from the night, . . .."

KJV Genesis 1:16     And God had made the two great lights, the greater light to govern הַיּוֹם "**the yom**," and the lesser light to govern the night; . . .."

KJV Genesis 1:18     And to rule בְּיוֹם over the "**yom**" and over the night, and to divide the light from the darkness: (Here the KJV translates בְּיוֹם "in yom" as "over the yom.")

The three forms used in these verses all refer to the time of illumination by the sun. Because the meaning is the same in all verses, these verses show that prefixing by בְּ "in" or by הַ "the" does not alter the meaning of the singular יוֹם "yom."

The remaining six uses of the singular יוֹם "yom" are in forms of the concluding phrase of each creative period. The meaning of this phrase will be studied carefully. The correct understanding of this phrase has been of concern from the beginning of the Christian era. A common understanding among Christians at this time is that the phrase represents a long period of time. There is another view advocated by some Christians who read the phrase as the 24-hour period of a day and a night. Again, note that the four uses of "yom" considered above did **not** refer to 24 hours.

To illustrate the antiquity of the question regarding the interpretation of this six-word phrase, consider several statements made by early Bible commentators. In about 411 A.D. Augustine wrote about the creative "yom,"

    "of what fashion of days (i.e., "yom") these were, it is either exceedingly hard
    or altogether impossible to think, much more to speak."

                                                            Augustine, *City of God*, 11.6, 411 A.D.

Philo, a Jewish writer, wrote in about 100 A.D.: [42]

> "And he says the world was made in six days (i.e., "six yom"), not because the creator stood in need of a length of time, . . . , but because the things created required arrangement, and number is akin to arrangement and of all the numbers six is by the laws of nature the most productive for all the numbers from the unit upwards, it is the most perfect one . . . and he allotted each of the six days to one of the portions of the whole . . . ."

Quoting ancient authors is **not** adequate to establish the meaning of the phrase. However, the quotes do establish that questions about how to read the phrases concluding each creative "yom" had existed long before the advent of Darwinism.

## How the study will now proceed

Before the meaning of the word יוֹם "yom" in the concluding phrases can be discussed it is important that the reader understand how the word יוֹם "yom" is actually used in the Hebrew of Genesis and the Hebrew Bible. The study will proceed in four sections which are:

1. **The use of יוֹם "yom" in the five Books of Moses and the Hebrew Bible**

    This seven-page section provides a preparation by reviewing the actual uses of יוֹם "yom" found in the Bible. Both "daytime" meanings and long time meanings are shown by verse examples. 24-hour meanings are also shown by examples.

2. **Translation and the time meaning of the creative "yom"**
    In this section the translation of the concluding phrases is discussed including the meanings of the words "evening" and "morning."

3. **Summary of Results for Genesis 1:1-5 and Comments Regarding 24-Hour "Day" Models**
    The creation models for יוֹם "yom" translated "time" and for the 24-hour day will be discussed.

4. **More About "... ...."**
    Additional sections will follow which give more extensive discussion of word meaning and translation issues which are relevant to the interpretation of the length of the creative "yom."

## The Use of יוֹם "Yom" in the Five Books of Moses and the Hebrew Bible

How is the singular word "yom" used elsewhere in the Books of Moses (the first five books of the Bible)? Consider:

KJV Numbers 3:1 These also *are the* generations of Aaron and Moses
        בְּיוֹם in the "yom" *that* the LORD spake with Moses in mount Sinai.
    **(KJV "in the day" )**

The word translated "in the yom" is the singular word (יוֹם) "yom" prefixed with the preposition בְּ (beth) meaning "in" and sometimes "on." In the Hebrew sentence shown below בְּיוֹם "in yom" occurs as the fifth word from the right. The prefix ה "*the*" does not appear in the Hebrew. The KJV has added "*are the*" and "*that*." The KJV often added words into the translation, which were indicated by italicization. In later translations these words are often no longer identified to the reader as being added words. The Hebrew of Numbers 3:1 follows.

**Numbers 3:1**

| סִינָי | בְּהַר | מֹשֶׁה | אֶת | יְהוָה | דִּבֶּר | בְּיוֹם | וּמֹשֶׁה | אַהֲרֹן | תּוֹלְדֹת | וְאֵלֶּה |
|---|---|---|---|---|---|---|---|---|---|---|
| Sinai | on mount (in) | Moses | dir. obj. marker | Yahweh | spoke | in "yom" | and Moses | Aaron | generations of | and these |

The KJV translates בְּיוֹם as "in the day." The New KJV translates בְּיוֹם as "when," and the NAS translates בְּיוֹם as "at the time." The word בְּיוֹם in this verse clearly does not refer to 24 hours; it refers to an extended period of time. The length of time which בְּיוֹם "in yom" represents can be determined by referring to Exodus 34:28.

In the KJV Exodus 34:28 shown below, the word "yom" has been inserted into the KJV as the translation of the Hebrew word יוֹם .

KJV Exodus 34:28     So he was there with the LORD forty "**yom**" and forty nights . . . .

| Exodus 34:28 | וַיְהִי | שָׁם | עִם | יְהוָה | אַרְבָּעִים | יוֹם | וְאַרְבָּעִים | לַיְלָה |
|---|---|---|---|---|---|---|---|---|
| ← Start English here. | and he had been (often translated "and it came to pass") | there | with | Yahweh (KJV "the LORD") | forty | yom | and forty | night |

The word יוֹם "yom" is in the singular, but as translated into KJV English יוֹם "yom" becomes "days." The word for night in the Hebrew is similarly in the singular, not the translated plural "nights." Also Exodus 34:28 shows that the singular word יוֹם "yom" did **not** include the night. יוֹם **"yom" did not mean 24 hours.**

For the Hebrew word "in yom" in Numbers 3:1, shown on the previous page, we now have the following result:

בְּיוֹם "in yom" means a time interval of more than a month, 40 "yom" and 40 nights. Because the יוֹם "yom" and the "night" are specifically included, this is 40 x 24 = 960 hours.

The study of Genesis 1:18, on page 59, established that the prefix בְּ does not alter the meaning of the word יוֹם "yom." Four Genesis verses were studied. In all of them יוֹם "yom" and its prefixed forms referred to the time of solar illumination (daytime). This meaning was independent of the use or non-use of a prefix.

Now consider Genesis 2:4. In this verse the singular בְּיוֹם "in yom" is used in the same manner as it is used in Numbers 3:1. The singular בְּיוֹם "in yom" refers to all six of the preceding creative "yom" as a group.

KJV Genesis 2:4     These *are the* generations of the heavens and of the earth when they were created,
                    in the "yom" that the LORD God made the earth and the heavens,

| Genesis 2:4 | אֵלֶּה | תוֹלְדוֹת | הַשָּׁמַיִם | וְהָאָרֶץ | בְּהִבָּרְאָם |
|---|---|---|---|---|---|
| ← Start English here. | these | generations of | the heavens | and the earth | in his creating |

| בְּיוֹם | עֲשׂוֹת | יְהוָה | אֱלֹהִים | אֶרֶץ | וְשָׁמָיִם |
|---|---|---|---|---|---|
| in "yom" of ("of" comes from the construct ) | making | Yahweh | Elohim | earth | and heavens |

The singular בְּיוֹם "in yom" is used here to refer to the entire sequence of six creative "yom" in the preceding chapter. Each of these creative "yom" were described by a version of the concluding phrase. As a consequence, the Hebrew word בְּיוֹם **"in yom" does not refer to a time period of 24 hours in Genesis 2:4.** The use in Genesis 2:4 is consistent with the many times the singular "in yom" is used to refer to extended periods of time. The singular "yom," as it is used in Genesis 2:4, does **not** refer to the period of solar illumination between sunrise and sunset. It refers to a longer period of time. This is the same usage as was considered in Numbers 3:1.

After Genesis 2:4, the singular word "yom" next occurs as בְּיוֹם "in yom" in Genesis 2:17.

KJV Genesis 2:17    But of the tree of the knowledge of good and evil, thou shalt not eat of it:
                    for בְּיוֹם in *the* "yom" that thou eatest thereof thou shalt surely die.

Genesis 2:17 has been the subject of much discussion and debate since the beginning of Christianity. The reason being that Genesis 5:5 states that Adam lived 930 years.

Two other verses which have figured in the many comments are Psalm 90:4 (which is attributed to Moses), and 2 Peter 3:8. These two verses use the word יוֹם "yom" in reference to a long period of time. In these verses יוֹם "yom" refers to about a **1,000 years**.

KJV Psalm 90:4   For a thousand years in thy sight are כְּיוֹם but as yesterday when it is past,
and as a watch in the night.

Here כְּיוֹם , literally "but yom" or "but a yom," is translated as "but as yesterday." (כְּ is the preposition "but.")

KJV 2 Peter 3:8   But, beloved, be not ignorant of this one thing,
that one (ἡμέρα) is with the Lord as a thousand years, and a thousand years as one (ἡμέρα).

The Greek word ἡμέρα (hemera), generally refers to the time between sunrise and sunset. This use can be clearly seen in Matthew 4:2 where the word ἡμέρα has added the plural ending ς.

KJV Matthew 4:2   And when he had fasted forty ἡμέρας days and forty nights, . . . .[43]

A different word νυχθήμερον (nuchthemeron) means 24 hours. The word "nuchthemeron" is literally "night-day" and was introduced into the Greek language in about 150 B.C. by Hipparchus.[44] Prior to that time the nighttime and the daytime were considered to be different and were divided differently. The practice of differing division is indicated in Psalm 90:4 by the Hebrew word וְאַשְׁמוּרָה translated as a watch in the night. A watch in the night would be about four hours as we reckon time. In 2 Peter 3:8 ἡμέρα (hemera) is used in the same manner as "yom" is used in Psalm 90:4. In Psalm 90:4 the Hebrew uses כְּיוֹם "like yom" which the KJV translates "as yesterday." It could just as well have been translated "like a daytime." 2 Peter 3:8 is essentially a reference to Psalm 90:4 and indicates 2 Peter's understanding of the meaning of the word "yom" in Psalm 90:4. Considered together, these verses indicate that the singular יוֹם "yom" does have the meaning **"time."** The length of the interval is **not** specified when used in this manner. The contrast is used to show that the eternal God does not view the passage of time as a limitation.

## The phrases "Day of the Lord" and "Day of ..." where יוֹם means long periods of time

The singular יוֹם "yom" is often used to refer to long periods of time when used in phrases which the KJV often translates "day of the Lord." "Day of the Lord" appears 17 times in the KJV translation of the Old Testament. Ezekiel 30:3 provides a clear example of this use. The phrase "the day of the LORD" is explicitly indicated to be a "time of" by using the Hebrew word עֵת meaning "time."

KJV Ezekiel 30:3   For the day *is* near, even the day of the LORD *is* near,
a cloudy day; it shall be the time of the heathen.

Ezekiel 30:3

| יִהְיֶה | גּוֹיִם | עֵת | עֲנָן | יוֹם | לַיהוָה | יוֹם | וְקָרוֹב | יוֹם | קָרוֹב | כִּי |
|---|---|---|---|---|---|---|---|---|---|---|
| it shall be | heathen (i. e., "nations") | time of | cloud | "yom" of | to Yahweh (KJV "the day of the LORD") | a "yom" | and near | a "yom" | near | For |

יוֹם "yom" also refers to other events which take place over long periods of time such as "day of vengeance," "day of calamity," etc. The word "yom" is used 25 times in phrases of this type. Isaiah 34:8 provides a clear example of this type of use where the יוֹם "yom" is indicated to be a long period of time by being used in parallel with the word שָׁנָה "year."

KJV Isaiah 34:8   For *it is* the day of the LORD'S **vengeance**,
*and* the year of recompences for the controversy of Zion.

| צִיּוֹן | לְרִיב | שִׁלּוּמִים | שְׁנַת | לַיהוָה | נָקָם | יוֹם | כִּי | Isaiah 34:8 |
|---|---|---|---|---|---|---|---|---|
| Zion | for controversy (or "strife") | recompences | year of | to Yahweh | vengeance | "yom" of | For | |

## The phrase בַּיּוֹם הַהוּא translated "in that day"

Another way the word "yom" is used in Genesis and in the Old Testament to describe a long period of time is the phrase בַּיּוֹם הַהוּא. Literally, the words in the Hebrew sequence are:

                                                 הַהוּא    בַּיּוֹם    ← Hebrew starts here.
                       (הַ is the prefix "the")   the that   in "yom"    ← Start English here.

The KJV usually translates בַּיּוֹם הַהוּא as "in that day." בַּיּוֹם הַהוּא refers to long periods of time more than 100 times. **More than 100 times is a frequent use.** In the KJV examples below "**in that yom**" is inserted for "in that day." The first example is KJV Deuteronomy 31:17:

KJV Deuteronomy 31:17: Then my anger shall be kindled against them בַּיּוֹם הַהוּא **in that "yom,"**
and I will forsake them, and I will hide my face from them, and they shall be devoured,
and many evils and troubles shall befall them; so that they will say בַּיּוֹם הַהוּא
**in that "yom,"** Are not these evils come upon us, because our God *is* not among us?

The term translated "**in that yom**" includes the time of the exile to Babylon and the difficulties with the Greeks and the Romans. This clearly amounts to a long period of time. This phrase is used often by the prophets. Isaiah alone uses the phrase 45 times. Consider Isaiah 11:10-11 which is widely accepted as a messianic passage referring to Christ as the "root of Jesse." Again, "yom" in the singular is used to refer to a long period of time.

KJV Isaiah 11:10-11    And בַּיּוֹם הַהוּא **in that "yom"** there shall be a root of Jesse, which shall stand for
an ensign of the people; to it shall the Gentiles seek: and his rest shall be glorious.
And it shall come to pass בַּיּוֹם הַהוּא **in that "yom,"** *that* the Lord shall set his hand
again the **second time** to recover the remnant of his people, which shall be left, from
Assyria, and from Egypt, and from Pathros, and from Cush, and from Elam, and from
Shinar, and from Hamath, and from the islands of the sea.

Here בַּיּוֹם הַהוּא **in that "yom"** refers to the Christian era of the church. The reference is to a period of time exceeding 2,000 years. Included in this time is "the **second time** to recover the remnant of his people." The reestablishment of the nation of Israel in our day has been in process for nearly 100 years and is still not completed. An additional example is KJV Amos 9:11-12.

KJV Amos 9:11    בַּיּוֹם הַהוּא In that "yom" will I raise up the tabernacle of David that is fallen, and
close up the breaches thereof; and I will raise up his ruins, and I will build it as in the
days of old:

KJV Amos 9:12    That they may possess the remnant of Edom, and of all the heathen, which are called
by my name, saith the LORD that doeth this.

In Isaiah 23:15 the phrase "**in that yom**" clearly means **more than 70 years**.

KJV Isaiah 23:15    And it shall come to pass בַּיּוֹם הַהוּא "**in that yom,**" that Tyre shall be forgotten
seventy years, according to the days of one king: after the end of seventy years
shall Tyre sing as an harlot.

**In an interim summary, this study has found:**

1. Four uses of the singular "yom" in Genesis One refer to the time between sunrise and sunset. These verses verified that the "time" indicated by יוֹם "yom," בְּיוֹם "in yom," and הַיּוֹם "the yom" was the same.

2. The singular "in yom" is used to refer to long periods of time, centuries, years, and many days. It is also used in Genesis 2:4 to refer to the entire previous six uses of the phrase for each creative "yom."

3. יוֹם means a long period of time in the phrases "Day of the Lord" and "Day of vengeance."

4. The singular בְּיוֹם "in yom" in the phrase בַּיּוֹם הַהוּא "in yom - the that" (KJV "in that day") is used to refer to long periods of time, centuries, years, and the ongoing perspective of the events after the second coming of Christ. This use is frequent and occurs more that 100 times.

Note: The most common use of the singular word "yom" is to refer to the time between sunrise and sunset. When "yom" is used in reference to activities which normally took place between sunrise and sunset, "yom" means daytime. Before the electric light and kerosene lanterns, activities were far more greatly restricted to the daytime.

**A reader of the Bible must not interpret "yom" as referring to 24 hours unless there is evidence in the text indicating that meaning.**

### Uses of הַיּוֹם "the yom"

Additional evidence about the meaning of the word "yom" is found in the uses of הַיּוֹם "the yom." הַיּוֹם "the yom" is יוֹם "yom" prefixed by ה "the." The clear use of הַיּוֹם "the yom" referring to the daytime between sunrise and sunset is found many times in the Bible. The most frequent KJV translation is "today," or the equivalent "this day." The text usually refers to events which have taken place, or are taking place, between sunrise and sunset. הַיּוֹם "the yom" is translated and used in this manner 70 times in Deuteronomy alone. The various translations of הַיּוֹם "the yom" are illustrated in the following examples:

KJV Genesis 40:6-7     And Joseph came in unto them in the morning, and looked upon them, and, behold, they *were* sad. And he asked Pharaoh's officers that *were* with him in the ward of his lord's house, saying, Wherefore look ye *so* sadly הַיּוֹם to day?

(הַיּוֹם "the yom" is the KJV "to day")

KJV Genesis 18:1     And the LORD appeared unto him (Abraham) in the plains of Mamre: and he sat in the tent door in the heat *of* הַיּוֹם "the yom"; (KJV "the day")

KJV Deuteronomy 9:25     Thus I fell down before the LORD forty הַיּוֹם "the yom" and forty nights as I fell down *at the first*; because the LORD had said he would destroy you.

*In Deuteronomy 9:25 both day and night are mentioned. The Hebrew word "the yom" does not include the night. If "the yom" included the night it would not be necessary to mention the night explicitly. Here "the yom" does not mean 24 hours. It refers to the time of illumination from the sun, about 12 hours.*

### The phrase "on to this day"

The word הַיּוֹם "the yom" is also used in often-repeated phrases such as "on to this day" (76 times) and "from the day that."

In these KJV phrases, the events referenced often extend over periods of years, months, or many days. הַיּוֹם "the yom" is in these cases equivalent to our expressions "from the time that," and "up to this time." In these expressions the Hebrew word "yom" has the meaning of the English word "time."

KJV Genesis 19:37     And the firstborn bare a son, and called his name Moab: the same *is* the father of the Moabites עַד הַיּוֹם **"unto this yom."** (עַד = till, until, unto)

KJV Exodus 10:6     And they (the locust) shall fill thy houses, and the houses of all thy servants, and the houses of all the Egyptians; which neither thy fathers, nor thy fathers' fathers have seen, מִיּוֹם **since the "yom" that they were upon the earth** עַד הַיּוֹם הַזֶּה **unto this "yom."** And he turned himself, and went out from Pharaoh. (הַזֶּה = **this**)

KJV Deuteronomy 9:24     Ye have been rebellious against the LORD מִיּוֹם **from the "yom"** that I knew you.

(מִ = preposition "from")

# The seventh "yom": A long period of time

Now consider the use of יוֹם "yom" in Genesis 2:2. This is the seventh "yom," often translated the "day of rest" in the KJV. The verse uses a singular form of "yom."

KJV Genesis 2:2   And on the seventh "yom" God ended his work which he had made;
and he rested on the seventh "yom" from all his work which he had made.

As already explained, the sixth "morning" in Genesis 1:31 marks the end of creative "yom" six and the start of the seventh "yom." Remember that concluding phrases read literally:

"and **had been** evening and **had been** morning, . . .."

The seventh "yom," which is not a creative "yom," is of specific interest in this study of the concluding phrases. It has been widely noted that the seventh "yom" is opened but is never closed. It is also widely held that the seventh "yom" continues to this very time because "and had been evening and had been morning, . . .." is never said for the seventh "yom." The Bible asserts that we will enter into God's "rest" of the seventh "yom." The following verses verify this position:

KJV Hebrews 4:9-11

9   There remains therefore a Sabbath rest for the people of God.
10  For the one who has entered His rest has himself also rested from his works, as God did from His.
11  Let us therefore be diligent to enter that rest, lest anyone fall through *following* the same example of disobedience.

The seventh "yom" is already thousands of years long by **any** reading. Placing the seventh "yom" into the creation week as a long period of time, the other six creative "yom" are, by analogy, also long periods of time. The Bible provides many indications that the seven-day cycle of the ordinary week is related to the seven "yom" creative sequence by analogy. For example, the six "yom" plus Sabbath "yom" sequence is commanded for years as well as for "yom" in Leviticus 25:2-8.[45] It was the failure to observe the Sabbath years of rest of the land (erets) which resulted in the exile to Babylon. The seven-year cycle was also commanded for the release of Hebrew bond servants.[46] Additionally there is a "Sabbath" of Sabbath years termed the Jubilee. The Jubilee is a 50th year when all debts of the Hebrews are to be canceled and indebted property returned to the original owners.[47]

The representation of heavenly realities by earthly analogies is well documented in the Bible. The New Testament is explicit in stating that the tabernacle, the ceremonies, and the sacrifices are but "shadows" representing the heavenly reality. All of these are commanded by God in the Books of Moses, as is the Sabbath. Consider the following verses:

KJV Hebrews 8:4-5   For if he were on earth, he should not be a priest, seeing that there are priests that offer gifts according to the law:
Who serve unto the example and shadow of heavenly things, as Moses was admonished of God when he was about to make the tabernacle: for, See, saith he, *that* thou make all things according to the pattern shewed to thee in the mount.

NAS Hebrews 10:1   For the Law, since it has *only* a shadow of the good things to come *and* not the very form of things, can never by the same sacrifices year by year, which they offer continually, make perfect those who draw near.

KJV Colossians 2:16-17   Therefore let no one act as your judge in regard to food or drink or in respect to a festival or a new moon or a Sabbath *days*:
things which are a *mere* shadow of what is to come; but the substance belongs to Christ.

**More verses which indicate that יוֹם "yom" and its forms do not include the "nighttime"**

There are more than 54 verses which use יוֹם "yom" or יוֹמָם "by yom" in a manner which indicates that the word יוֹם "yom" does not include the night. These are verses in which the word "yom" is used but where the Bible specifically includes the night. Some verses were considered earlier and several more examples are given below. In aggregate, they are convincing evidence that the word "yom" does not include the night. The inclusion of the night must be added in some manner. Consider Nehemiah 4:9.

KJV Nehemiah 4:9   Nevertheless we made our prayer unto our God, and set a watch against them **day** and **night**, because of them.

The actual Hebrew for the KJV "**day** and **night**" is יוֹמָם וָלַיְלָה , literally 'by "yom" - by night.'
                **and night  by "yom"** ← Start English here.

Nehemiah 4:9 specifically includes the night. Other phrases such as יוֹם בְּיוֹם "daily," or "every day," are not used, even though they are available. יוֹם בְּיוֹם "daily" is literally "yom - in yom" and refers to daytime activities.

The word יוֹמָם "by yom" is used 49 times, 43 of which mean "daytime." It means "daily" three times and refers to a long period of time two times. One use in Jeremiah 15:9 is uncertain as to whether it refers to daytime or to a longer period of time.[48] The "daytime" meanings are exemplified by Exodus 13:21.

YLT Exodus 13:21   and Jehovah is going before them יוֹמָם by day in a pillar of a cloud, to lead them in the way, and by night in a pillar of fire, to give light to them, to go יוֹמָם by day and by night;

Nehemiah 1:6 shows this exclusion of the night in the word הַיּוֹם "the yom." This part of the verse is translated differently in the KJV than it is in the YLT. Young's Literal Translation is a better representation of the Hebrew. The difference in the translations of the Hebrew words is shown below.

KJV Nehemiah 1:6   . . . which I pray before thee הַיּוֹם now, יוֹמָם day וָלַיְלָה and night, . . .
YLT Nehemiah 1:6   . . . that I am praying before Thee הַיּוֹם to-day, יוֹמָם by day וָלַיְלָה and by night, . . .

Esther 4:16 provides another example of the exclusion of the "nighttime" from the meaning of the word "yom." Here the word translated "days" is the plural word יָמִים "yoms." The prefix ו "and" is translated "or."

KJV Esther 4:16   Go, gather together all the Jews that are present in Shushan, and fast ye for me, and neither eat nor drink three יָמִים days, night or וָיוֹם day:

The author felt the need to expressly include the night. Even today in the Middle East fasts are carried out where those fasting do not eat in the daytime but feast after sunset. They do this on a daily basis.

The question now arises, "Does "yom" *ever* refer to 24 hours? " The answer is **seldom. WOW!**

**The word יוֹם "yom" and 24 hours**

When "yom" does refer to 24 hours, the use is most often connected with the Sabbath or the festivals and ceremonies which include a remembrance of the Exodus. That the Sabbath is a remembrance of the Passover and the departure can be verified by considering Deuteronomy 5:15.

KJV Deuteronomy 5:15   And remember that thou wast a servant in the land of Egypt, and *that* the LORD thy God brought thee out thence through a mighty hand and by a stretched out arm: therefore the LORD thy God commanded thee to keep the sabbath day.

As a remembrance, the ceremonial observance must include the night of the previous "yom," corresponding to the Passover. It must also include the daylight of the following "yom," remembering the departure. Because of this, terms like "Sabbath" and יוֹם הַשַּׁבָּת "yom the Sabbath" refer to 24 hours of ceremonial observance. יוֹם is also used infrequently regarding ceremonies which are specifically defined in other verses to include the night. The inclusion of the night is specifically added. An example of this is יוֹם הַכִּפֻּרִים "the Day of Atonement."

יוֹם הַכִּפֻּרִים translates literally as "yom of the atonement." Leviticus 23:27 defines the date and the activities of the daytime of the Day of Atonement.

Then in Leviticus 23:32 the יוֹם הַכִּפֻּרִים "yom of the atonement" is specifically said to be a שַׁבָּת "sabbath." The specific inclusion of the previous night is necessary for the phrase יוֹם הַכִּפֻּרִים "yom of the atonement" to include more than the daytime. In present day English this is referred to as "Yom Kippur."

KJV Leviticus 23:27   Also on the tenth *day* of this seventh month *there shall be* a day of atonement:
it shall be an holy convocation unto you; and ye shall afflict your souls,
and offer an offering made by fire unto the LORD.

KJV Leviticus 23:32   It *shall be* unto you a sabbath of rest, and ye shall afflict your souls:
in the ninth *day* of the month at even, from even unto even,
shall ye celebrate your sabbath.

How the Bible indicates when "yom" is used in a manner meaning 24 hours is treated extensively in the section "When 'Yom' Means 24 Hours" (page 84).

## Translation and the Time Meaning of the Creative יוֹם "Yom"

What does יוֹם "yom" mean in the concluding phrases of the creative "yom" of Genesis 1:3-31?

This is a question which has been vociferously argued in the last 40 years and which will now be considered. The study just completed has shown that the most common meanings of יוֹם is "daytime" and "time." The meaning "24 hours" was shown to be associated with ceremonial remembrance of the Passover and departure, an infrequent use. The use of יוֹם "yom" in Genesis 1:5 **does not** correspond to a ceremonial remembrance and so does not correspond to a 24-hour meaning. This leaves "time," the preferred translation of this study, and "daytime" as possible translations.

The reader should recall that the age of the Earth is **not** being determined by the time length of the creative periods. Genesis 1:1 and Genesis 1:2 describe the Earth in an existing (but unfinished) state before the start of the first creative period.

The concluding phrases of the six creative time periods are formal phrases. They differ only in the number which changes in the sequence of the six verses. The concluding phrase in Genesis 1:5 line (2) is:

**Genesis 1:5   line (2)**

| אֶחָד | יוֹם | בֹּקֶר | וַיְהִי | עֶרֶב | וַיְהִי | (2) | ← | Hebrew starts here. |
|---|---|---|---|---|---|---|---|---|
| one | "yom" | morning | "and had been," | evening | "and had been," | | ← | Start English here. |

KJV Genesis 1:5    . . . And the evening and the morning were the first day.†    ("were" indicates completed action)
† *Hebr. and euening was and morning was &c.* (KJV 1611 margin note.)

ASV Genesis 1:5    . . . And *there* was evening and *there* was morning, one day.    ("was" indicates completed action)

The KJV translation clearly does not reflect the Hebrew as it combines the completion of the evening and the morning into one event. The Hebrew indicates separate completions as translated in the ASV and as indicated in the KJV 1611 margin note. Because the phrases differ only in the final numerical word, the evidence that "yom" six is a long period of time is applicable to all the creative "yom."

### Evidence that "yom" six is a long period of time

The events described in Genesis 1:24-31 and Genesis 2:5-25 describe the activities of God, Adam, and Eve during the sixth creative "time." With "yom" translated "time" the events can be understood as occurring in an amount of time reflecting the usual meanings of the words. It is not necessary to "speed up" the performance rate of the events described in Genesis 1:24-31 and Genesis 2:5-25.

In brief, the events during the sixth creative "time" include:

1. God commands and the ground brings forth cattle.
2. God creates (bara) Adam.
3. God plants a garden.
4. Trees grow to sufficient maturity to bear fruit.
   (This requires at least a growing season, but often many seasons may pass before fruit is borne.)
5. Adam is given permission to eat from most of the trees.
6. Adam names the animals which are brought to him.
7. Adam sleeps and God removes tissue (KJV "rib") from Adam's side.
8. Eve is formed (cloned?) from the tissue (KJV "rib") and brought to Adam.

All the above suggest the passage of a considerable period of time. These are not the events of one "daytime"! The time of the growing season for the production of fruit is at least several months. This sense of time is contained in the ordinary meaning of the words and applies to all the actions, conveying a sense of the passage of considerable time. Genesis 2:15 indicates that Adam had performed gardening duties of some sort for a considerable period of time.

KJV Genesis 2:1  And the LORD God took the man, and put him into the garden of Eden to dress it and to keep it.

Those advocating a 24-hour creative time period often assert that the time between Genesis 1:3 and Genesis 1:31 is 144 hours (6 days x 24 hours). Because of this, they are forced into the absurd position of requiring all of the above events to take place at "warp speed." Everything listed above for creative "yom" six would take place in about 12 hours! This would also be required for the events of the other creative "yom." There is no indication in the language of these sections that the events were accomplished at an unusual rate. The translation "time" in the concluding phrases allows these sections to be understood more normally, consistent with the manner in which they were written. Evidence for a long sixth creative "yom" is found in Genesis 2:22-23 where Eve is brought to Adam. Adam's response in Genesis 2:23 is:

KJV Genesis 2:23      And Adam said, This *is* הַפַּעַם "now" bone of my bones, and flesh of my flesh: she shall be called Woman, because she was taken out of Man.

The word הַפַּעַם translated "now" carries a sense indicating the passage of a long period of time. This meaning can be seen in Genesis 29:34, in the statement of Leah, where the word הַפַּעַם is translated "this time."

KJV Genesis 29:34      And she conceived again, and bare a son; and said, Now הַפַּעַם "this time" will my husband be joined unto me, because I have born him three sons: therefore was his name called Levi.

The New KJV translates הַפַּעַם as "at last" in Genesis 2:23, indicating the passage of a considerable amount of time.

Next there is the question of how the "daytime" meaning of יוֹם yom is extended by the phrase "And *there* was evening and *there* was morning." The concluding phrases very carefully do not say "night"; they say "evening." "Evening" conveys a sense of gradual cessation or diminishing of activity. They say "morning," which conveys a sense of a new starting of creative activity. The use of morning and evening to represent long periods of time is evident in Psalm 90. This Psalm is commonly attributed to Moses, the writer of Genesis. It represents the youth of a person as the morning, and the old age of a person as the evening. Morning and evening are used here to represent long periods of time in a person's life.

ASV (American Standard Version) Psalm 90:3-6

3. Thou dost turn man back into dust, And dost say, "Return, O children of men."
4. For a thousand years in Thy sight Are like yesterday when it passes by, Or *as* a watch in the night.
5. Thou hast swept them away like a flood, they fall asleep;
   In the morning they are like grass which sprouts anew.
6. **In the morning it flourishes, and sprouts anew; Toward evening it fades, and withers away**.

Because this psalm represents the old age of a person as "evening" it shows that the phrase "And *there* was evening and *there* was morning" may indicate a long period of time.

Any assertion that "evening" in this phrase represents an ordinary "night" needs to be justified by biblical exegesis and should not be accepted on mere assertion. By not using the word "night" the phrase gives no indication of the total time of the "evening" and the "morning." The time interval between the "evening" and the "morning" may be longer than the ordinary "night." The Hebrew words translated "evening" and "morning" are discussed further in the section "More About Evening and Morning" (page 79). These words have other meanings.

With יוֹם "yom" translated "time," the absence of any specification of the time interval between the "evening" and the "morning" becomes evident. The translation "time" is consistent with the use of the word יוֹם "yom" to express long time periods as in:

יוֹם יְהוָה     **"day of the Lord"** (appears 14 times), יוֹם נְקָמָה **"a day of vengeance"** and other similar expressions

בַּיּוֹם הַהוּא     **"in that day"** (used more than 100 times referring to long periods of time)

עַד־הַיּוֹם     **"until this time"** (KJV "unto this day," used more that 82 times).

**How would the Hebrews at the time of Moses have interpreted "yom" in the concluding phrase?**

There is external evidence that they would have interpreted the "yom" as "time." This is how the symbol, ⊙, which is the symbol equivalent of "yom," was used in Egyptian hieroglyphic writing. Remember, the Hebrews had been under the influence of the Egyptians for about 400 years. Egyptian writing was, like the Hebrew, a language written using only the consonants of the words. Similarly to Hebrew, words with different spoken vowels were spelled the same. An additional complication was the use of several different symbols for each consonant. Different words which were spelled the same were identified by adding a "determinative" symbol to the word. The added determinative symbol represented a concept and was equivalent to a word representing that concept. For instance the word **NHH** which means eternity is written:

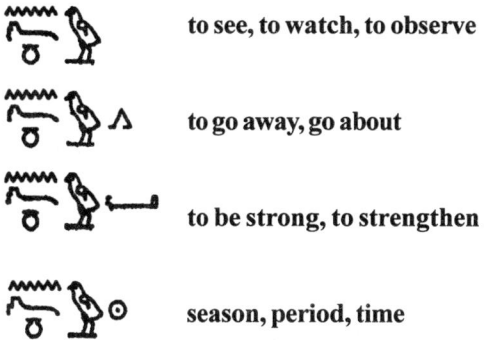

    N H H         N H H

The ⊙, the symbol equivalent to "yom," is added to identify that the intended word referred to time.

An additional example of the use of determinatives is given below for a hieroglyphic word, which without a determinative, means to see, watch, or observe.[49] The consonantal spelling of the words is the same. The determinative distinguishes between the words and so identifies the vowels. The determinatives are walking feet indicating motion, an arm holding a stick indicating power, and the sign ⊙ for day. The sign for day is the determinative for time.

    to see, to watch, to observe

    to go away, go about

    to be strong, to strengthen

    season, period, time

The concluding phrase "And *there* had been evening and *there* had been morning, one time" has a measure of similarity to the use of symbols to identify the meaning of words in Egyptian. Because of this, the Hebrews of the time of Moses would have been prepared to read the word "yom" at the end of a phrase as "time." That יוֹם "yom" frequently means "time" has already been shown. This may seem "unnatural" to an English reader and the argument is not definitive. But it does suggest that reading the concluding phrases as "long time periods" could have been expected more than 3,000 years ago immediately following the Exodus.

## Summary of Results for Genesis 1:1-5 and Comments Regarding 24-Hour "Day" Models

This section is a review of the results of the study of Genesis 1:1-5. Additional comments will also be made to prepare the reader for the following studies of the remaining creative "yom." The additional comments will concern issues which are relevant to the 24-hour interpretation of the word יום "yom."

**The study of Genesis 1:1-5 has determined that:**

1. Genesis 1:1 and Genesis 1:2 take place and describe actions completed before the "And God said..." of Genesis 1:3. As a consequence, Genesis 1:1 and Genesis 1:2 place no restriction on the age of the Earth or on the age of the Universe.

2. Genesis 1:3-4 describe the appearance of light at the surface of the earth in a manner consistent with ordinary physical principles.

3. The use of the word יום "yom" in Genesis 1:5 is consistent with and correctly translatable by the English word "time." The translation "time" is supported by the actual uses of the word יום "yom" found in the Bible. It is also supported by descriptions of the events occurring within the sixth creative period. The translation "time" is shown to be the most probable meaning of the word יום "yom" in Genesis 1:5.

However, the translation of יום as "day" cannot be conclusively excluded on the basis of only the analysis of the uses of the word יום "yom." Additional information is required. The analysis does show that the translation "day" is unlikely. The final exclusion of the translation "day" is based on the consideration of the events which occur in all the creative "yom" and consideration of the use of the word "yom" in Genesis 2:1-4. The translation "time" is also conclusively chosen based on the context and the events which take place within the creative periods.

Genesis 2:5-25, the story of Adam and Eve in the Garden, is part of the consideration. These verses relate events which take place within the sixth creative "yom."

The need to use additional information to determine the meaning of a word is a frequent requirement in translating biblical Hebrew. The ambiguity in meaning stems from the extremely small number of words in biblical Hebrew which leads to the same consonantal word having several meanings. This was explained in the early sections of this book (pages 4-6). The events of the remaining creative periods will be studied starting on page 90. There may be some readers who are not yet fully convinced that יום "yom" is to be translated "time" in the concluding phrases. These readers will need to consider the remaining creative periods which provide additional evidence supporting the translation "time."

### Additional Factors

There are two additional translation factors to be considered. These are involved with the determination of the "when" of actions and are listed below as (1) and (2).

(1) A Hebrew narrative will often include sentences that describe events which were already completed in the past, before the place where the sentence itself appears in the narrative. Said in another way, all the sentences do not describe actions which immediately follow the actions of the preceding sentence. Some sentences describe actions which had occurred prior to the preceding sentence.

In the following creative "yom" there are some Hebrew sentence structures which do indicate actions completed earlier. In a good English translation, these sentences would use the pluperfect. These sentences will be identified and the "when" of the actions will be discussed in detail.

(2) In Hebrew narrative, the time interval between the actions in successive sentences is also often unspecified. This is an important factor to consider when studying Genesis 1:1-31. Recall that biblical Hebrew verbs do not have tense, but rather express completed action or incomplete action. The Genesis One narrative is composed mostly of a sequence of sentences which begin with a "waw-consecutive" verb form. The "waw" is the prefix ו "waw" which

is translated "and." The "waw-consecutive" of an imperfect verb indicates only that the action is completed; it does not indicate that the actions follow immediately after the completed actions of the preceding sentence.

**Translation issues relevant to the 24-hour day interpretation**

Item (2) above and the phrase וַיְהִי כֵן which the KJV translates "and it was so," constitute constraints upon any 24-hour "day" interpretations of Genesis 1:3-35. These two constraints lead to a 24-hour day model where the assumed 24-hour creative "days" are separated by long periods of time. The time between Genesis 1:3 and Genesis 2:1 becomes a long period of time, not 144 hours (6 x 24 hours). Detailed consideration of how this comes about will now be given. Then the additional assumptions required to obtain a 144-hour interval will be discussed.

The issue described in item (2) will be considered first.

Often unnoticed, the time interval between each concluding phrase and the following "and God said . . ." is not stated and is not determinable from the Hebrew text of Genesis 1:1-31. This time interval cannot be assumed to be zero just because it is not stated. The figure below illustrates the placement of the unstated interval and the following example of Genesis 28:10-11 demonstrates that it cannot be assumed to not exist on the basis of not being stated.

Genesis 1:5        . . . and *there* was evening and *there* was morning, one time.

        ↑
        **a time interval of unstated length**
        ↓

Genesis 1:6.       And God said . . .

Genesis 28:10-11 provides an example of this pattern. Genesis 28:10-11 are about Jacob departing Beersheba to seek a wife from among his relations in Haran. Verses 10 and 11 begin with a "waw-consecutive" comprised of a "waw" prefixed to an imperfect verb, the usual pattern of the Hebrew narrative. The "and he lighted upon a certain place, . . . " does not specify the time interval between the verses.

KJV Genesis 28:10        And Jacob went out from Beersheba, and went toward Haran.
*(Literally "and had gone out Jacob . . .." The verb is the first Hebrew word.)*

        ↑
        **a time interval of unstated length**
        ↓

KJV Genesis 28:11        And he lighted upon a certain place, and tarried there all night, because the sun was set; and he took of the stones of that place, and put *them for* his pillows, and lay down in that place to sleep.

It is only later in Genesis 28:19, where the place is identified as Bethel, that the time interval can be estimated. Beersheba to Bethel is a distance of about 60 miles as the crow flies. This distance, given the terrain and travel conditions of the time, which would represent a journey of about four days. This estimate is based on the similar journey made by Abraham for the offering of Isaac.[50]

The study of this book concludes that the creative "yom" are long periods of time. Because of this, a time interval between the concluding phrase and the following "and God said . . ." is not a factor. The commands and their completion occur within the long creative time periods.

For those who wish to interpret the creative "yom" as 24 hours, the time interval is a factor which cannot be ignored. Additional evidence for the existence of a time interval is provided by frequent use of the phrase וַיְהִי כֵן which the KJV translates "and it was so." This phrase will be considered next.

The consonantal Hebrew phrase ויהי כן appears nine times in the Bible, six of which are in Genesis One. This phrase marked, וַיְהִי כֵן, is used in Genesis 1:3-31 to indicate the completion of the creative commands. The word וַיְהִי is the waw-consecutive of the imperfect verb "to be" and has the completed action meaning. The verb וַיְהִי is translated "and it came to pass" 320 times by the KJV. The next word כֵן, pronounced "ken," is the word usually translated "so." In Genesis One the KJV translates וַיְהִי כֵן as "and it was so." This phrase does **not** mean that the "so" was achieved immediately. The meaning of the phrase וַיְהִי כֵן can be determined from the three verses, not in Genesis One, which also use the phrase. 2 Kings 15:12 will be considered here as an example showing the meaning.

KJV 2 Kings 15:12    This *was* the word of the LORD which he spake unto Jehu, saying, Thy sons shall sit on the throne of Israel unto the fourth *generation*. וַיְהִי כֵן And so it came to pass.

The events that the words וַיְהִי כֵן describe in 2 Kings 15:12 do not take place immediately. They take place over an extended period of time, four generations. The Hebrew verb does indicate a completed action, but "when" the action is completed is not indicated by the וַיְהִי כֵן phrase. The other verses are discussed on page 95.

**Consequences of the Translational Issues, Time Models**

Because וַיְהִי כֵן does **not** indicate immediate command completion, it supports and fits well with the view that the creative times are long periods of time. These long periods of time allow for the later completion of the commands. For an *assumed* 24-hour day, because the completion of the commands does not take place immediately within the "daytime," a time interval is indicated. This leads naturally to a model where the 24-hour creative "days" are separated by long periods of time. The completion of the commands takes place within a long time interval between the creative "days" of command, between the "morning" and the following "and God said." The long creative times model and the 24-hour assumption model are pictured graphically below as an aid to understanding the differences.

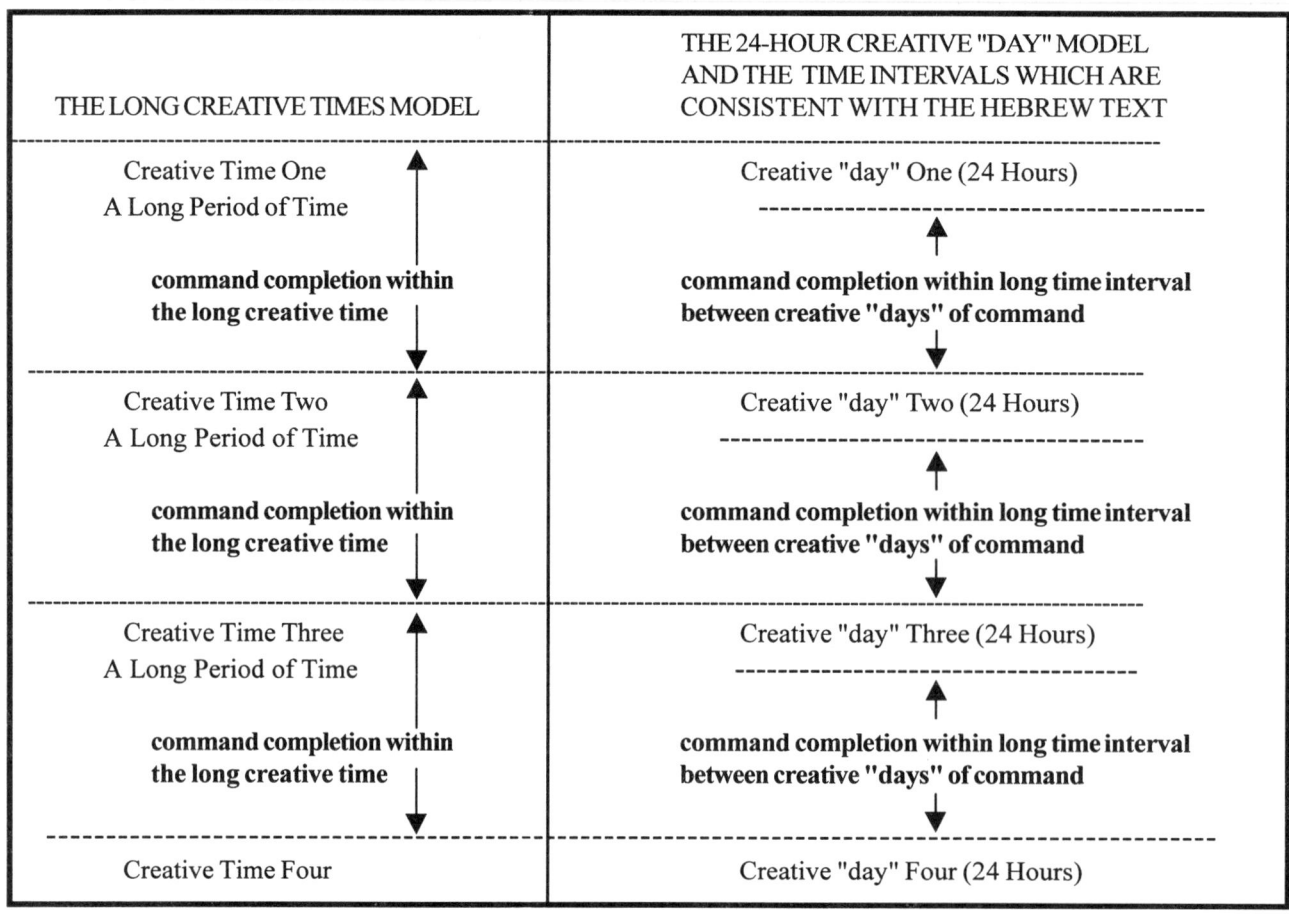

The 24-hour "day" model shown on the facing page is not the 24-hour model which is usually advocated. The usual 24-hour model asserts a 144-hour time interval (6 x 24) between Genesis 1:3 and Genesis 2:1. The 144-hour model requires two additional assumptions:

(1) That the commands are completed immediately within the 24-hour time period, an assumption contradicted by the example of 2 Kings 15:12. This assumption is also opposed by the many times וַיְהִי is translated "and it came to pass" by the KJV.

(2) That there is no time interval between the creative "days," an assumption contradicted and opposed by the example of Genesis 28:10-11. The presence of a time interval is also supported by the word וַיְהִי . When וַיְהִי has been translated "and it came to pass," it also often indicates that there has been a time interval, and that other events have also occurred which are not stated.

These additional assumptions are not generally stated and need to be justified for the Hebrew verses before being accepted. The evidences given in the examples cannot just be ignored.

**The marking of the time intervals and their duration**

For the creative times of Genesis One, the time intervals begin with the phrase translated "And God said." The phrases "and there was morning" mark the end of the preceding creative "yom." The mornings do not mark the start of the next creative "yom." The next creative "yom" begins with the following phrase "And God said."

Between these two markers there is a time interval of undetermined length, perhaps millions of 24-hour days. The 24-hour "day" interpretation asserts, without textual basis, that this time interval is zero. The assumption that the creative "yom" are immediately consecutive 24-hour days is just that, an assumption imposed upon the text. In accordance with the actual Hebrew text, the time intervals between successive "days" may be long.

The 24-hour day model also requires assuming an ordinary "daytime" followed by an ordinary "nighttime." That the phrase "and there was evening, and there was morning" indicates an ordinary "night" is also an assumption. This study earlier carefully discussed the use of evening and morning to mean long periods of time on page 68. The verses discussed were Psalm 90:3-6, a Psalm attributed to Moses, where evening and morning were clearly used to indicate long periods of time. Without this assumption the creative "yom" also become "daytimes" separated by long periods of time.

The usual 24-hour "day" interpretation requires acceptance of **all** the forgoing assumptions, and **all** the assumptions must be justified to obtain a 144-hour time interval (6 x 24) between Genesis 1:3 and Genesis 2:1.

# The Translation of Genesis 1:3-5

For the verses of Genesis One this study presents two translations. There is a Study Translation underneath the Hebrew which consistently uses "had" to translate the Hebrew completed action verbs. From this study translation there results a "Good English" translation which uses both the past and past perfect tenses. The Study Translation is used as an aid to determining the "when" of the actions from the context of the verb use. After the "when" of the actions has been determined, the "Good English" translation presents these results in the form expected in the English language. The "Good English" translation represents the results of this study, and represents the "when" determined for the actions in the creative times. Both translations for Genesis 1:3-5 will now be given followed by a discussion of the differences.

**Summary Study Translation of Genesis 1:3-5**

A summary Study Translation of Genesis 1:3-5 appears below which is derived from the translation which appeared under the Hebrew verses and the discussion. A "Good English" translation based on this study is given below the study translation.

| | |
|---|---|
| Genesis 1:3 | And God had said, Light shall exist; and light had existed. |
| Genesis 1:4 | And God had seen the light, as good; |
| | and God had separated between the light and between the dark. |
| Genesis 1:5 | And God had called the light "daytime" and the dark he had called "nighttime"; (1) |
| | and *there* had been evening and *there* had been morning, one time. (2) |

**The "Good English" Translation of Genesis 1:3-5**

| | |
|---|---|
| Genesis 1:3 | And God said, Light shall exist; and light existed. |
| Genesis 1:4 | And God **had seen** the light as good; |
| | and God **had separated** between the light and between the dark. |
| Genesis 1:5 | And God called the light "daytime" and the dark he **had called** "nighttime"; (1) |
| | **and *there* was evening and *there* was morning, one time. (2)** |

How did the words "had" come to be in the "Good English" translation? In the absence of any pluperfect indication found in the analyses, all the pluperfect verbs of the study translation would have been replaced by simple past tense verbs as is used in the KJV.

The "had separated" of Genesis 1:4 reflects the analysis on pages 56-57 where the separation was shown to occur simultaneously with the appearance of light in Genesis 1:3. The separation is past completed with respect to the place where the statement appears in the verse, therefore "**had separated**." The choice of "had separated" is made because of context, not on the basis of Hebrew grammatical construction. This analysis depended upon the translations "separated" or "divided" interpreted as a physical action.[51] The translation "had seen" has been chosen to make both of the verbs in Genesis 1:4 agree in tense. The translation "saw" would introduce a time ordering not in the Hebrew.

The use of the English past tense in Genesis 1:5 will now be explained. Genesis 1:5 line (1) is shown below.

KJV Genesis 1:5 (1) And God called the light Day, and the darkness he called Night.

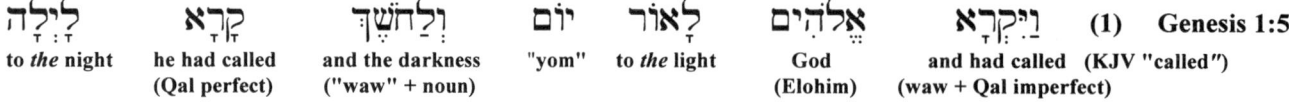

| לָיְלָה | קָרָא | וְלַחֹשֶׁךְ | יוֹם | לָאוֹר | אֱלֹהִים | וַיִּקְרָא | (1) Genesis 1:5 |
|---|---|---|---|---|---|---|---|
| to *the* night | he had called (Qal perfect) | and the darkness ("waw" + noun) | "yom" | to *the* light | God (Elohim) | and had called (waw + Qal imperfect) | (KJV "called") |

The first verb is the "waw + imperfect verb" which continues a narrative and is translated using the past tense as in the KJV. The initial "waw + imperfect verb" indicates that the namings, as a connected action, takes place after the events of Genesis 1:4. The sequence of the final three words is "waw + noun--perfect verb," followed by the noun "night." In this position the "waw + noun--perfect verb" construction refers to the sequence in which the two "namings" occurred in a nearly contemporaneous time interval.[52] It does not refer to a naming in the more distant past. The translation "and the dark he had called" is made by Z. Zevit in his book *The Anterior Construction In Classical Hebrew* on the basis of the "waw + noun--perfect verb" construction.[53] The "anterior construction" is Zevit's term for the "waw + noun--perfect verb" construction. Zevit holds that the "waw + noun--perfect verb" construction should be translated in a pluperfect sense. Most of Zevit's examples of this pluperfect construction involve events which are logically prior (anterior) to a preceding verb or sentence. The sequence of the naming the nighttime before the daytime is logically correct if importance is attached to the sequence of a dark planet surface becoming lighted. The "dark" existed before the light, and becomes nighttime when in contrast with the daytime.

For Genesis 1:5 line (2) the Study Translation and the "Good English" translation also differ. The "Good English" translation is the same as the most common English translations, which differ from the KJV.

Three final line translations are presented below for comparison:

                Study Translation:   And *there* had been evening and *there* had been morning, one time.
                               KJV:   "and evening and morning were, . . ."
ASV, NIV, NAS, RSV and "Good English":   "and *there* was evening and *there* was morning, . . ."

**Genesis 1:5 line (2)**

| אֶחָד | יוֹם | בֹּקֶר | וַיְהִי | עֶרֶב | וַיְהִי | (2) | ← Hebrew starts here. |
| one | "yom" | morning | "and had been," | evening | "and had been," | | ← Start English here. |

The literal Hebrew for the final phrase would read "and evening had been and morning had been." In the Study Translation, and in the "Good English" translation, the word order has been altered. "*There*" has been inserted to facilitate the flow of the English. This word order and the insertion of "*there*" reflects the word order and use of "*there*" in the ASV.

The KJV "And the evening and the morning were . . .." does not correctly represent the Hebrew. The KJV combines the completion of the evening and the morning into one event. The Hebrew relates their completions as being sequential. The KJV 1611 did acknowledge the Hebrew in a margin note: "†*Hebr. and euening was and morning was &c.*" The time interval between the completed evening and the completed morning is not stated.

The "Good English" translation does not use the "had been" of the Study Translation.

The "had been" of the Study Translation cannot be adopted because the concluding phrases are repeated at the end of all the creative times. In some of the creative times there are preceding verses which use the English past tense. The use of "had been" would introduce incorrect time ordering in these cases and so cannot be adopted. For this reason, the final "Good English" translation adopted will be **"and *there* was evening and *there* was morning, one time."**

The translation "time" is consistent with the verbs used in Genesis 1:5. In Genesis 1:5 line (2) the verb וַיְהִי is vowel marked as a "waw-consecutive Qal imperfect" which translates as the completed action. In this phrase the Study Translation can be "and had been," "and *it* had come to pass," or "and had become." The KJV translates the verb וַיְהִי as "and *it* came to pass" 320 times, a frequent translation. The translation "and it came to pass" has important consequences for "when" the "evening" and "morning" are completed. וַיְהִי often appears at the beginning of a sentence and the KJV phrase "and it came to pass" indicates that:

1.      There has been a time interval of unstated length.
2.      Events have occurred which may or may not have been stated.

The importance of this observation is in showing that the verb וַיְהִי does not include any sense of immediacy. As a consequence, the translation וַיְהִי "was" also cannot convey a meaning of immediacy. The lack of immediacy is consistent with the creative "yom" being long periods of time and is consistent with the translation **"and *there* was evening and *there* was morning, one time."**

In the "Good English" translation the word "*there*" is inserted and the verb וַיְהִי is translated "was." One advantage of the "*there*" is that it conveys a sense of "and *it* had come to pass," or "had become." The "*there*" also implies a change in condition but does not give a "when" or a duration.

## Exodus 20:11 Considered Again

Now Exodus 20:11 must be considered again. The verse is considered again because of incorrect attempts by others to apply these verses to determine the lengths of the six "creative times" and to assert that Genesis 1:3-31 is a 144-hour interval of time. Recall that the section Analysis of Exodus 20:11 (page 28) carefully showed that this verse did not refer to the "bara" creation of Genesis 1:1, but rather referred to the subsequent making (asah) of those things that had been created (bara) for making (asah). Exodus 20:10-11 cannot define the lengths of the six "creative times" for three reasons. Any one of these reasons is sufficient to defeat the attempt to assert that Genesis 1:3-31 is a 144-hour interval of time. The effect of the Hebrew "for six yoms" instead to the KJV "*in* six . . ." will be considered as reason number (3).

Reason (1): Exodus 20:11 is a reference to Genesis One. As a reference, Exodus 20:11 adopts the meaning of the word "yom" as used in the six concluding phrases of Genesis One. By adopting the meaning of a referenced word, a word cannot be used to define the referenced word. Genesis 1:5 is one of the phrases which defines the meaning which is adopted.

YLT Exodus 20:11
(1) for six days hath Jehovah made (asah) the heavens and the earth,
(2) the sea, and all that {is} in them, and resteth in the seventh day;
(3) therefore hath Jehovah blessed the Sabbath-day, and doth sanctify it.

| הָאָרֶץ | וְאֵת | הַשָּׁמַיִם | אֵת | יְהוָה | עָשָׂה | יָמִים | שֵׁשֶׁת | כִּי | (1) | Exodus 20:11 |
|---|---|---|---|---|---|---|---|---|---|---|
| the earth | and + dir. obj. marker | the heavens | dir. obj. marker | Yahweh | had made | "yoms" | six | for | | ← Start English here. |

Reason (2): Exodus 20:11 references and corresponds to the creative times by analogy. Correspondence by analogy cannot define the lengths of the six "creative times." That Exodus 20:11 references both the "seventh day" and the "Sabbath-day" by analogy will now be explained.

Exodus 20:11 (2) which refers to the "seventh yom" of Genesis 2:2-3 uses the Hebrew word וַיָּנַח which the YLT translates "resteth" and the KJV translates וַיָּנַח "rested." This word is **not** the word שָׁבַת (shabat) used in Genesis 2:3. The Hebrew of Exodus 20:11 (2) referring to the seventh "yom" is:

| ... הַשְּׁבִיעִי | בַּיּוֹם | וַיָּנַח | ... | (2) | Exodus 20:11 |
|---|---|---|---|---|---|
| the seventh | in "yom" | and rested ("waw" + Qal imperfect) | | | ← Start English here. |

The word וַיָּנַח = יָנַח + וַ is a form of the word נוח meaning "rest." The words used in Genesis 2:2 and Genesis 2:3 are וַיִּשְׁבֹּת "and had ceased," and שָׁבַת "had ceased." The change in words shows that the reference in Exodus 20:11 is by analogy and is not an exact correspondence. The reference of Exodus 20:11, YLT line (3), to the Sabbath-day is also an analogy because the Sabbath "yom" is itself a reference by analogy, as will now be discussed. This discussion will subsequently be shown to also apply to Exodus 31:16-17.

The KJV translates the word שָׁבַת (shabat) as "cease" (55 times) and as "rest" (11 times). In many cases the English translation "rest" is actually used to express a ceasing of work. We can easily misunderstand the KJV due to the changes in the connotation of the English word "rest" since the 1611 translation of the KJV. The English word "rest" also means to "stop" or "cease" work as when we take a "rest break." The Passover and the Exodus were the defining moments of the nation of Israel. The Sabbath **is** connected to the Exodus and **is** structured as a remembrance of the Passover and the departure from Egypt. As a remembrance, the ceremonial observance must include the night of the previous "yom," corresponding to the Passover. It must also include the daylight of the following "yom," remembering the departure. That the Sabbath is a remembrance can be verified by considering Deuteronomy 5:15.

KJV Deuteronomy 5:15   And remember that thou wast a servant in the land of Egypt, and *that* the LORD thy God brought thee out thence through a mighty hand and by a stretched out arm: therefore the LORD thy God commanded thee to keep the sabbath day.

There is further confirmation of the representative and analogous nature of the relationship of the sabbath day to the seventh "yom" of ceasing of Genesis 2:2-3. The phrase שַׁבָּת לַיהוָה which translates literally as "a ceasing to Yahweh" or "a Sabbath to Yahweh" occurs four times, one of which defines the "Sabbath" of the land.

KJV Leviticus 25:2　　　　Speak unto the children of Israel, and say unto them, When ye come into the land which I give you, then shall the land keep a שַׁבָּת לַיהוָה sabbath unto the LORD.

The Sabbath of the land can only be analogous of the pattern of the six creative times and the following seventh "yom" of Genesis 2:2. Here the KJV has translated שַׁבָּת לַיהוָה as "a Sabbath unto the LORD." This translation is in agreement with the earlier discussion of Exodus 20:10.

Correspondence by analogy is also shown in Exodus 31:16-17. In Exodus 31:16 and the first part of Exodus 31:17 the Sabbath is said to be a "covenant" and a "sign." A "sign" is not identical to the thing it represents. Following that statement there is again a reference to Genesis One and to the meaning of the word "yom" in the concluding phrases of Genesis One. That reference uses the word שָׁבַת.

KJV Exodus 31:16　　　　Wherefore the children of Israel shall keep הַשַּׁבָּת the sabbath, to observe הַשַּׁבָּת the sabbath throughout their generations, *for* a perpetual covenant.

KJV Exodus 31:17　　　　It *is* a sign between me and the children of Israel for ever:

(A reference to Genesis One then follows; note that *in* does not appear in the Hebrew.)

　　　　for *in* six days the LORD עָשָׂה made heaven and earth, [עָשָׂה (asah) "made" is not "bara"]

　　　　and on the seventh day he שָׁבַת **rested**, and וַיִּנָּפַשׁ was **refreshed**. (שָׁבַת is "ceased.")

The word translated "rested" is שָׁבַת which means "ceased." The following word וַיִּנָּפַשׁ is a form of the word נָפַשׁ meaning "to take breath." The word וַיִּנָּפַשׁ appears three times and the KJV always translates it "refreshed." The American idiomatic expression to "take a breather," used by people to indicate a "rest break" from manual labor, is an example of "breathing" being related to rest or ceasing work. In this reference the KJV again inserts the word "*in*" which does **not** appear in the Hebrew. The Hebrew reads "for six 'yoms' " just as in Exodus 20:11. **Correspondence by analogy cannot define the lengths of the six creative times.**

Reason (3):　A third reason that Exodus 20:11 cannot determine the total time of the creation is that line (1) does not refer to the entire time interval.

Exodus 20:11 **does not** refer to any of the creative action (bara) of God referenced in Genesis 1:1 or to any creative action בָּרָא "bara" of God which preceded Genesis 1:3. It cannot make this reference because עָשָׂה "asah" (made) is different from "bara" (create).

Exodus 20:11 and Exodus 31:17 also do not include the time referred to in the concluding phrases "and *there* was evening and *there* was morning." These verses therefore cannot determine the time interval between Genesis 1:3 and Genesis 1:35. The word which the KJV translates "days" is יָמִים "yoms," the plural of the word יוֹם "yom." יָמִים most often means "daytime," and does not include the nighttime. That יָמִים "yoms" refers to "daytimes" can be seen by reference to Exodus 16:26 below which refers to the gathering of the manna. The manna is known from the associated text to have been gathered in the "daytime."

Exodus 16:26

KJV　　Six יָמִים days ye shall gather it; but on the seventh day, *which is* the sabbath, in it there shall be none.

YLT　　six יָמִים days ye do gather it,　　and in the seventh day　　— the sabbath — in it there is none.

The argument that the יוֹם "yom" of the ordinary human week can be used to define the יוֹם "yom" of the concluding phrases of the creative times fails. The translation 'For six "yom" or "for six days" has an important difference in meaning. Correctly translated, Exodus 20:11 and Exodus 31:17 are consistent with long creative times. This is just the opposite of the conclusion claimed by the 144-hour, six 24-hour day advocates.

Line (2) of Exodus 31:17 is shown below in the YLT which translates the line correctly and in the KJV which inserts an "*in*" which is not in the Hebrew.

YLT Exodus 31:17 (2) . . . for six days Jehovah made the heavens and the earth, . . .
KJV Exodus 31:17 (2) . . . for *in* six days the LORD made heaven and earth, . . .

Exodus 20:11 and Exodus 31:17 refer to the makings (asah) commanded in Genesis One in all of the creative times. The pattern in Genesis One is that after an initial "And God said," the commands spoken by God (Elohim) are related. Evidence for long creative times comes about because some of the makings (asah) can be shown to have not taken place immediately. This is because of the use of the phrase וַיְהִי כֵן "and it did come to pass so." וַיְהִי כֵן is translated "and so it came to pass" by the KJV in 2 Kings 15:12, a verse where the completion occurs over four generations. This phrase וַיְהִי כֵן occurs in three of the creative times. Genesis 1:11-12, Genesis 1:14-18 and Genesis 1:24-25 all provide textual evidence that the completions did not take place within 24 hours. A discussion of the grammar and the repetition principles which apply to all these verse sequences is given later on page 98. The three verses which define the meaning and use of וַיְהִי כֵן are discussed on page 95.

The 144-hour, six 24-hour day model requires that the commands be completed within the assumed 24-hour "day" in which they are spoken. For "long creative times" a later completion of the commanded makings (more than 24 hours later) presents no difficulty and is evidence that the creative times are long. The advocates of the 24-hour model must either:
1. Assert that the commands are completed within the daytime hours, or
2. Assert that the "made" (asah) refers to the commands which God spoke within the six creative times.

Assertion (1) lacks evidence. The evidence most commonly asserted for command completion within 24 hours is the "*in* six days" of Exodus 20:11 and Exodus 31:17. This evidence does not exist because "*in*" does not appear in the Hebrew. The KJV "*in*" has played a significant role in the advocacy of the creation being completed within 144 hours (6 times 24). An "in yom" does appear with the word "asah" in Genesis 2:4. There the בְּיוֹם עֲשׂוֹת 'in "yom" of making' uses the singular בְּיוֹם "in yom" to refer to all six creative times, a long period of time.

Assertion (2) can fit the speaking of the commands within the daytime of an assumed 24-hour day. It is the completions which are not indicated to occur within the assumed 24-hour day. As a consequence, assertion (2) does not lead to a 144-hour interval for the six creative times. Correctly translated, Exodus 20:11 and Exodus 31:17 are consistent with long creative times or with 24-hour days of command which are separated by longer time periods of unspecified length.

## Choices

For readers who want additional information about the translation "time" and the word "yom" there are four sections that follow immediately. These sections continue the study of the word "yom" and provide additional evidence supporting the translation "**time**" in the concluding phrases. These section are:

More About "Evening" and "Morning".................. page 79
"Yom" as a Marker of the Passage of Time .............. page 81
When "Yom" Means 24 Hours................................ page 84
History of the English Genesis One Text ................ page 88

The reader who fully accepts the translation "time" may wish to "fast forward" to the section **The Second Creative Yom: Genesis 1:6-8**, which starts on page 90.

The study of the remaining creative "yom" will provide information which relates to all the issues already discussed relative to Genesis One. These sections have application as support for the long creative times model and they have relevance to the model of 24-hour "days" separated by long periods of time.

**This study does not advocate any 24-hour day model. This study's analysis supports the long time interpretation of the creative "yom."**

# More About "Evening" and "Morning"

Consider the phrase, "and *there* had been evening and *there* had been morning, one 'yom'."
The phrase being translated is:

| אֶחָד | יוֹם | בֹּקֶר | וַיְהִי | עֶרֶב | וַיְהִי | ← Hebrew starts here. |
|---|---|---|---|---|---|---|
| one | "yom," time | morning | and *there* had been | evening | and *there* had been | ← Start English here. |

Notice that the phrase does not say "and had been night"; the words used are "evening" and "morning."

The words "evening" and "morning" do not involve passage of a specific amount of time. The word "evening" also does not have a defined time length. The word "evening" conveys a sense of the gradual diminishing of the activity of the day which merges into the reduced activity of the coming night. Specifically, note the concept of blending. The word עֶרֶב translated evening is a vowel marked word derived from the unmarked consonantal word ערב. Remember that the original Hebrew was written without vowel markings. The consonantal word cannot be distinguished from the vowel marked word עֵרֶב which is translated "mixed" or "mingled" six times in the Old Testament. The word ערב is also translated "woof" nine times. "Woof" refers to the crossing over and under of fibers in a woven fabric. The meaning of עֵרֶב carries a sense of mixing or intermingling. Exodus 12:38 provides an example of the translation "mixed."

KJV Exodus 12:38    And a עֵרֶב mixed multitude went up also with them; and flocks, and herds, *even* very much cattle.

| וְגַם | עֵרֶב | רַב | עָלָה אִתָּם וְצֹאן וּבָקָר מִקְנֶה כָּבֵד מְאֹד | Exodus 12:38 |
|---|---|---|---|---|
| and also | mixed | many | | |

The choice of "evening" cannot be accidental. Within the series of creative "yom" there are a series of creative acts. The creative acts do not stand alone. Each act requires integration of all which has preceded to form a complete compatible whole. The use of "evening" may be to convey a sense of both this integration and the transition to a period of time of much reduced activity.

Notice that the word "morning" cannot be limited to meaning the observation of the physical rising of the sun above the horizon. Morning speaks to the moment of dawn as either the start of the day or, metaphorically, of the start of some action. A light-dark cycle can be observed even during heavily-clouded overcast weather. Sunrise and sunset are not observable when there is heavy cloud cover. Under such conditions, a visually observed sunrise does not mark the beginning of the day, but we still speak of the "morning." The light and dark periods blend gradually.

The light-dark cycle started during the first creative "yom." However, there is no indication of a clear atmosphere before the fourth creative "yom." It is in the fourth creative יוֹם "time" that the two מְאֹרֹת "lights" are commanded to perform the function of marking the years and dividing the day from the night. By then, a version of the same concluding phrase has already been used three times.

The cyclical pattern is the important content of the concluding phrases. The concluding phrases may suggest an initially high level of creative activity, then a subsequent decrease and blending of creative activity, and then a low level of activity followed by a fresh and notable increase in creative activity at the start of the next creative "yom." Nothing in the language of "evening" and "morning" implies a limit on the length of time involved in a creative "yom." This study has already shown, by biblical verse examples, reasons for the creative "yom" being long periods of time.

The creative actions of the creative times often describe changes that are planet-wide in effect. The darkness of Genesis 1:2 is usually presumed to be planetary in scope. The separation of the waters, the appearance of the sky, and the appearance of the "dry" are planetary in scope. On a planet-wide scale there is no planet-wide day or night. Day and night exist simultaneously at all times on the surface of planet Earth. The careful avoidance of "night" in the concluding phrases must be respected. The phrase is not to be construed as representing an ordinary night.

This Page Intentionally Blank

## "Yom" as a Marker of the Passage of Time

The word "yom" is used as a marker to count the passage of time. This practice is also used in English. However, the practice in biblical Hebrew is not identical to the practice in English. The biblical Hebrew use will be investigated and will be found to not support a 24-hour meaning of "yom."

In Hebrew יוֹם "yom" is most often used in the two ways represented by the KJV examples below.

Counting: Genesis 7:24   And the waters prevailed upon the earth an hundred and fifty יוֹם "yom." (KJV "days")

Dating:   Genesis 7:11   In the six hundredth year of Noah's life, in the second month,
the seventeenth יוֹם "yom" (KJV "day") of the month,. . ..

The counting measurement of the passage of time and dating are procedures compatible with the "daytime" meaning of the word "yom." The reader must understand that some specific event is used in the count. In measuring the passage of time by numbering "days" the most typical events used are the "time" near sunrise and the "time" near sunset. In some cases both sunrise and sunset may be used at the same time. This is demonstrated in the following illustration:

Suppose a man worked two days painting his house.

A friend asks:   "How long did it take to paint your house?"

He answers:   "Two days. I started Monday morning and finished late Tuesday afternoon."

The passage of time has been indicated using the word "days," with the meaning being "daytime." Both the start and the end of the "daytime" have been used as markers. This occurs even in modern society where work is not restricted to the "daytime" by the absence of light.

In Genesis 7:12 and Genesis 7:17 there are two closely related uses of the word "yom" describing the passage of time.

KJV Genesis 7:12   And the rain was upon the earth forty יוֹם days and forty nights.
**("yom")**

KJV Genesis 7:17   And the flood was forty יוֹם days upon the earth; . . ..
**("yom")**

The singular יוֹם "yom" is used in both verses, not the plural used by the KJV. In Genesis 7:12 the presence of the "night" indicates that יוֹם "yom" means "daytime." Genesis 7:17 refers to the same event and conveys the meaning of the same time interval. The KJV "40 days" (40 יוֹם) expresses a measurement of the passage of time by counting the number of יוֹם "yom" using the "daytime" meaning. The specific events "morning" or "evening" used in starting and ending the count are not given here.

In the case where it is the end of a period of time that is being marked, the period of time ends with the morning of the day which follows that period of time. This is the pattern which is evident in the concluding phrases used for the creative times of Genesis One.

The Bible uses two different methods for specifying the "daytime" to which the "nighttime" is considered to be attached. The "nighttime" may be attached to the preceding "daytime," (most evident in Genesis), or the "nighttime" may be attached to the following "daytime." Attachment to the following daytime is founded on the ceremonial purposes of the Sabbath and of the festivals as a remembrance of the Exodus, a subject which will be discussed later in the section entitled "When 'Yom' Means 24 Hours" (page 84).

Additional verses relevant to the marking of the passage of time will now be considered.

In Genesis 7:4 (the story of Noah), the passage of time is indicated by counting the number of יוֹם "yom" which have passed. The first line in the verse is relevant to the counting of the passage of time.

KJV Genesis 7:4      For yet seven יוֹם "yom," and I will cause it to rain
upon the earth (erets) forty "yom" and forty nights; . . ..

| Genesis 7:4 | כִּי | לְיָמִים | עוֹד | שִׁבְעָה | אָנֹכִי | מַמְטִיר |
|---|---|---|---|---|---|---|
| | for (since, when, surely, etc.) | at by "yom" | repeat | seven | I | will cause rain |

| | עַל | הָאָרֶץ | אַרְבָּעִים | יוֹם | וְאַרְבָּעִים | לַיְלָה |
|---|---|---|---|---|---|---|
| | above | the land (erets) | forty | "yom" | and forty | night |

Look carefully at the literal English translation under the Hebrew. The second word לְיָמִים is composed of the prefix לְ "at" or "to" and the word יָמִים "by yom" meaning "daytime." What is being counted is the number of times that the daytime ("yom") repeats. The actual "daytime" hours of the seven "yom" are not involved in this use as a counting marker to indicate the passage of time. At the seventh repeat of the daytime, rain will be caused to occur. The word "yom," used in this manner, clearly does not mean 24 hours because in the same verse we are explicitly told that the rain will come down both "yom" and night. This pattern is again repeated in Genesis 7:12.

KJV Genesis 7:12 And the rain was upon the earth forty days and forty nights.

| Genesis 7:12 | וַיְהִי | הַגֶּשֶׁם | עַל | הָאָרֶץ | אַרְבָּעִים | יוֹם | וְאַרְבָּעִים | לַיְלָה |
|---|---|---|---|---|---|---|---|---|
| | and had been or (and had existed) | the rain | over | the land (erets) | forty | "yom" | and forty | night |

In Genesis 7:17 the forty "yom" are again counted. The "yom" and night pattern is not used; the night is not mentioned.

KJV Genesis 7:17      And the flood was forty days upon the earth; and the waters increased, and bare up the ark, and it was lift up above the earth.

| Genesis 7:17 | וַיְהִי | הַמַּבּוּל | אַרְבָּעִים | יוֹם | עַל | הָאָרֶץ | וַיִּרְבּוּ |
|---|---|---|---|---|---|---|---|
| | and had been | the flood | forty | "yom" | above | the land (erets) | and had become much |

| | הַמַּיִם | וַיִּשְׂאוּ | אֶת | הַתֵּבָה | וַתָּרָם | מֵעַל | הָאָרֶץ |
|---|---|---|---|---|---|---|---|
| | the waters | and had lifted | dir. obj. marker | the ark | and had risen | from off | the land (erets) |

Genesis 7:17 shows clearly that the counting of a number of "yom" to mark the passage of time does not indicate that "yom" means 24 hours. The counting operates in the same manner as in Genesis 7:4. Some feature of the "yom" is used as a reference marker which is noted at each occurrence by adding one to the count. That the time between the marking events is 24 hours is incidental. Typically, the event counted will be the sunrise or the sunset. The same method of marking the passage of time occurs in Genesis 7:24.

KJV Genesis 7:24      And the waters prevailed upon the earth an hundred and fifty days.

| Genesis 7:24 | וַיִּגְבְּרוּ | הַמַּיִם | עַל | הָאָרֶץ | חֲמִשִּׁים | וּמְאַת | יוֹם |
|---|---|---|---|---|---|---|---|
| | and had prevailed | the waters | above | the land (erets) | fifty | and hundred | "yom" |

In this verse no indication is given of the specific event which is used as the marker for the count. The event can be determined using another verse. The same 150 יוֹם "yom" are again referenced in Genesis 8:3 where the Hebrew text indicates that "sundown" was the event which was counted.

KJV Genesis 8:3      And the waters returned from off the earth continually:
and after the end of the hundred and fifty days the waters were abated.

YLT Genesis 8:3      And turn back do the waters from off the earth, going on and returning;
and the waters are lacking at the end of a hundred and fifty days.

Genesis 8:3

| וַיָּשֻׁבוּ | הַמַּיִם | מֵעַל | הָאָרֶץ | הָלוֹךְ | וָשׁוֹב |
|---|---|---|---|---|---|
| and had returned | the waters | from off | the land (erets) | going | and returning |

| וַיַּחְסְרוּ | הַמַּיִם | מִקְצֵה | חֲמִשִּׁים | וּמְאַת | יוֹם |
|---|---|---|---|---|---|
| and had lacked, (KJV *were abated*) | the waters | from end (KJV *at the end of*) | fifty | and hundred | "yom" |

The same type of counting is also indicated in Genesis 8:6.

KJV Genesis 8:6      And it came to pass at the end of forty days, that Noah opened the window of the ark which he had made:

Genesis 8:6

| וַיְהִי | מִקֵּץ | אַרְבָּעִים | יוֹם | וַיִּפְתַּח | נֹחַ | אֶת | חַלּוֹן |
|---|---|---|---|---|---|---|---|
| and had been (and had existed) | from end (KJV *at the end of*) | forty | "yom" | and had opened | Noah | dir. obj marker | window (literally "piercing") |

| הַתֵּבָה | אֲשֶׁר | עָשָׂה |
|---|---|---|
| the ark | which | he had made |

There is another procedure for the counting of the "yom" which is used in defining a passage of time. In this procedure the years, months, and "yom" are all counted. This procedure is also used when referring to calendar dates. Genesis 7:11 provides an example of this. It has already been shown that יוֹם "yom" means "daytime" in these passages.

KJV Genesis 7:11      In the six hundredth year of Noah's life, in the second month,
the seventeenth day of the month, the same day were all the fountains of the great deep broken up, and the windows of heaven were opened.

Genesis 7:11

| בִּשְׁנַת | שֵׁשׁ | מֵאוֹת | שָׁנָה | לְחַיֵּי | נֹחַ | בַּחֹדֶשׁ | הַשֵּׁנִי | בְּשִׁבְעָה | עָשָׂר | יוֹם | לַחֹדֶשׁ |
|---|---|---|---|---|---|---|---|---|---|---|---|
| In year | six | hundredth | year | to life of | Noah | in month | the second | in seventh | ten (KJV "seventeenth") | "yom" | to month |

| בַּיּוֹם | הַזֶּה | נִבְקְעוּ | כָּל | מַעְיְנוֹת | תְּהוֹם | רַבָּה | וַאֲרֻבֹּת | הַשָּׁמַיִם | נִפְתָּחוּ |
|---|---|---|---|---|---|---|---|---|---|
| in "yom" (KJV "same day") | this | break up | all | fountains of | deeps | many (KJV "great") | and windows of | the heavens | had been opened |

**Summary**

In conclusion, this section has shown that the use of "yom" as a counting marker for the passage of time or the specification of calendar dates does not imply the word "yom" has the meaning of 24 hours. As a counting marker, it is the repeating of some portion of the "yom" which is used. Commonly used markers are the sunrise or sunset. That the counted interval is 24 hours does not require, imply, or depend upon the word "yom" having a meaning of 24 hours.

## When "Yom" Means 24 Hours

As stated earlier, there are times when the word יוֹם "yom" does refer to 24 hours. In these cases the meaning of the word יוֹם "yom" is not established by the word יוֹם "yom" itself. It acquires this meaning because it has an associated modifying word which has been defined as indicating a 24-hour time period. Examples of this are יוֹם הַשַּׁבָּת "yom the Sabbath" and יוֹם כִּפֻּרִים "yom of atonements." When יוֹם "yom" does refer to 24 hours, the use is almost exclusively connected with the Sabbath or the festivals and ceremonies which include a remembrance of the Exodus. Understanding this requires a review of the establishment of the Sabbath in relationship to the Exodus.

As previously noted, the Passover and the Exodus were the defining events of the nation of Israel. The Sabbath is connected to the Exodus and is structured as a remembrance of the Passover and the departure from Egypt. As a remembrance, the ceremonial observance must include the night of the previous "yom" corresponding to the Passover. It must also include the daylight of the following "yom" remembering the departure. This can be verified by considering Deuteronomy 5:15 which is shown below as preparation for the discussion which follows.

KJV Deuteronomy 5:15   And remember that thou wast a servant in the land of Egypt, and *that* the LORD
thy God brought thee out thence through a mighty hand and by a stretched out
arm: therefore the LORD thy God commanded thee to keep the sabbath day.

Consider the events of the Passover and departure as recorded in Exodus 12:1-51. Briefly, the Israelites selected lambs on the tenth "yom" of the month. At sunset on the fourteenth "yom" the lambs were slaughtered and subsequently roasted and eaten that night.

KJV Exodus 12:6   And ye shall keep it (the lamb) up until the fourteenth "yom" of the same month:
and the whole assembly of the congregation of Israel shall kill it in the evening.

Then on the next "yom," the fifteenth "yom" of the month, they departed in the light of day.

KJV Numbers 33:3   And they departed from Rameses in the first month, on the fifteenth "yom"
of the first month; on the morrow after the Passover the children of Israel
went out with an high hand in the sight of all the Egyptians.

The Feast Of Unleavened Bread is similarly described in Exodus 12:18. (1) and (2) have been added to this verse to identify the two separate uses of "at even."

KJV Exodus 12:18   In the first *month*, on the fourteenth "yom" of the month **at even (1)**, ye shall
eat unleavened bread, until the one and twentieth "yom" of the month **at even (2)**.

"**At even**" (1) is the evening before the fifteenth "yom," the evening starting at sunset of the fourteenth. In the Sabbath ceremonies of remembrance, the evening represents the evening of the Passover. In Exodus 12:18 and in Exodus 12:6 the evening is ascribed to the "yom" which precedes the "yom" which has just ended at sunset. In Exodus 12:6 the evening is explicitly attached to the "yom" which follows.

The same formula is repeated for the Day of Atonement. The Day of Atonement, the tenth day of the month, is mentioned in this verse as being a "Sabbath."

KJV Leviticus 23:32   It *shall be* unto you a sabbath of rest, and ye shall afflict your souls:
in the ninth *day* of the month at even, from even unto even,
shall ye celebrate your sabbath.

The attachment of the previous evening, in an explicit manner, to the ceremonial "yom" of remembrance is consistent with "yom" meaning the time between sunrise and sunset. In the absence of a ceremonial inclusion (such as the sabbath), the Bible has other verses which attach the night to the day ("yom") which has just ended at sunset. One of these, about Lot and his daughters, will be discussed next.

KJV Genesis 19:33-34

33.     And they made their father drink wine that night: and the firstborn went in, and lay with her father; and he perceived not when she lay down, nor when she arose.

34.     And it came to pass on the מִמָּחֳרָת morrow, that the firstborn said unto the younger,

Behold, I lay אֶמֶשׁ yesternight with my father: let us make him drink wine this night also; and go thou in, *and* lie with him, that we may preserve seed of our father.

אֶמֶשׁ yesternight is used four times in the Bible. The Septuagint translates the word אֶמֶשׁ using the Greek word ἐχθές meaning "yesterday."

Now consider the ceremonial use of "yom." Specific inclusion of the nighttime into a ceremony is shown in the verses of Leviticus 8:33-35. This study has shown that the most common meaning of "yom" is the time between sunrise and sunset. Moses first specifies a seven "yom" ordination ceremony for Aaron and his sons. Then Moses specifically instructs Aaron that the nights are to be included. The inclusion is specified because "yom" does not by itself include the night. This is effectively saying, "Aaron, do not go home at night and return before dawn."

In verse 35 the suffixed form יוֹמָם "by yom" occurs with the singular וָלַיְלָה "and night" in the phrase translated "by day and *by* night." The word יָמִים is the plural of יוֹם "yom," literally "yoms." The YLT is used because it closely follows the Hebrew word order.

YLT Leviticus 8:33-35

33.     and from the opening of the tent of meeting ye go not out seven יָמִים "yoms", till the יוֹם "yom" of the

fulness, the יְמֵי "yoms" of your consecration -- for seven יָמִים "yoms" he doth consecrate your hand;

34.     as he hath done בַּיּוֹם "in yom" this, Jehovah hath commanded to do, to make atonement for you;

35.     and at the opening of the tent of meeting ye abide, יוֹמָם by day וָלַיְלָה and *by* night seven

יָמִים "yoms", and ye have kept the charge of Jehovah, and die not, for so I have been commanded.

In this case, the ceremony did not start the night of the preceding "yom" as is specified for the Sabbath and the Passover. The ceremony had started that day, in the "daytime," and was already in progress when this statement was made. There are events concluding the ceremony on the eighth "yom," so presumably, the included nights are the nights following each "yom."

It has now been established that the Sabbath, a ceremonial remembrance of the Passover and the Exodus, is a 24-hour period of time. This 24-hour period starts at sundown of the sixth "yom" and ends at sundown of the seventh "yom" of the week.

Now consider the KJV Leviticus 23:27-32. These verses are about the "yom" of atonement. The two Hebrew words הַכִּפֻּרִים and כִּפֻּרִים, which are usually translated "atonement," are actually plural words.

27.     Also on the tenth *day* of this seventh month *there shall be* a day of atonement:     i.e. הַכִּפֻּרִים   יוֹם

it shall be an holy convocation unto you; and ye shall afflict your souls,         *the atonements*   *"yom" of*

and offer an offering made by fire unto the LORD.

28.     And ye shall do no work in that same day: for it *is* a day of atonement,     i.e. כִּפֻּרִים   יוֹם

to make an atonement for you before the LORD your God.                    *atonements*   *"yom" of*

29.     For whatsoever soul *it be* that shall not be afflicted in that same day,

he shall be cut off from among his people.

30.     And whatsoever soul *it be* that doeth any work in that same day, the same soul will I destroy

from among his people.

31.     Ye shall do no manner of work: *it shall be* a statute for ever throughout your generations in all your dwellings.

32.     It *shall be* unto you a שַׁבַּת שַׁבָּתוֹן "sabbath of rest," in the ninth *day* of the month at even,

from even unto even, תִּשְׁבְּתוּ "shall ye celebrate" שַׁבַּתְּכֶם "your sabbath."

        **(תִּשְׁבְּתוּ literally "you shall cease," a Qal imperfect verb)**

In Leviticus 23:32 the two Hebrew words שַׁבַּת שַׁבָּתוֹן are translated "a sabbath of rest." The first word שַׁבַּת (shabat) is from the root meaning "to cease" and is used here as a noun translated "Sabbath." The second word שַׁבָּתוֹן "shabbton" is derived from שָׁבַת. The KJV translates שַׁבָּתוֹן "rest" but the Septuagint translates it as σαββάτων meaning a "ceasing." The Septuagint translation reflects the derivation of the word שָׁבַת (shabat). The English word "rest" also means to "stop" or "cease" work as when we take a "rest break." It is in the sense of stopping work that the "rest" of the KJV is to be understood in connection with the Sabbath.

תִּשְׁבְּתוּ, translated "celebrate" in the KJV, is actually a form of the verb שָׁבַת (shabat). The word שָׁבַת (shabat) means "to cease." Literally, תִּשְׁבְּתוּ is "you shall cease."

Leviticus 23:27-32 concerns the יוֹם כִּפֻּרִים "day of the atonements." Leviticus 23:27 describes the activities of the "daytime" of the event. Five verses later, in Leviticus 23:32, this term יוֹם כִּפֻּרִים "Yom Kippur" is defined as "your שַׁבַּת Sabbath." The defining was necessary because the word יוֹם "yom" did not carry the 24-hour meaning. The root word שָׁבַת (shabat) does carry this meaning and was used in defining the time interval of the observance. Standing alone, the term יוֹם כִּפֻּרִים "Yom Kippur" would have referred to the "daytime" observance (the convocation) of the שׁבת (shabat). Notice that the בָּעֶרֶב "at even" is said to be in the "ninth of the month." The "day of atonement" is the tenth of the month.

It was shown earlier that the word יוֹם "yom" generally carries two meanings, i.e., the meaning of "daytime" and the meaning of "time" when referencing activities taking place over a long period of time.

The word יוֹם "yom" is used in connection with ceremonies or the Sabbath about 40 times. These are events known to be associated with a 24-hour period of time, but the word "yom" does not always mean 24 hours when used in connection with these events. This has now been shown for the ordination ceremony of Aaron and is apparent in the instructions about the "Day of Atonement" (Yom Kippur). The question is:

What does יוֹם "yom" mean in the phrases יוֹם הַשַּׁבָּת "yom the Sabbath" and בְּיוֹם הַשַּׁבָּת "in yom the Sabbath" ?

יוֹם הַשַּׁבָּת is used nine times in the Old Testament and בְּיוֹם הַשַּׁבָּת is used 13 times. The KJV translations are the phrases יוֹם הַשַּׁבָּת "the sabbath day" and בְּיוֹם הַשַּׁבָּת "on the sabbath day."

The יוֹם "yom" in these two phrases often refers to activities which take place during the "daytime," i.e., the time of solar illumination. In fact, all 22 of the verses can be read as referring to the time of solar illumination. The use of "yom" in this fashion is entirely consistent with the use of "yom" in all the other cases discussed.

As an example, consider KJV Nehemiah 13:15-17, modified below to show some of the Hebrew words and their literal translations.

KJV Nehemiah 13:15-17

15. In those days saw I in Judah *some* treading wine presses בַּשַּׁבָּת "in sabbath," and bringing in sheaves, and lading asses; as also wine, grapes, and figs, and all *manner of* burdens, which they brought into Jerusalem בְּיוֹם הַשַּׁבָּת "in yom the sabbath": and I testified *against them* בְּיוֹם "in yom" wherein they sold victuals.
16. There dwelt men of Tyre also therein, which brought fish, and all manner of ware, and sold בַּשַּׁבָּת "in sabbath" unto the children of Judah, and in Jerusalem.
17. Then I contended with the nobles of Judah, and said unto them, What evil thing *is* this that ye do, and profane יוֹם הַשַּׁבָּת "yom the sabbath" ?

The term בַּשַּׁבָּת "in sabbath" and the term יוֹם הַשַּׁבָּת "yom the sabbath" are both used in these three verses. Nehemiah 13:15 references the bringing of agricultural items and burdens into Jerusalem. This is an activity which would normally take place during the "daytime," i.e., the time of solar illumination. This activity also would require that the gates of the city be open. Remember, they did not have the luxury of electric lights which we now take for granted. The treading of the winepresses "in sabbath" is not restricted to the "daytime" by the text and is not restricted to Jerusalem. This activity may have taken place in the daytime and later into the evening after the official start of the sabbath. Oil lamps may have been sufficient illumination to allow this work of harvest to continue after sundown.

In verse 16, "and sold in sabbath" is said to take place in Jerusalem and could continue to take place after the start of the sabbath at sundown. The gate of the city need not be open, because the men of Tyre dwelt in Jerusalem. This may account for the use of the term "in sabbath" and not the use of the term "yom the sabbath." Nehemiah 13:19 also indicates that the "sabbath" is differentiated from the phrase "yom the sabbath."

KJV Nehemiah 13:19

> And it came to pass, that when the gates of Jerusalem began to be dark before הַשַּׁבָּת the sabbath, I commanded that the gates should be shut, and charged that they should not be opened till after הַשַּׁבָּת the sabbath: and *some* of my servants set I at the gates, *that* there should no burden be brought in בְּיוֹם הַשַּׁבָּת "in yom the sabbath."

In this verse the meaning of בְּיוֹם הַשַּׁבָּת "in yom the sabbath" is equivocal. The burdens would normally be brought in during the "daytime" when the gates would be open. But here the gates are closed the entire Sabbath, a time which includes the "daytime." Considering בְּיוֹם הַשַּׁבָּת "in yom the sabbath" to mean the "daytime" has to be made based upon its use in other verses. The meaning "daytime" is supported here because the term "Sabbath," used twice, is not repeated. The different term בְּיוֹם הַשַּׁבָּת "in yom sabbath" is used and must have a meaning different than the entire "sabbath."

**Summary**

It has been found that the term יוֹם הַשַּׁבָּת "yom the sabbath" and בְּיוֹם הַשַּׁבָּת "in yom the sabbath" generally refer to that part of the sabbath that is the "daytime" i.e., the time of solar illumination. If the reference is to more than the time of solar illumination, the term used is שַׁבָּת (shabbat). In the KJV the word שַׁבָּת (shabbat) is translated "sabbath." Clearly, the Hebrews needed to be able to refer to the entire שַׁבָּת sabbath and the "daytime" of the sabbath when there was solar illumination. To not have been able to do so would have made communication very primitive. The Hebrews of that time were not primitive. This interpretation is consistant with בְּיוֹם הַשַּׁבָּת being a "construct," which is the way in which biblical Hebrew indicates the word "of." Considered a "construct," the translation would be "in yom of the sabbath" or "in daytime of the sabbath."

## History of the English Genesis One Text

For Genesis One, the history of the entire English Bible is not of primary interest. The primary interest is the transmission history of the first chapter and the first four verses of the second chapter. This is less complicated than the history of the entire English Bible.

Starting with the Hebrew text as it existed in about 300 B.C., the transmission of Genesis One to the English proceeds along two paths. One path is the transmission and translation of the Hebrew text. The second path is one that starts with the Greek Septuagint translation of the Hebrew and proceeds through the Latin Vulgate and then through a sequence of English translations.

All the current English translations are critically dependent upon the Tyndale translation of 1526 – 1534. Even though Tyndale translated the Pentateuch using the Hebrew text of his time, there is evidence that his translation of Genesis One was primarily based upon the Latin Vulgate. One clear piece of evidence is his introduction and use of the word "firmament." He defines the word "firmament" in this manner: "Firmament is skies." The Latin Vulgate uses the Latin word "firmamentum." Firmament is thus seen to be an Anglicization of the Latin word "firmamentum."

Tyndale's intent was both to correct the errors of the Vulgate and to make it possible for the common man to possess and read the Bible in English. In this effort Tyndale was the successor to Wycliffe and his followers. The Wycliffe English Bible was completed about 1384. It was replicated by making hand-written copies. When a well-known translation exists, a second translator will change and correct that which he believes to be in error or to be poorly translated. In the case of Genesis One there would have been, at that time, little reason to view the tense translation of the verbs in Genesis One as being of great significance. Galileo and his astronomical investigations would not take place for almost another 70 years. The tendency would have been to translate the English tenses in correspondence with the familiar Latin, and to correct the errors which were considered to be of theological significance.

This is what Tyndale apparently did in Genesis One. The verb tenses are translated in correspondence with the Latin Vulgate. This is easy to do as there is an almost one-to-one correspondence between the Latin and the English tenses. The Latin Vulgate used the simple past for the Hebrew verbs which expressed completed action. Tyndale continued this practice. The Latin Vulgate was based on the Septuagint, the Old Latin translations, and the Hebrew text. The Septuagint had used the Greek "aorist" for these verbs. The Greek "aorist" is a past verb form which is said to be "undefined." "Undefined" means that the action is either completed or continuing, but is **not** specified as to which of the two possibilities is intended. The verbal action is simply stated to have happened. As such, the "aorist" is an appropriate translation of the Hebrew completed action but at the cost of introducing an ambiguity. This ambiguity may lead to misinterpretation of the meaning of the text.

A comparison of the action nature of several of the verb forms (or tenses) in Hebrew, Greek, Latin, and English is given on the next page. These are the verb forms which have been used in translations to translate the biblical Hebrew completed action verbs.

### Comparison of Verb Tense and Meaning in Hebrew, Greek, Latin, and English

The next page lists a comparison of the "action nature" the Hebrew perfect verb form and the verb forms (or tenses) by which it has been translated in Greek, Latin, and English.

| Language | Verb Form (tense) | Meaning |
|---|---|---|
| Hebrew | Hebrew perfect | completed action<br>    does **not** specify "when" the action took place<br>    does **not** specify the length of time of the action (duration) |
| Greek | Aorist | past action, says action happened<br>action is either completed or continuing in the past<br>    does **not** specify if action is completed<br>    does **not** specify if action is continuing |
| Latin | Perfect | past action, can be equivalent to the English past tense<br>    example: walked (completed action)<br>    or can be equivalent to English present perfect<br>    example: has walked (completed action)<br>the present perfect type reading is not fully equivalent to the Hebrew perfect because it introduces an element of time location |
| English | Past | past action: example: walked |
| | **Hebrew equivalence** | can be read as completed action — OK: completed action<br>can be read as continuous action — Not OK: not completed action<br>can be read as punctiliar action — Not OK: violates requirements that no time location and no duration be specified |
| English | Pluperfect | past action: example: had walked |
| | **Hebrew equivalence** | **is** read as completed action — OK: completed action<br>Location in time and duration **not** specified by Hebrew verb<br>Location in time and duration **determined by context and Hebrew word order.** |

The question is, "What happened to the Hebrew perfect (completed action) meaning as it was transmitted through the historic sequence of translations?"

If the Greek aorist is read as a completed action, it is an appropriate translation of the Hebrew perfect. If the aorist is read as a continuing action it is not an appropriate translation. The Latin perfect is an appropriate translation of the aorist (completed action) used in the Septuagint and of the perfect (completed action) used in the Hebrew.

The next step in the chain of translation is the translation into English. The Latin perfect, because it can be read as equivalent to the English present perfect, naturally lent itself to the narrative type of translation adopted for Genesis One. The completed nature of the actions and their lack of explicit location in time in the Hebrew text are obscured in the narrative style. Once this obscuring has happened, the misreading of the English past as punctiliar type action, action that occurs quickly at a specific point in time, becomes more likely. The punctiliar reading is clearly wrong as it violates the meaning of the Hebrew perfect by introducing a specification of "when" and a specification of "duration."

## Chapter Four  THE REMAINING CREATIVE "YOM"

## The Second Creative "Yom": Genesis 1:6-8   The Sky and the Waters

The second creative "yom" is described in three verses, Genesis 1:6 through Genesis 1:8. Phrases previously discussed in detail will not be reanalyzed in detail, specifically the three Hebrew phrases "and God had said," "and God had called," and the phrases concluding each creative "yom." The parts of speech and the verb forms will be provided only for those words which are of particular interest. Detailed attention will be directed only to new issues.

Genesis 1:6-8 describe modification of the atmosphere. There are differing interpretations as to the physical model of the sky, atmosphere, and the "heavens" which is being described. The reader should understand that the physical model of הַמַּיִם "the waters," the רָקִיעַ (raqia), and the atmosphere described in these verses has been the subject of much controversy. The following study of Genesis 1:6-7 will:

(1) Discuss translation issues for Genesis 1:6-7 and present clarified translations.
(2) Present a physical model of the sky and the waters.
(3) Present an extensive analysis supporting the translation מֵעַל as "from off."

**Translation issues in Genesis 1:6:** רָקִיעַ (raqia), וִיהִי "and *there* shall be," and מַבְדִּיל "*a* separating"

The Hebrew of Genesis 1:6 is:

| הַמַּיִם | בְּתוֹךְ | רָקִיעַ | יְהִי | אֱלֹהִים | וַיֹּאמֶר | (1) | **Genesis 1:6** |
|---|---|---|---|---|---|---|---|
| the waters | in midst of | (firmament, sky) or (expanse) | shall be | God (Elohim) | and had said | | ← Start English here. |

| לְמָיִם | מַיִם | בֵּין | מַבְדִּיל | וִיהִי | (2) |
|---|---|---|---|---|---|
| to waters | waters | between | (a) separating (Hiphil participle) | and *there* shall be | |

KJV Genesis 1:6   And God said, Let there be a firmament in the midst of the waters,
and let it divide (Hebrew: *a* separating) the waters from the waters.

In Genesis 1:6 line (1) the meaning of the Hebrew word רָקִיעַ (raqia) is of particular interest. The word רָקִיעַ (raqia) is translated "firmament" in the KJV and is an English word derived from the Latin word "firmamentum" used in the Vulgate. Tyndale, in his 1534 translation defined "firmament" as "Firmament, the skies."[54] "Sky" is the translation which will be adopted later in this study and will be discussed when the model is presented. The meaning of רָקִיעַ (raqia) as sky will be developed in the analysis which follows.

In Genesis 1:6 line (2) the verb וִיהִי and the following participle מַבְדִּיל are of interest. The verb וִיהִי has two possible interpretations. It could be the jussive command יְהִי prefixed by ו "and" or it could be the Qal imperfect of יִהְיֶה prefixed by the ו which also results in the form וִיהִי.[55] The KJV translates this word as the jussive command and inserts an "it" which is not in the Hebrew. The command וִיהִי could be translated "and let *there* be" referring to the following commanded action "a separating." In this translation the "it" of the KJV does not appear. The KJV translates the first command "Let there be" and "let there be" is an appropriate translation for the second command. For example, the KJV translates וִיהִי as "that there may be" in Exodus 9:22, Exodus 10:21, and Malachi 3:10. Exodus 10:21 is presented below as an example where וִיהִי has been inserted to identify its translation, which is printed in bold.

KJV Exodus 10:21   And the LORD said unto Moses, Stretch out thine hand toward heaven,
וִיהִי **that there may be** darkness over the land of Egypt, even darkness *which* may be felt.

The word מַבְדִּיל in line (2) of Genesis 1:6 is a participle. In English, the participle can be made by adding "ing" to a verb. The verb root בדל means "to separate," so the singular participle becomes "a separating." The participle

מַבְדִּיל is in the Hiphil, a form used to express a causation where the objects participate in the action. The י added just before the final Hebrew letter and the prefix מ is the method by which the Hiphil participle is formed.[56] Translation of the word מַבְדִּיל as "a dividing" or "a separating" is closer to the Hebrew.

The KJV translation "let it divide" imposes a physical model by inserting the word "it." The KJV model assumes that the רָקִיעַ (raqia) is the divider between the two waters, something not stated in the Hebrew text. The jussive command translations "and let *there* be a dividing," "and *there* shall be a dividing," or "that there may be a dividing" do not impose a model but allow a model to be determined from the text of both Genesis 1:6 and Genesis 1:7. This model is also consistent with other uses of the word "raqia." The study of Genesis 1:7 will support the correctness of the three foregoing translations.

The study translation of Genesis 1:6 is:
(1) And God said, *There* shall be a sky in the midst of the waters
(2) and *there* shall be a separating between *the* waters to *the* waters.

**Translation issues in Genesis 1:7: Words not translated by the KJV and the translation מֵעַל "from off"**

Genesis 1:7 indicates the completion of the actions commanded in Genesis 1:6. The KJV Genesis 1:7 adds confusion by not translating the word בֵּין meaning "between" and by not translating the preposition ל (the Hebrew letter lahmed) which appears twice. The most important translation issue is the word מֵעַל which will be shown to mean "from off."

| אֲשֶׁר | הַמַּיִם | בֵּין | וַיַּבְדֵּל | הָרָקִיעַ | אֵת | אֱלֹהִים | וַיַּעַשׂ | (1) Genesis 1:7 |
|---|---|---|---|---|---|---|---|---|
| those | the waters | between | and had separated | the (firmament, sky) | dir. obj. marker | God (Elohim) | and had made | |

| כֵּן | וַיְהִי | לָרָקִיעַ | מֵעַל | אֲשֶׁר | הַמַּיִם | וּבֵין | לָרָקִיעַ | מִתַּחַת | (2) |
|---|---|---|---|---|---|---|---|---|---|
| so | and had been ("waw"+ imperfect verb) | in reference to firmament, or sky | from off | those | the waters | and between | in reference to firmament, or sky | from under | |

KJV Genesis 1:7    And God made (Hebrew: had made) the firmament, and divided the waters which *were* under the firmament from the waters which *were* above the firmament: and it was so.

There are two important words to consider in Genesis 1:7 line (2).

The second word of line (2) includes the preposition ל which occurs in the word לָרָקִיעַ prefixing the word רָקִיעַ "raqia" (KJV "firmament"). The preposition ל is not translated by the KJV in Genesis 1:7 and thereby introduces a great deal of difficulty. The basic meaning of the ל is "in reference to," "to," "at," "from," and other meanings which define the relationship between specified objects represented by words in a sentence.

Note: Both of the "waters" are specified in reference to the **same** "firmament," "sky," or "expanse."

The second important word is מֵעַל which has been translated "from off." מֵעַל is a word composed of two prepositions, מִן meaning "from" and עַל which indicates a directional reference. The translation "from off" will be carefully justified by analysis of other verses which use the word מֵעַל. The analysis will follow the presentation of the physical model so that the relevance of the verses, and why they are being considered, is clear. The KJV translates מֵעַל "from off" 21 times in the Books of Moses. To facilitate an understanding of the issues, a modified KJV translation of Genesis 1:7 is given on the next page with the following four modifications.

(1) "Firmament (sky)" will be used to replace the "firmament" of the KJV.[57]
(2) "From off" will replace the "above" by which the KJV translates מֵעַל.
(3) The preposition ל will be translated "in reference to." The KJV does not translate the preposition ל.
(4) The words בֵּין "between" will be translated. The KJV does not translate the two בֵּין "between."

Genesis 1:7 (KJV modified)  And God had made the firmament (sky) and had separated
between those waters **from under** in reference to the firmament (sky).
and between those waters **from off** in reference to the firmament (sky).

In this translation there is both a "**from under**" and a "**from off**." Both these distances are measured in reference to the "firmament (sky)." The word מִתַּחַת is translated "from under," the same as in the KJV. This word also appears in Genesis 1:9 where it refers to the location of the waters which are gathered and subsequently called seas. The word מֵעַל which is translated "from off" is the word translated "above" in the KJV. The translation "above" has fueled considerable academic controversy relating to the physical model. The critics of Genesis thrive on the controversy. The translation "from off" is justified by analysis on pages 93-94.

## A Model of the Sky and the Waters

When מֵעַל is translated "from off" the picture is phenomenologically understandable. With this translation the "waters from under" (the surface waters or seas) are placed **far below** as measured by their separation from the "firmament (sky)." The clouds ("the waters from off") are below the "sky," but in appearance and in fact are in more close proximity to the sky than the waters "from under." Both of the "waters" are below the sky. They differ in being at substantially different quantitative measures of "below" as described by a person standing on the surface of the ground. To a person on the ground, both the clouds (the waters from off) and the seas (the waters from under) are below the sky. The "sky" is not yet the "blue sky" which we often see now, but a continually overcast cloudy layer with additional clouds visible below this sky. The רָקִיעַ "sky" is the underside of the continually overcast cloudy layer as seen from below. Because this layer contains water, the רָקִיעַ "sky" is in "midst" of the waters. The clearing of the atmosphere which will allow the stars, sun, and moon to be seen has not yet occurred. This clearing occurs and is described in Genesis 1:14-18.

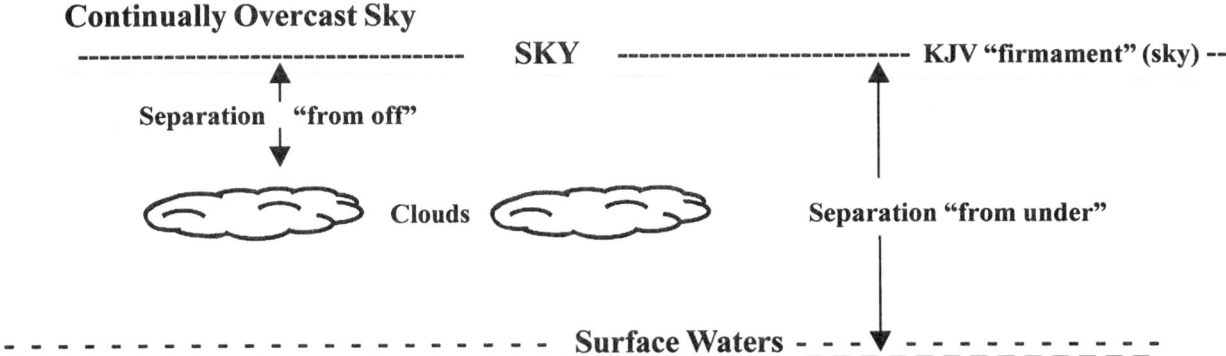

The creation account of Genesis One describes a progression of changes in the atmosphere of planet Earth. It starts with clouds so thick and dark that the surface of the waters of the "deep" is described as being in darkness. Then the clouds become sufficiently less dark so that light can be discerned at the surface. Then a further progression is described where the continuous cloud layer lifts from the surface, and a space appears between the continuous cloud layer and the surface of the planet. It is in this space that other clouds appear below the continuous layer. These lower clouds are the "waters from off." The underside of the continuous cloud layer is the רָקִיעַ (raqia), which translates as "sky." Sky is a word which we use to describe the underside of a continuous cloud layer stretching out from horizon to horizon. We see this on stormy days, and in the winter often such a condition persists for weeks. Additional clouds underneath the stretched out continuous layer are often seen moving across the "face of the sky."

Under the conditions just described, the stars, sun, and moon are not seen. This is not surprising because the sky is cloudy or clouded over, but it is still called the sky. When the sky is clear we can see the stars, sun, and moon. We then say that the stars are visible in the sky, or that the sun can be seen in a blue sky. The light blue sky of the daytime and the dark blue sky of the nighttime are still sky, just as a gray, continually overcast layer is sky.

**How the word מֵעַל is used: the translation "from off."** The following study will show that "from off" or "off of" is the preferred translation of the Hebrew word מֵעַל and will also show that the translation "above" cannot be justified from the

Hebrew text. The word מֵעַל is used in 205 verses in the Bible and 55 times in the Books of Moses. The same consonantal form is also the consonantal spelling of a word translated "trespass" in the KJV. The words are distinguishable by context and are vowel marked differently. The KJV, in the Books of Moses, translates the word מֵעַל as "from off" (21 times), "from" (17 times), translations involving "away" (4 times), translations involving "above" or "over" (5 times), and other translations (7 times). The question is, "How should the word מֵעַל be translated in verse Genesis 1:7?"

The use of מֵעַל in Genesis 24:64 shows a meaning "from off." The direction of the "from off" is determined by the context. In Genesis 24:64 the direction of מֵעַל is clearly down. Therefore, "from off" or "off of" are both appropriate. "From off" appears in the YLT shown following.

KJV Genesis 24:64    And Rebekah lifted up her eyes, and when she saw Isaac, she lighted off the camel.

YLT Genesis 24:64    And Rebekah lifteth up her eyes, and seeth Isaac, and alighteth from off the camel;

| הַגָּמָל | מֵעַל | וַתִּפֹּל | אֶת יִצְחָק | וַתֵּרֶא | עֵינֶיהָ אֶת | רִבְקָה | וַתִּשָּׂא | Genesis 24:64 |
|---|---|---|---|---|---|---|---|---|
| the camel | from off (KJV "off") | and cast down (KJV "lighted") | Isaac dir. obj. marker | and saw | her eyes dir. obj marker | Rebekah | and lifted up | |

As another example where מֵעַל means "from off" consider KJV Exodus 3:5.

KJV Exodus 3:5    And he said, Draw not nigh hither: put off thy shoes from off thy feet, for the place whereon thou standest is holy ground.

| רַגְלֶיךָ | מֵעַל | נְעָלֶיךָ | שַׁל | הֲלֹם | תִּקְרַב | אַל | וַיֹּאמֶר | Exodus 3:5 |
|---|---|---|---|---|---|---|---|---|
| your feet | from off | shoes | slip off | hither | come near | not | and he had said | |

| הוּא | קֹדֶשׁ | אַדְמַת | עָלָיו | עוֹמֵד | אַתָּה | אֲשֶׁר | הַמָּקוֹם | כִּי |
|---|---|---|---|---|---|---|---|---|
| it (is) | holy | ground | above | standing | thou (you) | which | the place | for |

Deuteronomy 9:17 provides another example where the direction of מֵעַל "from off" is ultimately down. מֵעַל is not translated "above," but is translated "out of."

KJV Deuteronomy 9:17    And I took the two tables, and cast them מֵעַל out of my two hands, and brake them before your eyes.

| לְעֵינֵיכֶם | וָאֲשַׁבְּרֵם | יָדָי | שְׁתֵּי | מֵעַל | וָאַשְׁלִכֵם | הַלֻּחֹת | בִּשְׁנֵי | וָאֶתְפֹּשׂ | Deuteronomy 9:17 |
|---|---|---|---|---|---|---|---|---|---|
| before your eyes | and had broken | hands | two | from off (KJV "out of ") | and had thrown | the tablets | in two (KJV "the two") | and I had laid hold (KJV "And I took") | |

Genesis 7:17 provides an example where the context indicates that מֵעַל "from off" is in an upward direction.

KJV Genesis 7:17    And the flood was forty days (yom) upon the earth; and the waters increased, and bare up the ark, and it was lift up above the earth.

YLT Genesis 7:17    And the deluge is forty days (yom) on the earth, and the waters multiply, and lift up the ark, and it is raised up from off the earth;

| הַמַּיִם | וַיִּרְבּוּ | הָאָרֶץ | עַל | יוֹם | אַרְבָּעִים | הַמַּבּוּל | וַיְהִי | Genesis 7:17 |
|---|---|---|---|---|---|---|---|---|
| the waters | and had increased | the land | above (KJV upon) | yom (KJV "days") | forty | the flood | and had been (KJV "was" ) | |

| הָאָרֶץ | מֵעַל | וַתָּרָם | הַתֵּבָה | אֶת | וַיִּשְׂאוּ |
|---|---|---|---|---|---|
| the land | from off (KJV above) | had lifted up | the ark | dir. obj marker | and rose up |

In Genesis 7:17 two different words meaning "lifted" or "rose up" are used in close proximity, leading to different translations, although the meanings are very similar. The important point for our consideration is that "from off" is a clearly correct translation in context. The KJV translation "above" in Genesis 7:17 is based on additional information already known about boats and the rising water of floods. There is no similar information for Genesis 1:7. The translation "from off" is correct and represents all the information contained in the Hebrew.

The final verse of the second creative "yom" is Genesis 1:8. It is in this verse that the רָקִיעַ (raqia) is identified as the שָׁמַיִם "heavens." Here this study translates רָקִיעַ "sky" and the word לָרָקִיעַ = רָקִיעַ + לְ is translated "to *the* sky." לְ (le) is the preposition meaning "to." The concluding phrase has already been discussed.

| שֵׁנִי | יוֹם | בֹּקֶר | וַיְהִי | עֶרֶב | וַיְהִי | שָׁמַיִם | לָרָקִיעַ | אֱלֹהִים | וַיִּקְרָא | Genesis 1:8 |
|---|---|---|---|---|---|---|---|---|---|---|
| a second | yom | morning | and had been | evening | and had been | heavens | to *the* "sky" (KJV "firmament") | God (Elohim) | and had called | |

Here, the collective meaning of the first four Hebrew words is to be considered. The literal translation is "And God had called to *the* sky heavens." The root word קָרָא "called" is used to name things and people. Does this mean that the "sky" and the "heavens" are the same? The answer is, "No." This answer is clear from verses Genesis 1:14, 15, and 17.

In these verses רָקִיעַ (raqia) appears in the phrase: בִּרְקִיעַ הַשָּׁמַיִם i.e., literally "in sky of the heavens."
                                                        the heavens   in sky of

The two Hebrew words are in the construct relationship which indicates the "of" used in the English translation. The "sky" is here associated with, and indicated to be, a *part of the* heavens." The רָקִיעַ "sky" is not identical to the entire "heavens." The difficulty in understanding the meaning is traceable to the small Hebrew vocabulary which requires a broad range of meanings be ascribed to individual root words. Genesis 1:14, 15, and 17 indicate that Genesis 1:8 is best translated, "And God had called the sky *a part of the* heavens. . . ." The words in italics (*a part of the*) do not appear in the Hebrew.

## The Translation of Genesis 1:6-8

The goal now is to provide a "Good English" translation of Genesis 1:6 through Genesis 1:8 with רָקִיעַ translated "sky." "Sky" means either the pale blue "sky" of the daytime and/or the dark blue "sky" of the nighttime. In both cases the blue "sky" has the appearance of a hemispherical dome to a person on the ground below. The translation "sky" is in agreement with the Tyndale 1534 translation. The word מֵעַל is translated "off of" because it more smoothly gives the meaning of the Hebrew. Both "from off" and "off of" are appropriate in these verses.

### A "Good English" translation of Genesis 1:6-8

Genesis 1:6    And God said, *There* shall be a sky in the midst of the waters
                  and *there* shall be a separating between *the* waters from *the* waters.

Genesis 1:7    And God made the sky, and separated between the waters under the sky,
                  and between those waters off of the sky; and *it* did come to pass so.   (KJV "and it was so")

Genesis 1:8    And God called the sky *a part of the* heavens;
                  and *there* was evening and *there* was morning, a second time.

Most of the commands translated "There shall be . . ." in Genesis One are commands for actions which continue to the present time. The command in Genesis 1:6 may not indicate a condition that continues uniformly to the present time. For example, when the sky is fully overcast by a cloud layer, the "sky" which is seen is the underside of the clouds. Under these conditions the "sky" could be aptly described as being "in the midst of the waters." There is another sky condition which is often seen. This condition is a fully overcast sky with additional lower individual clouds below the fully overcast layer. This condition would exhibit a sky "in the midst of the waters" and at the same time exhibit lower clouds, the "waters from off the sky." The extreme brevity of the description leaves some remaining uncertainty about the intended meaning of the first line of Genesis 1:6.

# The translation "and *it* did come to pass so"

There is one additional point to consider regarding the "Good English" translation of Genesis 1:7. This is the translation of the Hebrew words וַיְהִי כֵן which have been translated by the phrase "and *it* did come to pass so." This phrase indicates that the commands have been completed and does not imply an immediacy of the completion. The KJV translations of "and it was so" or the translation "and so it came to pass" are satisfactory translations provided the reader does not impute an immediacy to the completion. The Hebrew phrase וַיְהִי כֵן uses the verb וַיְהִי which is the "waw-consecutive" of the imperfect verb יְהִי. The action of the וַ "waw" is to change the imperfect meaning to be that of the completed action. (See pages 10-11 for a review.)

The Hebrew consonantal phrase ויהי כן appears nine times in the Bible, six of which are in Genesis One. The three verses which are not in Genesis One are those from which insight into the correct translation must be obtained. Two of these are vowel marked as in Genesis One. The two verses are 2 Kings 15:12 and Judges 6:38, both presented below.

KJV 2 Kings 15:12    This *was* the word of the LORD which he spake unto Jehu, saying, Thy sons shall sit on the throne of Israel unto the fourth *generation*. וַיְהִי כֵן And so it came to pass.

The events that the words וַיְהִי כֵן describe do not take place immediately. They take place over an extended period of time and are confirmed by other verses in the Bible. This is an example of a completed action Hebrew verb asserting a completion which lies in the future of the statement to which the phrase applies. The translation "and *it* did come to pass so" could be made here, and properly state the completion, and **not** indicate that the completion was immediate.

In Judges 6:37-38, in the story of Gideon, there is again a period of time.

KJV Judges 6:37    Behold, I will put a fleece of wool in the floor; *and* if the dew be on the fleece only, and *it be* dry upon all the earth *beside*, then shall I know that thou wilt save Israel by mine hand, as thou hast said.

KJV Judges 6:38    וַיְהִי־כֵן And it was so: for he rose up early on the morrow, . . .

The completion does not take place immediately, the completion takes place on the day following. A translation "and it did come to pass so" would have correctly expressed the meaning of the phrase וַיְהִי כֵן in this verse. The translation "and it did come to pass so" is also consistent with the 320 times that the KJV translates וַיְהִי as "and it came to pass."

The phrase ויהי כן also appears in Amos 5:14 where it is vowel marked differently. Remember that the vowel markings were not in the original text and are a later interpretation. The KJV splits the phrase and translates ויהי כן in two parts as "and so . . .    . . . shall be . . .    . . .." The phrase וִיהִי כֵן contains the only Hebrew verb in the clause of line (2).

KJV Amos 5:14    Seek good, and not evil, that ye may live:

(2) **and** כֵן so the LORD, the God of hosts, וִיהִי **shall be** with you, as ye have spoken.

| אֲמַרְתֶּם | כַּאֲשֶׁר | אִתְּכֶם | צְבָאוֹת | אֱלֹהֵי | יְהוָה | כֵן | וִיהִי (2) | Amos 5:14 |
| ye have spoken | as (like which) | with you | hosts | God of | The LORD (Yahweh) | so | and it came to pass (KJV "shall be") | |

The KJV interprets the verb as a certain future result dependent on actions which those being spoken to have not done and have yet to do. Again, the dependent completion is not immediate. Viewed as the "waw-consecutive," this would be an example of the prophetic use of a completed action verb to apply to a future action. The KJV translates the verb as a jussive. A translation "and it shall come to pass so" would be equivalent to the KJV.

The foregoing three verses show that the phrase ויהי כן does not indicate immediate completion of the commands in Genesis One. Consistent with the absence of tense in Hebrew, it indicates completion but does not specify a "when." The וַיְהִי which the KJV commonly translates "and it came to pass" also indicates a later, not immediate completion. The actual "when" is not indicated. The examples have shown time intervals until completion of four generations, the next day, and a conditional completion in the future. The important fact for Genesis One is that completion is not indicated to be immediate.

# The Third Creative "Yom": Genesis 1:9-13 — The Land and the Land Plants

The verses describing the events of the third creative "yom" divide into two groups. Genesis 1:9-10 deal with the modification of the physical environment to provide dry land. Genesis 1:11-12 deal with plant life which the land is commanded to produce. The verses will first be considered individually, explaining the words and verb forms. Then the verses will be considered as a unit in an English translation to determine the "when" of the actions.

**Genesis 1:9** ← Start English here.

| הַשָּׁמָיִם | מִתַּחַת | הַמַּיִם | יִקָּווּ | אֱלֹהִים | וַיֹּאמֶר |
|---|---|---|---|---|---|
| the heavens | from beneath | the waters | shall be gathered (Niphal imperfect) | God (Elohim) | and had said |

| וַיְהִי כֵן | הַיַּבָּשָׁה | וְתֵרָאֶה | אֶחָד | מָקוֹם | אֶל |
|---|---|---|---|---|---|
| so and *it* did come to pass | the dry | and had appeared or and had been seen (Niphal imperfect) | one, same | place | into |

KJV Genesis 1:9    And God said, Let the waters under the heaven be gathered together unto one place, and let the dry *land* appear: and it was so.

The verb יִקָּווּ commanding the gathering of the waters is in the Niphal imperfect and is translated "shall be." The Niphal is a verb form which is used to express passive action.[58] Passive action means that the subject of the action, "the waters," do not act. "The waters" receives the action of some other agent which does the gathering. What this agent is, or a description of how the gathering was accomplished, is not specified. The action was at the command of God. The verb is usually translated as a "jussive" command. This is a translator's choice because, for this word, the Niphal jussive and the Niphal imperfect are written the same way. The subsequent verb וְתֵרָאֶה translated "and had appeared" or "and had been seen" is also in the Niphal, a passive form of the verb meaning, "to see." Because the "who" doing the seeing is not stated, the translation "had appeared" might be better expressed as "had become able to be seen."

Note that it is the waters which are gathered. In the next verse, Genesis 1:10, the "gathered waters" are named "seas," a plural word. The הַיַּבָּשָׁה "the dry" is not said to be in one landmass. A number of land masses is consistent with the "one place" and with the plural seas of Genesis 1:10. The existence of islands in an ocean is not considered to separate the ocean into separate bodies of water. The Pacific Ocean remains "gathered into one place" and is considered a connected unity even with the presence of islands.

In Genesis 1:9-10 the KJV has italicized the word *land*. The word אֶרֶץ "land" does not appear in the Hebrew text. The word used is הַיַּבָּשָׁה which is derived from the root word יבשׁ meaning "dry." "*Land*" is inserted because "the dry" is called (or given the name) אֶרֶץ "land" or "ground" in Genesis 1:10. The word יַבָּשָׁה "dry" is used in 14 verses, seven of which refer to the "dry" on which the sea was crossed during the Exodus or the crossing of the Jordan. As a consequence "dry" is considered to refer to land which has been under water and which has become dry.[19]

**Genesis 1:10**

| הַמַּיִם | וּלְמִקְוֵה | אֶרֶץ | לַיַּבָּשָׁה | אֱלֹהִים | וַיִּקְרָא |
|---|---|---|---|---|---|
| the waters | and to *the* gathered | land | to *the* dry | God (Elohim) | and had called |

| טוֹב | כִּי | אֱלֹהִים | וַיַּרְא | יַמִּים | קָרָא |
|---|---|---|---|---|---|
| good | as | God (Elohim) | and had seen | seas | he had called (Qal perfect) |

KJV Genesis 1:10    And God called the dry *land* Earth; and the gathering together of the waters called he Seas: and God saw that *it was* good.

The word אֶרֶץ (erets), which has previously been used to refer to the entire planet, is now being restricted to its most common meaning of dry ground or land. The author is explicitly telling the reader of this restriction for the following verses. The word is used with the meaning "land" in all the following verses of Genesis One. The next two verses describe the appearance of some plants which now appear on the dry ground.

| | | | | | | | | | |
|---|---|---|---|---|---|---|---|---|---|
| פְּרִי | עֵץ | זֶרַע | מַזְרִיעַ | עֵשֶׂב | דֶּשֶׁא | הָאָרֶץ | תַּדְשֵׁא | אֱלֹהִים | וַיֹּאמֶר Genesis 1:11 |
| fruit | tree | seed | yielding (seeding) | grass (KJV herb) | plant (grass) | the land | shall bring forth (Hiphil imperfect) | God (Elohim) | and had said |

| | | | | | | | | |
|---|---|---|---|---|---|---|---|---|
| כֵּן | וַיְהִי | הָאָרֶץ | עַל | בוֹ | זַרְעוֹ | אֲשֶׁר | לְמִינוֹ | פְּרִי | עֹשֶׂה |
| so | and *it* did come to pass | the land | upon | *is* in it | seed | which (whose) | to *its* kind | fruit | bearing |

KJV Genesis 1:11    And God said, Let the earth (land) bring forth דֶּשֶׁא grass, the עֵשֶׂב herb yielding seed, *and* the fruit tree yielding fruit after his kind, whose seed *is* in itself, upon the earth: and it was so.

The verb תַּדְשֵׁא "shall bring forth" is a command in the Hiphil representing incomplete action. The Hiphil is a verb form which is used to indicate causation and indicates that the land is to be the agent producing the action of sprouting. The command of the action is translated using "shall."

The verse ends with the phrase וַיְהִי כֵּן "and *it* did come to pass so," which was discussed on page 95. This phrase indicates that the commanded actions had been completed, but does not indicate how much time had elapsed between the command and the completion. As discussed earlier, the phrase does not indicate immediate completion. The stated completion does imply that the grass had produced seed and that the fruit tree had yielded fruit, processes which require a considerable amount of time. The time required would be a season for grass and could be many years for newly sprouted fruit trees. The time required is internal evidence that this verse and the "creative yom" represent long periods of time. A completion within 24 hours would require that the meanings of the words describing the actions could not represent their usual meanings. There is no textual evidence to indicate anything but the usual meanings.

## The "When" of Genesis 1:12: A Pluperfect Reference to Past Actions

Genesis 1:12 is a verse which repeats much of Genesis 1:11 verbatim but also includes two differences. "And had brought forth" replaces the "And had said God" of Genesis 1:11; and "and it was so" is replaced by the phrase כִּי טוֹב which the KJV translates as "and God saw that *it was* good."

| | | | | | | | |
|---|---|---|---|---|---|---|---|
| וְעֵץ | לְמִינֵהוּ | זֶרַע | מַזְרִיעַ | עֵשֶׂב | דֶּשֶׁא | הָאָרֶץ | וַתּוֹצֵא Genesis 1:12 |
| and tree | after his kind | seed | yielding (seeding) | grass (KJV herb) | plant (grass) | the land | and had brought forth ("waw" + Hiphil imperfect) |

| | | | | | | | | |
|---|---|---|---|---|---|---|---|---|
| טוֹב | כִּי | אֱלֹהִים | וַיַּרְא | לְמִינֵהוּ | בוֹ | זַרְעוֹ | אֲשֶׁר | פְּרִי | עֹשֶׂה |
| good | as | God (Elohim) | and had seen | of his kind | in it | seed | which | fruit | bearing (making) |

KJV Genesis 1:12 And the earth brought forth grass, *and* herb yielding seed after his kind, and the tree yielding fruit, whose seed *was* in itself, after his kind: and God saw that *it was* good.

The first word תּוֹצֵא is again a verb in the Hiphil and indicates that the subject (the land) was the cause of the resulting actions. The verb form is in the imperfect but because of the prefix ו "waw" represents the perfect completed action. In Genesis 1:11 God had commanded the land to be the agent causing the sprouting or bringing forth of the desired plants. Genesis 1:12 verifies that the land had performed as commanded and had been the agent producing the desired plants. This verification comes after the actions are stated to have been completed. The question to be considered is: When did the actions of Genesis 1:12 take place with respect to the phrase "and *it* did come to pass so" which concluded Genesis 1:11? Recall that "and *it* did come to pass so" does not indicate immediate completion (page 95).

The two phrases "and *it* did come to pass so" followed by "and God had seen *it* as good" are an indicator that the verbs which occur between these two phrases are to be translated by the pluperfect. The pluperfect meaning of this phrase pattern is most easily demonstrated in the paired verses Genesis 1:11-12. This pattern occurs four times in Genesis One and is important to the understanding of the sequence of events in those occurrences. Genesis 1:11-12 will be analyzed in detail on the next page to demonstrate the pattern.

The analysis of Genesis 1:11-12 will later be applied to justify the pluperfect translation of verbs in Genesis 1:16-18 and pluperfect translation in Genesis 1:25. The pluperfect translation of Genesis 1:16-18 has been the subject of considerable controversy. Genesis 1:11-12 will now be repeated using the usual English word order, i.e., subject followed by the verb.

| | |
|---|---|
| Study Translation of Genesis 1:11 | And God had said the land shall bring forth plants, grass yielding seed and fruit tree bearing fruit of its kind whose seed is in it upon the land; and *it* did come to pass so. (KJV "and it was so") |
| Study Translation of Genesis 1:12 | And the land had brought forth plants, grass yielding seed after its kind, and tree bearing fruit whose seed is in it of its kind; and God had seen (*it*) as good. |

The question is "When do the events of Genesis 1:12 take place?" Clearly, the "had brought forth" of Genesis 1:12 takes place before the "and *it* did come to pass so" of Genesis 1:11 (KJV "and it was so"). The Hebrew phrase וַיְהִי כֵן "and *it* did come to pass so" is a perfect completed action. Schematically, the time sequence of the actions in Genesis 1:11 is:

Genesis 1:11         And God had said . . . (commands) . . . (events of Genesis 1:12) . . . and *it* did come to pass so.
                     **(KJV "and God said")**                                                 **(KJV "and it was so")**

Genesis 1:12 returns to a time after the commands of Genesis 1:11 by means of a partial repetition of those commands as completed actions. Genesis 1:12 provides additional information about the events of Genesis 1:11. This is called "epexegesis" and is a known pattern in biblical Hebrew. Genesis 1:12 tells of actions completed **before** the place where Genesis 1:12 occurs in the narrative. The "waw + imperfect verb" וַתּוֹצֵא translates as "and had brought forth," a pluperfect. This verb is not a continuation of the narrative sequence of events; it supplies epexegetical information about events already completed in the past. The use of a "waw + imperfect verb" in epexegesis to supply pluperfect information is well-known and is the subject of continuing research leading to improved understanding. Grammars which discuss the Hebrew verb document this pattern.

A quote from Driver's *A Treatise on the Use of the Tenses in Hebrew and Some Other Syntactical Questions* is useful for establishing the correctness of the pluperfect translation of the "waw + imperfect verb" וַתּוֹצֵא in Genesis 1:12. Referring to a "waw + imperfect verb" at the beginning of a sentence, Driver says the following:[59]

> 75. But the chronological sequence, though the most usual, is not the sole principle by which the use of ו is regulated. Where, for example, a transaction consists of two parts closely connected, a Hebrew narrator will often state the principal fact first, appending the concomitant occurrence with the help of ו; or again, in describing a series of transactions, he will hasten at once to state briefly the issue of the whole, and afterwards, as though forgetting that he had anticipated, proceed to annex the particulars by the same means: in neither of these cases is it implied that the event introduced by the ו is subsequent to that denoted by the previous verb: . . .

Application of the above quotation requires identifying the word and phrases which correspond with the descriptions used by Driver. For Genesis 1:11-12 the correspondences are:

1. The previous verb is the verb translated "and *it* did come to pass so."
2. "The issue of the whole" is the verse Genesis 1:11 telling of the commands and of their completion.
3. The commands and their completion are "the series of transactions."
4. The "annexed particulars" corresponds to Genesis 1:12.

In accordance with Driver's statement, Genesis 1:12 (the annexed particulars) is not subsequent to "and *it* did come to pass so." This quote from Driver supports the interpretation of this study that the events of Genesis 1:12 take place before the "and *it* did come to pass so."

The pattern described by Driver is also discussed by Zevit in *The Anterior Construction In Classical Hebrew*.[60] Zevit describes the Hebrew word sequence as being of the form: "and he-fell    John    and he-pushed him    Max."
                                                                            **Hebrew verb    Noun    Hebrew verb    Noun**

The Hebrew verb-noun "and he-pushed him Max" is a pluperfect reference to the antecedent cause of John falling. This is the pattern described by Driver, and the pattern in Genesis 1:11-12. In the examples which Zevit presents, the verbs are the "waw-consecutive" imperfect verbs of ordinary narrative discourse. Examples of pluperfect references which have no indication by means of word order or topic sequence are also known.[61]

Waltke and O'Connor, in *An Introduction to Biblical Hebrew Syntax*, discuss epexegetical use and give examples.[62] The references indicate that the use of the "waw + imperfect verb" to refer to past completed events occurs in many passages in the Bible. Now it is possible to understand one use which Genesis One makes of the phrases numbered (1) and (2) below, when phrase (1) is followed by verses that are a substantial repeat of a preceding verse.

(1)  "and *it* did come to pass so"  (KJV "and it was so")
(2)  "and God had seen (*it*) as good"  (KJV "and God saw that *it was* good")

Phrase (1) acts to indicate that the next sentence may describe events which were already completed in the past. This possibility is verified if the following sentence or sentences are a substantial repeat of already partially described events. This use is clearly shown in Genesis 1:12.

Phrase (2) following phrase (1) acts to indicate that the description of past events will end. This function is clearly shown in Genesis 1:10. Genesis 1:11-12 clearly must take place after Genesis 1:9-10.

Part of the above pattern appears in Genesis 1:10. The question is where to place the events of Genesis 1:10. The "Good English" translation of the four verses Genesis 1:9-12 is shown below. The events of Genesis 1:10 are identified as to the proposed time sequence of their occurrence.

Genesis 1:9  And God had said, the waters from beneath the heavens shall be gathered into one place and the dry shall be seen;
and *it* did come to pass so.  (KJV "and it was so")

**Back in time before "and it did come to pass so"**
{ *Genesis 1:10*  *And God had called the dry "land" and the gathered waters he had called seas; and God had seen (it) as good;*

Genesis 1:11  And God had said the land shall sprout grass, plants yielding seed *and* fruit tree bearing fruit of its kind whose seed is in it upon the land;
and *it* did come to pass so.  (KJV "and it was so")

**Back in time before "and it did come to pass so"**
{ *Genesis 1:12*  *And the "land" had brought forth grass, plants yielding seed after its kind and tree bearing fruit whose seed is in it of its kind; and God had seen (it) as good.*

The events of Genesis 1:12 take place before the "and *it* did come to pass so" of Genesis 1:11. The analysis of Genesis 1:11 and Genesis 1:12 has clearly shown that this time location is correct. Genesis 1:12 does not advance the story in time; it refers to actions which have already taken place.

Genesis 1:9-10 is a more difficult translation issue than Genesis 1:11-12. Genesis One contains four distinct pairs of "and *it* did come to pass so" followed by a sentence or sentences which end with וַיְהִי כֵן which the KJV translates "and God saw that *it was* good." The pattern used for three of these pairs is a partial repetition of events which have previously been related, such as occurs in Genesis 1:12. Partial repetition, as just discussed, is a known pattern for inserting pluperfect information into Hebrew. The Genesis 1:9-10 pair differs.

Genesis 1:10 does not repeat any verb or events of Genesis 1:9. The phrase **called the dry "land"** may take place before the "and *it* did come to pass so," but the verb form itself does not require this placement. In the Hebrew of the second clause **"and the gathered waters he had called seas,"** the subject הַמַּיִם "the waters" precedes the verb קָרָא . This is the "waw + noun--perfect verb" construction by which Hebrew indicates the pluperfect, and informs of the sequence in which the seas and "dry" were named. Because Genesis 1:10 does not repeat events or commands of Genesis 1:9, the pluperfect verb translation **And God had called the dry "land"** is based on the presence of the "and *it* did come to pass so" followed by a sentence which ends with וַיְהִי כֵן "and God had seen (*it*) as good." The pattern, which is clear in three cases, is applied here based on the evidence of the three cases.

It is important to recognize the existence of verses referring back to past events in Genesis One. Some interpretations assume that all the events recorded in Genesis One take place one after another in the sequence in which the verses are written. This study has shown that this is not so. Past events are described. Remember, the correct determination of the "when" and duration of the events of Genesis One is the subject of this study.

## The Words Translated Grass and Tree

The issue for the reader of Genesis One is how to correctly translate and understand the Hebrew words דֶּשֶׁא "deshe," עֵשֶׂב "eseb," and עֵץ "ets." These Hebrew words are not as well defined as a reader of the English translation might suppose.

There are two words in Genesis 1:11 which can be translated "grass." The words are דֶּשֶׁא "deshe" and עֵשֶׂב "eseb." In Genesis 1:11 the KJV translates דֶּשֶׁא "grass" and עֵשֶׂב "herb." The problem with the KJV translation is that in other verses (such as Deuteronomy 32:2) the KJV translates עֵשֶׂב "grass" and דֶּשֶׁא "herb." The poetry of Deuteronomy 32:2 provides an example of the reversed translation and also verifies that the two words have a measure of equivalence. By the rules of Hebrew poetry two or more lines are to repeat the same general (but not identical) meaning. The KJV translation of the two words is reversed as compared to that of Genesis 1:11.

KJV Deuteronomy 32:2    My doctrine shall drop as the rain, my speech shall distil as the dew,

                as the small rain upon the tender דֶּשֶׁא herb, and as the showers upon the עֵשֶׂב grass.

In Genesis 1:11 this study concludes that עֵשֶׂב "eseb" should be translated "grass." The reason for translating עֵשֶׂב "grass" lies in the great importance grass has in the agricultural economy which provides food for human society. Genesis One, as a whole, tells about preparation and provision made for Adam and Eve. This provision includes food for man and food for animals. Grasses provide food for humans because the grains which people eat are the seeds of grasses. The part of Genesis 1:11 dealing with plants and trees is shown below for reference.

Genesis 1:11    And God said, The land shall bring forth דֶּשֶׁא plant, עֵשֶׂב grass yielding seed,

        *and* fruit tree yielding fruit after its kind, whose seed *is* in itself, . . .

The translation of singular word דֶּשֶׁא "deshe" as "plant" results in the following words "grass yielding seed after its kind" being an additional specification identifying the type of plant intended. This same pattern is repeated in identifying the "fruit tree" as a type (kind) whose seed is in its fruit. Genesis 1:11 may refer to only one type (kind) of plant called דֶּשֶׁא "deshe." By its nature the word grass is a plural, and the singular Hebrew word עֵשֶׂב "grass" is interpreted as a plural. The singular, however, must be allowed to the extent it relates to type (kind). It should not be inferred that דֶּשֶׁא "deshe," and עֵשֶׂב "eseb" refer to all plant life, or to all the different species of grasses as they are known today.

The Hebrew word עֵץ (ets), translated tree, also needs to be considered because of the much broader meaning of the Hebrew word. The main emphasis is on the seed being in the fruit of the "fruit tree." The actual nature of the plant which first appeared on the land and which bore fruit cannot be determined. The Hebrew word עֵץ (ets) is used to refer to any plant which has a woody branch or stalk. In Joshua 2:6, the passage in which Rahab hid the spies in Jericho, the KJV translates the word הָעֵץ as stalks. Literally, the word הָעֵץ is "the tree" or "the wood." The ה is the attached prefix meaning "the."

KJV Joshua 2:6    (1) But she had brought them up to the roof of the house,

        (2) and hid them with הָעֵץ the stalks of flax, which she had laid in order upon the roof.

| הַגָּג | עַל | לָהּ | הָעֲרֻכוֹת | הָעֵץ | בְּפִשְׁתֵּי | וַתִּטְמְנֵם | הַגָּגָה | הֶעֱלָתַם | וְהִיא | (1) Joshua 2:6 |
|---|---|---|---|---|---|---|---|---|---|---|
| roof | above | by her | the arranged | the tree (the wood) | from flax | and hid | the roof | caused to ascend | and she | |

Another illustration of the use of עֵץ "tree" is found in Ezekiel 15:2-3.

KJV Ezekiel 15:2-3    Son of man, What is the vine עֵץ tree more than any עֵץ tree, *or than* a branch which is

        among the trees of the forest? Shall עֵץ wood be taken thereof to do any work? or will

        *men* take a pin (peg) of it to hang any vessel thereon?

That the vine is to be considered a עֵץ "tree" is further illustrated in Judges 9:12 and surrounding verses which relate the parable of the trees seeking a king. Brambles are also invited to be king in another verse.

KJV Judges 9:12  Then said the הָעֵצִים trees unto the vine, Come thou, and reign over us.

| Judges 9:12 | וַיֹּאמְרוּ | הָעֵצִים | לַגֶּפֶן | לְכִי | אַתְּ | מָלוֹכִי | עָלֵינוּ |
|---|---|---|---|---|---|---|---|
| | and had said | the trees | to the vine | come | you | reign | above |

In Genesis 1:11 words for tree and for fruit are in the singular. The singular Hebrew word "tree" is usually translated into English as the plural. But again, even though the word may be translated as the plural trees, the singular must be allowed. Genesis 1:11 may only intend one specific type of plant called a tree.

In the "Good English" translation below, the singular Hebrew word דֶּשֶׁא "deshe" has been translated "plant." The translation of עֵשֶׂב as "grass" which follows introduces the existence of multiple copies of this plant. The singular Hebrew word עֵץ (ets) for tree has been translated "tree." The word עֵץ does not include the prefix ה "the" added by the KJV. The plural meaning flows naturally from the English without introducing a plural "trees" which could be interpreted as indicating multiple kinds of trees. The text does not specify how many types of "trees" are in view. In the sixth creative "yom" there are many types of grass and trees. The text of the sixth creative "yom" refers to "every tree" and "every grass yielding seed."

**The "Good English" Translation of Genesis 1:9-13**

Genesis 1:9    And God said, The waters under the heavens shall be gathered together unto one place, and the dry shall be seen; and *it* did come to pass so.  (KJV "and it was so")

Genesis 1:10   And God **had called** the dry "land," and the gathering together of the waters he **had called** Seas; and God had seen *it* as good.    (KJV "and God saw that *it was* good)

Genesis 1:11   And God said, The land shall bring forth plant, grass yielding seed, *and* fruit tree yielding fruit after its kind, whose seed *is* in itself, upon the land; and *it* did come to pass so.   (KJV "and it was so")

Genesis 1:12   And the land **had brought** forth plant, grass yielding seed after its kind, and tree yielding fruit, whose seed *was* in itself, after its kind: and God had seen *it* as good.   (KJV "and God saw that *it was* good)

Genesis 1:13   And *there* was evening and *there* was morning, a third time.

In Genesis 1:12 the words translated "and God had seen *it* as good" are a phrase which is used seven times in Genesis One. The phrase expresses that God considered the results of the commands and the response of the land to be as intended. The "*it*" does not appear in the Hebrew. Here, again, the completed action has been translated using "had." The meaning of "good" is dependent upon context but is an appropriate translation. The reader will understand that the word is to be interpreted in context. The usual translation follows the KJV and is "and God saw that it was good." The verb "saw" is formally a completed action but is subject to being misinterpreted as previously explained.

The final Hebrew verse of the third creative "yom" is a repetition of the concluding phrase already discussed extensively and shown to be a long period of time. This phrase marks the conclusion of creative "yom" three.

| Genesis 1:13 | וַיְהִי | עֶרֶב | וַיְהִי | בֹקֶר | יוֹם | שְׁלִישִׁי |
|---|---|---|---|---|---|---|
| | and had been | evening | and had been | morning | "yom" | third |

# The Fourth Creative "Yom": Genesis 1:14-19 — The Lights in the Sky

The verses of the fourth creative time describe modification of the physical environment of the heavens. These verses also include another pair of the phrases וַיְהִי כֵן "and *it* did come to pass so" and "and God saw that *it was* good." In this case there are three intervening sentences between the two phrases. These sentences explain events completed before the וַיְהִי כֵן (KJV "and it was so"). This study will first consider the verses individually, explaining the words and verb forms. Then the verses will be considered as a unit in English translation, to determine the "when" of the actions. The first verse of this section is Genesis 1:14.

| Genesis 1:14 | וַיֹּאמֶר | אֱלֹהִים | יְהִי | מְאֹרֹת | בִּרְקִיעַ הַשָּׁמַיִם | לְהַבְדִּיל | בֵּין |
|---|---|---|---|---|---|---|---|
| | and had said | God (Elohim) | shall be | lights | in sky of (KJV "firmament of") the heavens | to separate | between |

| הַיּוֹם | וּבֵין | הַלַּיְלָה | וְהָיוּ | לְאֹתֹת | וּלְמוֹעֲדִים | וּלְיָמִים | וְשָׁנִים |
|---|---|---|---|---|---|---|---|
| the daytime "yom" | and between | the nighttime | and shall be | for signs | and for seasons | and for days "yoms" | and years |

KJV Genesis 1:14      And God said, Let there be lights in the firmament of the heaven to divide the day (yom) from the night; and let them be for signs, and for seasons, and for days, and years:

The first two Hebrew words וַיֹּאמֶר אֱלֹהִים are the familiar "And God had said" (KJV "And God said") which has been discussed. The verb יְהִי is the Qal imperfect incomplete action which is translated "shall be." The יְהִי verb form can also be considered a "jussive" command leading to the KJV translation "Let there be." The same verb also appears in the second line as the "waw-consecutive" in the form וְהָיוּ. This construction is וְהָיוּ the perfect form of the verb "to be" with a plural ending prefixed by ו. As a consequence of the ו, the verb represents the incomplete action and is translated "and shall be." The וְהָיוּ is **not a jussive** or an imperative form which can be translated as the command "let them be." The "let them be" of the KJV is, in this case, a stylistic choice of the translator. The "shall be" does not require an immediate fulfillment. The "shall be" is also consistent with the continuing of the commanded functions to the present time.

The event which is being described is the visible appearance of the sun and the moon in the sky (heavens). The "to separate" is not the same event as the separation between the light (yom) and the dark (night) which took place in Genesis 1:4. Here the lights are to appear in the sky which did not appear until Genesis 1:6

These two **newly visible** light sources are also given new functions. These functions are "for signs, and for seasons, and for days, and years." "Yom" is clearly and unambiguously used in the sense of the time of solar illumination. Because the meaning is clear, "yom" has been translated "daytime" in this passage and the Hebrew word הַלַּיְלָה has been "nighttime."

The new functions for the sun and the moon are to mark the passage of time as described by several types of intervals. Remember the context is the time of Moses. The lunar month measured by the cycle and phases of the moon was an important cycle used to measure and describe the passage of time. The passage of time was also measured by counting the number of occurrences of a clearly definable event such as the sunrise or sunset. Sundials divided the day into intervals. The time length of the solar day, and the divisions of the day, vary with the season of the year. They are shorter in the winter and longer in the summer. The longer intervals of years, seasons, and signs were of religious significance in Egypt and the surrounding cultures. The word לְאֹתֹת translated "for signs," is prefixed with the preposition ל meaning "for," "to," "at," etc. The KJV translates the root word אוֹת as sign (60 times), as token (14 times), and as miracle (2 times).

The word וּלְמוֹעֲדִים is the plural word מוֹעֲדִים "seasons" prefixed by two prepositions. The prepositions are ו "and," and ל meaning "for" or "to." The root word מוֹעֵד is translated by the KJV as congregation (150 times), feast (23 times), season (13 times), and time (12 times).

What is at issue here?

The Law of Moses commands or specifies the observances of days (the Sabbath), months (the new moons), and seasons. The seasons are the annual feasts such as the Passover. Also special multiples of the years are to be observed such as the Sabbath year of rest of the land, and the Jubilee. The text refers to these functions. This terminology is also used in the New Testament. In Galatians 4:10 Paul refers to days, months, and times, and years.

KJV Galatians 4:9-11   But now, after that ye have known God, or rather are known of God,
how turn ye again to the weak and beggarly elements,
whereunto ye desire again to be in bondage?
Ye observe days, and months, and times, and years.
I am afraid of you, lest I have bestowed upon you labour in vain.

The next verse, Genesis 1:15, specifies a second function for the newly visible light sources. This function is to give light to the surface of the land.

| Genesis 1:15 | וְהָיוּ | לִמְאוֹרֹת | בִּרְקִיעַ | הַשָּׁמַיִם | לְהָאִיר | עַל | הָאָרֶץ | וַיְהִי | כֵן |
|---|---|---|---|---|---|---|---|---|---|
| | and *they* shall be | for lights | in sky of (KJV "firmament") | the heavens | to give light | over | the land | and *it* did come to pass | so |

KJV Genesis 1:15   And let them be for lights in the firmament of the heaven to give light upon the earth: and it was so.

The verb וְהָיוּ is the perfect form of the verb "to be" with a plural ending prefixed by וְ. As a consequence of the וְ, the verb represents the incomplete action and is translated "and shall be." The וְהָיוּ is **not a jussive** or an imperative form which can be translated as the command "let them be." The "let them be" of the KJV is again a stylistic choice of the translator; it is not in the Hebrew text or in the Latin Vulgate. The imperative translation does appear in the Septuagint. The incomplete action "and they shall be" refers to the function of the sun and the moon to illuminate the surface of the land. These functions continue to the present time.

Another important verb in this verse occurs in the phrase וַיְהִי כֵן "and *it* did come to pass so" (KJV "and *it was* so"). This completed action phrase confirms that the sun and moon had performed each of the functions commanded in Genesis 1:14-15. It indicates that each of the functions of signs, seasons, and years **had completed** at least one cycle. **This is an additional indication that the "creative yom" are long periods of time.** This implication is also clear when translated "and *it was* so" as does the KJV or "and *it* did come to pass so," as does the "Good English" translation of this study. Recall that וַיְהִי כֵן "and *it* did come to pass so" does not indicate immediacy of fulfillment.

Notice the sun and the moon are not mentioned by name, they are called "lights." The sun and the moon are referred to as objects, not as gods. The sun and the moon were worshiped as gods by the other peoples of the region. Genesis 1:16 continues the denial that the sun and moon are gods; Genesis 1:16 states that the sun and moon were made (asah). These statements were of great theological significance to the people at the time of Moses, which can easily be overlooked because the sun and moon are not presently considered to be gods. It is also of importance today, but for a different reason. This reason has to do with the controversy advanced by critics of the Bible about when the sun and moon were made. This controversy arose primarily through not understanding the completed action meaning of the verb form וַיַּעַשׂ (asah) for the making of the sun and the moon. The issue of "when" will be discussed after considering the meanings of the Hebrew words of Genesis 1:16-18. It will then be shown that these three verses are a past narrative describing events completed before the וַיְהִי כֵן "and *it* did come to pass so" of Genesis 1:15. Genesis 1:16-18 will also be shown to span a considerable amount of time.

The Hebrew of Genesis 1:16 is:

| הַגָּדֹל | הַמָּאוֹר | אֶת | הַגְּדֹלִים | הַמְּאֹרֹת | שְׁנֵי | אֶת | אֱלֹהִים | וַיַּעַשׂ | Genesis 1:16 |
|---|---|---|---|---|---|---|---|---|---|
| the great | the lights | dir. obj. marker | the great | the lights | two | dir. obj. marker | God (Elohim) | and had made | |

| וְאֵת הַכּוֹכָבִים | הַלַּיְלָה | לְמֶמְשֶׁלֶת | הַקָּטֹן | הַמָּאוֹר | וְאֵת | הַיּוֹם | לְמֶמְשֶׁלֶת |
|---|---|---|---|---|---|---|---|
| the stars and + dir. obj. marker | the nighttime | for rule of | the small | the light | and + dir. obj. marker | the daytime | for rule of |

KJV Genesis 1:16   And God made two great lights; the greater light to rule the day, and the lesser light to rule the night: *he made* the stars also.

YLT Genesis 1:16   And God maketh the two great luminaries, the great luminary for the rule of the day, and the small luminary -- and the stars -- for the rule of the night;

The first word וַיַּעַשׂ (asah) means to make or to fashion. This is not the word בָּרָא "bara" used in the first verse of Genesis. בָּרָא "bara" means to create a new thing. The significance of the use of a different word in this verse is that the sun and moon are **not** described as new things.

Recall that Genesis 2:3 says that God "created" (bara) "for making" (asah). This was already discussed on page 28 and on pages 32-35. The phrase "the heavens and the earth" of Genesis 1:1 includes the creation of the sun and the moon. In Genesis 1:16 the verb יַעַשׂ is in the Qal imperfect, but is prefixed with the וַ "and." The effect of the וַ is to make the action of the verb the completed (perfect) action. The critics of Genesis have not translated the verb וַיַּעַשׂ as the completed action. They have seized upon the usual translation "and God made," and have read the verb as indicating immediate action. That is to say, they take the "made" as having occurred just an instant before the visual appearance of the sun and the moon. The Hebrew does not allow that interpretation. That interpretation arises because of the style used by the usual English translations, a style derived from the Latin Vulgate. The "making" (asah) must precede the completion indicated by the וַיְהִי כֵן "and *it* did come to pass so" in Genesis 1:15. The "making" (asah) refers to an action completed in the past and is correctly translated by the pluperfect "and had made."

The translation "made" is also an impediment to understanding this verse as a theological statement. "Asah" expresses the concept of doing, and is translated "do" more than 1300 times by the KJV. "Do" is the most common translation, but the translations "shew" and "dress" are also made. The KJV translation "shew kindness" could have been translated "do kindness." "Asah" is translated "dress" as in preparing meat for cooking 13 times and is translated "prepare" 37 times. "Asah" translated "had prepared" in Genesis 1:16 would reveal more clearly the theological content of Genesis 1:16-17. This content is twofold: (1) God did it and (2) the sun, moon, and stars are not gods as supposed by the pagan religions of the day.

Genesis 1:16 also includes indication of future purposes which are not accomplished by the "and had made." The purposes are the ruling of the daytime and the ruling of the nighttime. These purposes are accomplished by the actions described in Genesis 1:17.

The next verse, Genesis 1:17, is a partial repetition of Genesis 1:15. There are interesting changes made in the partial repetitions. The command "and shall be" of Genesis 1:15 is replaced by "and had given." The word translated given is also often translated "placed" or "set." The verb form is different, indicating that actions which are to accomplish the purposes stated in Genesis 1:15 have now been taken and are completed actions.

| הָאָרֶץ | עַל | לְהָאִיר | הַשָּׁמַיִם | בִּרְקִיעַ | אֱלֹהִים | אֹתָם | וַיִּתֵּן | Genesis 1:17 |
|---|---|---|---|---|---|---|---|---|
| the land | over (upon) | for giving light | the heavens | in sky of (KJV "firmament") | God (Elohim) | them + dir. obj. marker | and had given (set) | |

KJV Genesis 1:17 And God set (placed) them in the firmament of the heaven to give light upon the earth,

The first word יִתֵּן is a verb in the Qal imperfect form. Because it is prefixed by ו "and," the meaning is the completed (perfect) action. This action is translated using had. The second word is the direct object marker in a form not encountered before. The pronoun suffix ם meaning "them" has been added indicating that the object of the verb is the sun and the moon.

The verb לְהָאִיר translated "for giving light" is in the form called the Hiphil infinitive. The verb is prefixed by ל meaning "to" or "for." The insertion of the י "yod" just before the last letter of the three-letter word root is how the Hiphil is written. This form is generally translated as "to" followed by a word expressing the action or is translated using the "ing" form of the verb. The translation "for giving light" has been adopted. The Hiphil is the verb form which is used to indicate causation by means of the action of an intermediary agent (means).[63] God is the source cause of the light on the land. The action is accomplished by means of the sun and the moon. The infinitive has the sense of continuing action. Had the KJV translation been "for giving light," the continuing future nature of the meaning would have been more explicit.

Genesis 1:18 continues explaining the results flowing from the "and had given" of Genesis 1:17. Genesis 1:18 also uses the Hiphil infinitive (the -ing verb form) for the words which the KJV translates "and to rule" and "and to separate." These actions continue into the future. The word וְלִמְשֹׁל translated "and to rule" by the KJV is prefixed with the preposition ל "to" or "for." The KJV translates the consonantal word משׁל as dominion (10 times) and as rule (4 times). Genesis 1:18 in Hebrew is:

| Genesis 1:18 | וְלִמְשֹׁל | בַּיּוֹם | וּבַלַּיְלָה | וּלְהַבְדִּיל | בֵּין | הָאוֹר | וּבֵין |
|---|---|---|---|---|---|---|---|
| | and for ruling | in day (yom) | and in night | and to separate | between | the light | and between |

| הַחֹשֶׁךְ | וַיַּרְא | אֱלֹהִים | כִּי | טוֹב |
|---|---|---|---|---|
| the dark | and had seen | God (Elohim) | as | good |

KJV Genesis 1:18    And to rule over the day and over the night, and to divide the light from the darkness: and God saw that *it was* good.

God is the cause of the actions. Each of the verb forms is prefixed by ו meaning "and." With the Hiphil infinitive, the ו does not alter the nature of the action of the verb. The translation can be "and to rule" or "and for ruling." When the "ing" form is used, "to" is best replaced by "for" to indicate purpose and the continuing action in the English translation.

Now the question of the "when" of the actions of Genesis 1:14-18 will be considered starting on the next page.

# The "When" of the Actions of Genesis 1:14-18, the Pluperfect References to Past Actions

The first step in identifying and explaining the "when" of the actions of Genesis 1:14-18 is to present a "Good English" translation of these verses in summary form below. This is based on the translation which appeared below the Hebrew during the study of these verses. The sequence of five verses begins with the usual "And God said."

Genesis 1:14 And God said, there shall be lights in the sky of the heavens
   **(2)** to separate between the daytime and the nighttime, **(2)**
   and *they* will be for signs and for seasons and for days and years.

Genesis 1:15 **(1)** And *they* shall be for lights in the sky of the heavens for giving light upon the land; **(1)**
   and *it* did come to pass so.

Genesis 1:16 And God had made (prepared) the two lights;
   the great for rule of the daytime and the small for rule of the nighttime,
   and the stars.

Genesis 1:17 And God had given (set) them in the sky of the heavens
   for giving light upon the land

Genesis 1:18 And for ruling in the daytime and in the nighttime,
   and to separate between the light and the dark;
   and God had seen *it* as good.

The pattern of Genesis 1:14-15 is: commands of functions and purposes followed by a statement of completed fulfillment. The phrase translated "and *it* did come to pass so" is the statement of completed fulfillment.

Genesis 1:16-18 follows the statement "and *it* did come to pass so" and concludes with "and God had seen *it* as good." Genesis 1:16-18 are translated with the pluperfect using "had." The pluperfect translation is based on two indicators. One indicator is the repetition of words from commands of Genesis 1:14-15. These repetitions are:

   Genesis 1:17 which repeats words from of Genesis 1:15 line **(1)**.
   Genesis 1:18 which repeats words from of Genesis 1:14 line **(2)**.

The second indicator of the pluperfect is the bracketing of these repeated words by the phrases "and *it* did come to pass so" and "and God had seen *it* as good." This is the pattern that was found to be an indicator of already completed past actions. This was covered in the discussion of Genesis 1:11-12 (pages 97-99).

Genesis 1:16 indicates new functions not mentioned earlier, the ruling of the daytime and the nighttime. These new functions are made possible by the "had given (set)" of Genesis 1:17.

Genesis 1:16 says that God "had made (prepared)" the two lights and that the action was completed. This "asah" does **not** indicate the creation (bara) of the sun and the moon during the fourth creative yom. The sun and moon are created in Genesis 1:1. Recall Genesis 2:3 says that God "had created" (bara) "for making" (asah), a subsequent action. Nothing requires or indicates that the "had made (prepared)" take place within the fourth creative "yom." The "had made" statement functions as background information preparatory to the subsequent action "had given." As a background statement it may refer to unspecified actions occurring to prepare the sun and the moon for the intended functions. Recall that the daytime and nighttime both occur and are named in Genesis 1:4-5, in the first creative time. The daytime does not just suddenly appear here in Genesis 1:16.

The "had made" statement of Genesis 1:16 is primarily theological. It is a reminder that the sun and moon are things subject to God. They are spoken of as being equivalent to lamps. There is no indication that the sun and the moon are alive, an important factor at the time of Moses when they were considered to be alive and were worshiped as gods.

There is a time progression of the actions. The creation (bara) of the sun and moon in Genesis 1:1 precedes the "had made" of Genesis 1:16, which in turn precedes the "had given" of Genesis 1:17. The "when" of the "had given" is before the "and *it* did come to pass so" which appeared at the end of Genesis 1:15. The final phrase "and God had seen it as good" of Genesis 1:18 indicates that the next verse will again advance the time sequence of the story line.

Many of the commanded functions require a clear atmosphere. The function "for signs and for seasons" requires the visibility of the sun and the moon. The function of the moon in giving light on the land also requires a clear atmosphere. The light-dark cycle of Genesis 1:2 did not require a clear atmosphere, only that visible light penetrate to the surface of planet Earth.

The present understanding of the natural history of planet Earth asserts that early in its history there would have been a dense, permanent, cloud cover. This is not merely a secular model; the Bible in Job 38:9 indicates that the first ocean was wrapped (swaddled) in a darkness due to clouds. Genesis 1:2 describes a water surface (the deep) which was in darkness.

KJV Job 38:9   When I made the cloud the garment thereof, and thick darkness a swaddlingband for it,

YLT Job 38:9   In My making a cloud its clothing, And thick darkness its swaddling band,

| | | | | | Job 38:9 |
|---|---|---|---|---|---|
| חֲתֻלָּתוֹ | וַעֲרָפֶל | לְבֻשׁוֹ | עָנָן | בְּשׂוּמִי | |
| swaddling band of it | thick darkness | its garment | cloud | In My making of | |
| | | | | (an infinitive prefixed by ב "in") | |

Recall that under heavy cloud cover the night is very dark. Most people will have experienced the "blackest of nights" under these conditions. The illumination of the land by the moon is not discerned nor is the moon visible under these conditions. In the absence of a clear atmosphere, the lunar cycle would not have been observable. Because the phases of the moon would not have been visible, the function of marking signs, seasons, and years would not have been possible.

Genesis 1:15 tells us that there was a change, that the atmosphere had become clear enough for the moon to give noticeable illumination to the surface of the land. The phrase "and *it* did come to pass so" is assurance of the completion of this change.

This analysis of the verses of creative "yom" four yields evidence of some remarkable truths in the Bible. This is just the opposite of what critics of the Bible claim for the events of the fourth creative "yom."

One often-advanced objection claims that the Bible says that the sun and the moon first come into existence during the fourth creative "yom," after the introduction of plants. To make this objection they must assume that made (asah) and create (bara) are identical in meaning. They must further assume that the sun and moon are not included in the creation in the beginning.

This objection fails because that is **not** what the text says. The sun and the moon are included in the "bara" creation of the heavens and the Earth of Genesis 1:1. The cycle of light ("yom") and dark (night) were introduced in Genesis 1:3-5. No mention is made in those verses of the visibility of the sun and the moon. The initial cloud cover is proposed to have gradually diminished. At some point the cloud cover would have become sufficiently thin that a noticeable amount of light reached the surface. At that time the light and dark cycle would have commenced. The start of the daytime-nighttime cycle is what is described in Genesis 1:4. A light and dark cycle can be observed even when the sky is continually overcast with clouds. The source of the light is not visible under such conditions.

The land plants are introduced in Genesis 1:11-12 after the start of the light and dark cycle. Light **was** available, at that time, to provide for the photosynthesis of land plants. Again, the sequence of events described in Genesis One is in accord with the natural history sequence, as it is now understood. The sequence of events described in Genesis One was, of course, written long before there was any scientific knowledge about the natural history of planet Earth.

## About the "Patterning" of Genesis One

Proposals made by others suggest that Genesis One is arranged topically and not chronologically. These proposals have not carried the day but have forced recognition that the patterns of Genesis One indicate more than a simple chronological sequence. The actual pattern of Genesis One does not fit into a purely chronological or topical organizational pattern. **Genesis One is so masterfully constructed that it is easy to forget that it is written using less than 100 Hebrew root words plus pronouns and prepositions.** The verses of Genesis 1:14 through Genesis 1:19 exhibit a topical pattern of arrangement within the overall pattern of relating the events.

The "Good English" translation is repeated below with additional annotations to show this patterning. These annotations are dotted lines connecting corresponding topics or phrases showing a pattern of symmetry about the middle verse, which is Genesis 1:16.

The overall topical patterning of Genesis 1:14-18 is relevant to the question of the "when" of the actions in the verses. The overall topical pattern is additional evidence that the sentence sequence is not a purely chronological sequence. This is in agreement with the placement of the "when" of the actions found in the earlier analysis of these verses.

**Genesis 1:14-18 "Good English" Translation, with lines showing patterning:**

And God **said, there shall be lights in the sky of the heavens**

to separate **between the daytime and the nighttime,**

**and *they* will be for signs and for seasons and for days and years.**

**And *they* will be for lights** in the sky of the heavens
for giving light upon the land;
**and *it* did come to pass so.**

**And God had made (prepared) the two lights;**
**the great for ruling the day, and the small for ruling the night,**
**and the stars.**

**And God had given (set) them** in the sky of the heavens

for giving light upon the land.
**And for ruling in the daytime and in the nighttime,**
**and to** separate **between the light and the dark;**

and God **had seen *it* as good.**

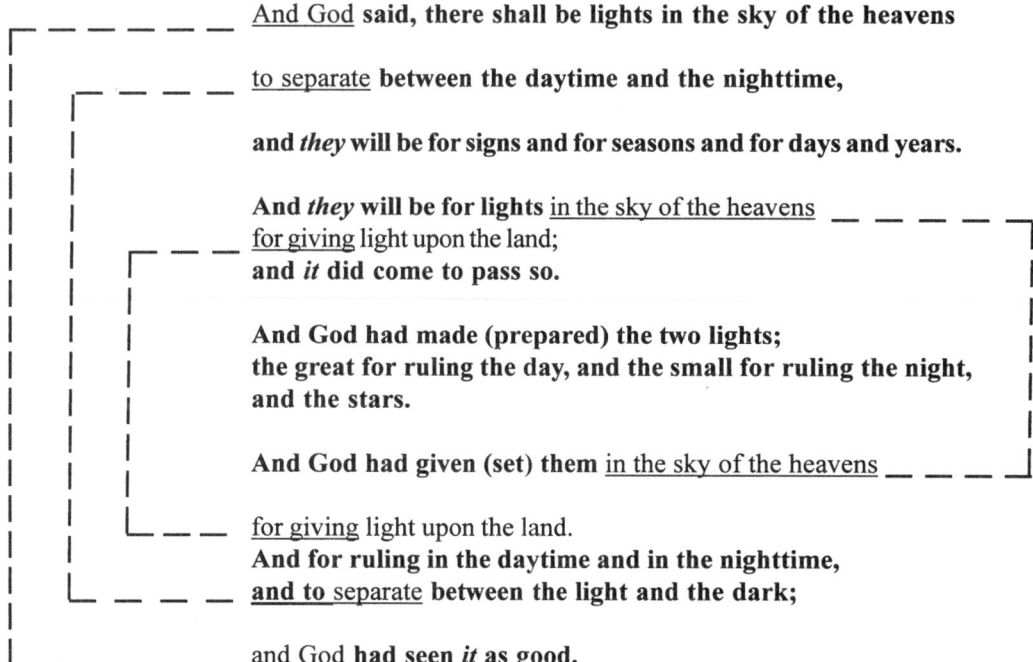

The final phrase of the Genesis 1:18, translated here "and God had seen it as good" uses the completed action form of the verb "to see." This is the fourth time this concluding phrase has appeared. It has already been discussed extensively in reference to Genesis 1:5.

The final verse of the fourth creative "yom" is a repetition of the phrase we discussed extensively showing the time referred to was a long period of time.

| רְבִיעִי | יוֹם | בֹקֶר | וַיְהִי | עֶרֶב | וַיְהִי | **Genesis 1:19** |
|---|---|---|---|---|---|---|
| **fourth** | **yom** | **morning** | **and *there* had been** | **evening** | **and *there* had been** | |

Again, a "Good English" translation is given which includes Genesis 1:19 and has no dotted lines showing the patterning. This "Good English" translation is based on the discussion and the translation appearing under the Hebrew verses in the preceding sections.

**"Good English" Translation of Genesis 1:14-19**

Genesis 1:14   And God said, *There* shall be lights in the sky of the heavens
to separate between the daytime and the nighttime,
and *they* will be for signs, and for seasons, and for days, and years.

Genesis 1:15   And *they* will be for lights in the sky of the heavens
for giving light upon the land; and it did come to pass so.   (KJV "and it was so")

Genesis 1:16   And God **had made** (prepared) the two great lights; the great for rule of the daytime,
and the small for rule of the nighttime, and the stars.

Genesis 1:17   And God **had given (set)** them in the sky of the heavens
for giving light upon the land,

Genesis 1:18   And for ruling in the daytime and in the nighttime, and to separate between
the light and the dark: and God had seen *it* as good.   (KJV "and God saw that *it was* good)

Genesis 1:19   And *there* was evening and *there* was morning, a fourth time.

# The Fifth Creative "Yom": Genesis 1:20-23      Air-Breathing Creatures in the Waters

The events of the fifth creative time period are described in Genesis 1:20-23. The events contain information which can easily be overlooked if the verses are not studied carefully. Questions and issues which will be considered in this section are:

1. What is the nature of the creatures which are commanded to "swarm" in the waters? They are described by the Hebrew phrase נֶפֶשׁ חַיָּה pronounced "nephesh khay-yah." They will be shown to be air breathing.

2. What is the order of the creative events within creative "yom" five?

3. What methods did God use to introduce plant life and animal life? It will be shown that God has revealed three methods which He has used to accomplish His creation.

It is imperative that a Bible defender know what the Bible does and does not say about the introduction of living things. A defender should be able to identify misrepresentations of the Bible by Darwinists and by other well-meaning but confused defenders of the Bible.

## Creatures in the Waters

Question (1) is "What is the nature of the creatures which are commanded to "swarm" in the waters"?
Genesis 1:20 will be considered first. The YLT is used because it follows the Hebrew more closely than does the KJV. The YLT translates the noun שֶׁרֶץ (sherets) and the verb יִשְׁרְצוּ using forms of the English word "teem." The KJV does not translate these words in a consistent manner, thereby introducing considerable confusion.

The verb יִשְׁרְצוּ = וּ + שְׁרְץ + יִ and the noun שֶׁרֶץ are both derived from the same root שֶׁרֶץ (sherets). The Hebrew spellings somewhat obscure this connection because שׁ and ץ indicate the same letter. Consistent translation reveals the relationship of the noun and the verb. The KJV translates the noun שֶׁרֶץ as "creeping thing" or "creep" 13 of the 15 times it appears. However, in Genesis 1:20 the KJV translates the verb as "bring forth abundantly" and the noun as "moving." These translations obscure the connection between the verb and the noun. The study translation under the Hebrew will translate the verb יִשְׁרְצוּ as "swarm" and the singular noun שֶׁרֶץ as "a swarm of" which explicitly displays the singular nature of the word. The YLT translates שֶׁרֶץ "teem." The ASV and NAS translate the verb "teem" and the noun "swarms."

The words שרץ "swarm" and רמשׂ (ramas) "creep," will be considered in more detail in a later section on page 118.

YLT Genesis 1:20 And God saith, 'Let the waters יִשְׁרְצוּ **teem** (KJV "bring forth abundantly") with the שׁרץ **teeming** living creature, and fowl let fly on the earth on the face of the expanse of the heavens.'

| חַיָּה | נֶפֶשׁ | שֶׁרֶץ | הַמַּיִם | יִשְׁרְצוּ | אֱלֹהִים | וַיֹּאמֶר | (1) Genesis 1:20 |
|---|---|---|---|---|---|---|---|
| YLT "living" | nephesh | a swarm of | the waters | shall swarm | God (Elohim) | and had said | |
| (singular) | (singular) | (singular) | | (incomplete action) | | (completed action) | |

| הַשָּׁמָיִם | רְקִיעַ | פְּנֵי | עַל | הָאָרֶץ | עַל | יְעוֹפֵף | וְעוֹף | (2) |
|---|---|---|---|---|---|---|---|---|
| the heavens | firmament of | face of | over | the land (erets) | above | shall fly (singular) | and a flyer (singular) | |

The word נֶפֶשׁ translated phonetically as "nephesh," and חַיָּה (ḥayyâ) translated "living" will now be studied in detail. The transliteration (ḥayyâ) with the dotted "ḥ" is used to distinguish חַיָּה from the word הָיָה "haya" which was discussed earlier. Hebrew has two "h" type letters ה "heh" and ח "ḥeth." ח "ḥeth" is pronounced somewhat like "kh" but written "ch" in the transliterations of *Strong's Concordance*. The word חַיָּה (ḥayyâ) is pronounced somewhat like "khay-yah." "Khay-yah" will be used in brackets to represent this word in the following discussion.

The word נֶפֶשׁ (nephesh) includes the connotation of air breathing. נֶפֶשׁ (nephesh) is usually translated "soul" or "creature," but is also translated "breath." The connection between breathing and being alive was present in the Greek and Latin languages as well as in the Hebrew. The words נֶפֶשׁ חַיָּה "nephesh khay-yah" used together are usually translated "living thing" or "living soul" in the KJV. In the following study, the relationship between נֶפֶשׁ חַיָּה and "breathing" will first be shown to apply to man and to creatures. Then two additional verses are considered showing that נֶפֶשׁ חַיָּה "nephesh khay-yah" is consistently used to refer to air breathing creatures. The importance will be to show that the Genesis definition translated "living" or "life" is far more restricted than a reader would expect based on the English words. This will also result in the observation that Genesis does not indicate when fish were created.

## נֶפֶשׁ חַיָּה And "Breathing"

Genesis 2:7 will be considered next with the Hebrew words נֶפֶשׁ חַיָּה inserted into the KJV translation. The various translations of נֶפֶשׁ חַיָּה by other versions are explicitly displayed following the Hebrew words.

KJV Genesis 2:7   And the LORD God formed man *of* the dust of the ground,
and breathed into his nostrils the breath of life;

and man became לְנֶפֶשׁ חַיָּה
- "a living soul."      KJV
- "a living being."     NAS
- "a living creature."  YLT
- "a nephesh living."   A literal translation

The word לְנֶפֶשׁ is the word נֶפֶשׁ prefixed by ל "to." The addition of the prefix ל "to" indicates the achievement of the condition described by נֶפֶשׁ חַיָּה "nephesh the living." These words are translated "a living soul" in the KJV. The Hebrew of the verse, and a translation, is given below.

(1) Genesis 2:7 — and had formed / Yahweh / God (Elohim) / dir. obj. marker / the man / dust / from / the ground

(2) and had breathed / in face / breath of / life / and had become / the man / to a nephesh (KJV "a living soul") / living

The Hebrew word נִשְׁמַת "neshawma" translated "breath" appears in the line (2) of the Hebrew. This word is used 24 times in the Bible and of those is translated breath 17 times.[64] The phrase נִשְׁמַת חַיִּים "breath of life" is of primary importance. The word חַיִּים = חַי + ים is a masculine plural noun formed by adding the plural suffix ים to חַי. The word חַי "hay," pronounced "khah'-ee," is derived from the word חָיָה (khay-yah) meaning "living." In the KJV חַיִּים "kahy-yim" is often translated "life," "live," or "alive."

**Man is called חַיָּה "living" because he has been given the "breath of life" and breathes.**

Now consider the translation of Genesis 1:30 shown below. Here breathing is associated with the "life" of land animals. The YLT translates נֶפֶשׁ (nephesh) as "breath" in the phrase נֶפֶשׁ חַיָּה "breath of life." The KJV and some other versions do not translate the word נֶפֶשׁ (nephesh), they translate only the חַיָּה (khay-yah) as "life."

KJV Gen. 1:30    And to every beast of the earth (land), and to every fowl of the air, and to every thing
that creepeth upon the earth (land), wherein *there is* נֶפֶשׁ חַיָּה "life," ( נֶפֶשׁ *is not translated* )
*I have given* every green herb for meat: and it was so.

YLT Gen. 1:30    and to every beast of the earth (land), and to every fowl of the heavens, and to every
creeping thing on the earth, in which {*is*} נֶפֶשׁ חַיָּה "breath of life," ( נֶפֶשׁ *is translated* )
every green herb {*is*} for food: and it is so.

The Hebrew of Genesis 1:30 follows. All the creatures in Genesis 1:30 are air breathing.

| וְעַל הָאָרֶץ | רֹמֵשׂ | וּלְכֹל | הַשָּׁמַיִם | עוֹף | וּלְכָל | חַיַּת הָאָרֶץ | וּלְכֹל | Genesis 1:30 |
|---|---|---|---|---|---|---|---|---|
| the land on | creeping | and to all | the heavens | flyer of | and to all | the land life of (KJV "beast of") | and to all | |

| וַיְהִי כֵן | לְאָכְלָה | עֵשֶׂב | יֶרֶק | כָּל | אֶת | חַיָּה | נֶפֶשׁ | בּוֹ | אֲשֶׁר |
|---|---|---|---|---|---|---|---|---|---|
| so and it did come to pass | for food | grass | green | all | dir. obj. marker | life | breath of (nephesh) of | in which | those |

The עוֹף (owph) flyer of the "heavens" are air breathing because of the restriction "of the heavens" and because they are נֶפֶשׁ חַיָּה "nephesh living." The word עוֹף "flyer," when unrestricted, includes flying insects. Flying insects are not said to be נֶפֶשׁ חַיָּה "nephesh living." This will be discussed more extensively later. The three English translations (NIV, RSV, and YLT) which do translate נֶפֶשׁ (nephesh), all translate נֶפֶשׁ as "breath." The Greek Septuagint translation uses ψυχήν which means "breath."

**It has now been established that man, and creatures described by נֶפֶשׁ חַיָּה, are <u>air breathing</u>.**

## Additional verses showing the use of נֶפֶשׁ חַיָּה

Consider Genesis 9:10. This verse refers to the covenant God makes with Noah. The term נֶפֶשׁ הַחַיָּה "nephesh the living" is applied to the creatures with Noah in the Ark. The הַחַיָּה = חַיָּה + הַ (the) is a noun of the same root as חַיָּה (khay-yah) translated "living" used in Genesis 1:20. All the creatures in this verse are described as being נֶפֶשׁ הַחַיָּה "nephesh the khay-yah." The KJV here translates נֶפֶשׁ הַחַיָּה as "living creature."

KJV Genesis 9:10

And with every נֶפֶשׁ הַחַיָּה living creature that *is* with you, בְּעוֹף of the fowl, בַּבְּהֵמָה of the cattle, and of every חַיַּת הָאָרֶץ beast of the earth (land) with you; from all that go out of the ark, to every חַיַּת הָאָרֶץ beast of the earth (land). (The KJV in this verse translates בְּ as "of.")

| בַּבְּהֵמָה | בְּעוֹף | אִתְּכֶם | אֲשֶׁר | הַחַיָּה | נֶפֶשׁ | כָּל | וְאֵת | (1) Genesis 9:10 |
|---|---|---|---|---|---|---|---|---|
| of cattle ("in cattle") | of flyer ("in flyer") | with you | which | the life breath of (KJV "living creature") | | all | and with | |

| הָאָרֶץ | חַיַּת | לְכֹל | הַתֵּבָה | יֹצְאֵי | מִכֹּל | אִתְּכֶם | הָאָרֶץ | חַיַּת | וּבְכֹל | (2) |
|---|---|---|---|---|---|---|---|---|---|---|
| the land life of (KJV "beast of the earth") | | and to all | the ark | going out | from all | together with | the land life of (KJV "beast of the earth") | | and of all | |

In line (1) the translation under the Hebrew translates נֶפֶשׁ "breath of" in the phrase נֶפֶשׁ הַחַיָּה. This same word was translated "breath of" in Genesis 1:30. In Genesis 9:10 the phrase נֶפֶשׁ הַחַיָּה is translated "breath of the life." הַחַיָּה is חַיָּה "life" prefixed with הַ meaning "the." The phrase נֶפֶשׁ הַחַיָּה clearly refers to "air breathing" creatures.

In line (2) חַיַּת הָאָרֶץ has been translated "life of the land." The word חַיַּת is a form of the word חַיָּה (khay-yah) meaning "live," or "have life." A simpler translation of חַיַּת הָאָרֶץ would be "land life." The "life of the land" are clearly "air breathing" creatures for which the term נֶפֶשׁ הַחַיָּה "breath of the life" is appropriate. In the KJV, חַיַּת is translated "beast" and חַיַּת הָאָרֶץ is translated "beast of the earth." The KJV also refers clearly to "air breathing" creatures. The use of נֶפֶשׁ חַיָּה "breath of life" to refer to "air breathing" creatures continues in the other verses concerning the covenant with Noah. Genesis 2:19 also provides clear evidence that נֶפֶשׁ חַיָּה refers to "air breathing" creatures.

KJV Genesis 2:19

> And out of the ground the LORD God formed every beast of the field, and every עוֹף fowl (flyer) of the air (הַשָּׁמַיִם "the heavens"); and brought *them* unto Adam to see what he would call them: and whatsoever Adam called every נֶפֶשׁ חַיָּה "living creature," that *was* the name thereof.

The "beast of the field" are air breathing. The עוֹף (owph) flyer of the "heavens" are also air breathing and because of the addition of "of the heavens" do not include insects. Birds are categorized as עוֹף "flyer," but all the עוֹף "flyer" are not birds. The categorization of some insects as עוֹף (owph) "flyer" will be considered in detail later in this section.

**Genesis One does not tell us when fish were created.**

Many commentaries on Genesis One make the assumption that the creatures commanded to swarm in the waters in Genesis 1:20 include fish. This has lead some to assert Genesis is in conflict with the geological record because it indicates the fish and water dwelling mammals appear at the same time.

The foregoing verses have shown that the phrase נֶפֶשׁ חַיָּה "nephesh khay-yah" refers to air breathing creatures. The creatures which שֶׁרֶץ "swarm" the waters in Genesis 1:20 are described as נֶפֶשׁ חַיָּה and therefore air breathing. Recall that Genesis 1:20 line (1) is:

| חַיָּה | נֶפֶשׁ | שֶׁרֶץ | הַמַּיִם | יִשְׁרְצוּ | אֱלֹהִים | וַיֹּאמֶר | (1) Genesis 1:20 |
|---|---|---|---|---|---|---|---|
| *"the living"* | nephesh | a swarm of (YLT "the teeming") | the waters | shall swarm (YLT "shall teem") | God (Elohim) | and had said | |

The final three words of Genesis 1:20 line (1) are singular and are not a general reference to all creatures which swarm in the waters. Line (1) refers **only** to the נֶפֶשׁ חַיָּה "nephesh *the living*" which "shall swarm the waters." The creatures referred to are **not** "fish"; they are "air breathing" creatures.

The Bible uses the words חַיָּה (khay-yah) and חַי (khah'-ee) to refer to "living" air breathing creatures. These words are applied to God, mankind, and to other soulish creatures.[65] The KJV translates חַיָּה "living" and translates נֶפֶשׁ הַחַיָּה "living thing." Our present day category "living" is different from that of the Hebrew חַי (hay) and includes things which are not in the Hebrew category. The Hebrew Bible does not call plants חַיָּה, KJV "living." We do. The Bible never calls fish חַיָּה (khay-yah) or נֶפֶשׁ הַחַיָּה "nephesh the khay-yah." There are four verses where fish are said to die or to be slain. These verses **do not** constitute an assertion that a fish is a נֶפֶשׁ הַחַיָּה "nephesh the khay-yah." The KJV translation "living thing" includes things (fish and plants) not included in the Hebrew, thereby introducing a distortion of meaning. The translation "air breathing," which will be adopted in the "Good English" translation, avoids this distortion.

The waters are not commanded to swarm with fish. Genesis One does not indicate when fish were created. The Hebrew words usually translated fish are דָּג "dag" or דָּגָה "dagâ." The word דָּגָה "dagâ" is used in Genesis 1:26 and Genesis 1:28 where man is given dominion over the "dagâ" of the sea. The meaning of the word דָּגָה "dagâ" will be considered in the discussion of Genesis 1:28.

**The Order of Creative Events Within Creative יוֹם "Yom" Five**

What is the order of the creative events of creative "yom" five? The answer to this question provides much-needed understanding of God's introduction of these air breathing creatures. Genesis 1:20 and Genesis 1:21 together provide an answer. When considered as a unit they show that all the air breathing life was **not** introduced at one time; the introduction was not like a bolt of lightning. These verses indicate a gradual increase in the number of different created creatures during the fifth creative "yom." This may be surprising to some readers; it was to me. **These verses attribute the increase in the number of the individual "kind" to the creative (bara) action of God. This is not Darwinism.** God acts directly to create the additional kinds. Be warned that the following analysis is very tedious and starts at the top of the next page.

The Hebrew must be followed carefully. There is a change from singular to plural meaning which is obscured in the usual English translation. The important singulars and plurals are indicated below the nouns. The study translation under the Hebrew translates the singular noun שֶׁרֶץ as "a swarm of." [66] Genesis 1:20 refers to a singular kind of "air breathing creature" and a singular kind of "flyer." The swarm is singular in kind, but a swarm is composed of many individual creatures of that kind. The lines are numbered on the left side of the page for easy reference.

(1) Genesis 1:20

| חַיָּה | נֶפֶשׁ | שֶׁרֶץ | הַמַּיִם | יִשְׁרְצוּ | אֱלֹהִים | וַיֹּאמֶר |
|---|---|---|---|---|---|---|
| "air breathing creature" (singular) | (singular) | a swarm of (singular) | the waters | shall swarm (Qal imperfect) | God (Elohim) | and had said (completed action) |

*(i. e., a swarming "air breathing creature")*

(2)

| הַשָּׁמָיִם | רְקִיעַ | פְּנֵי | עַל | הָאָרֶץ | עַל | יְעוֹפֵף | וְעוֹף |
|---|---|---|---|---|---|---|---|
| the heavens | sky of | face | over | the land (erets) | above | shall fly (singular) | and a flyer (singular) |

(3) Genesis 1:21

| וְאֵת | הַגְּדֹלִים | הַתַּנִּינִם | אֵת | אֱלֹהִים | וַיִּבְרָא |
|---|---|---|---|---|---|
| and + dir. obj. marker | the great | the "tanniym" (plural) | dir. obj. marker | God (Elohim) | and had created (bara) (completed action) |

(4)

| לְמִינֵהֶם | הַמַּיִם | שָׁרְצוּ | אֲשֶׁר | הָרֹמֶשֶׂת | הַחַיָּה | נֶפֶשׁ | כָּל |
|---|---|---|---|---|---|---|---|
| by kinds or to kinds (plural) | the waters | "had swarmed" (completed action, plural) | which | the creeping (singular) | "the living nephesh" (i. e., "air breathing creature") (singular but of plural effect) | | all |

(5)

| טוֹב | כִּי | אֱלֹהִים | וַיַּרְא | לְמִינֵהוּ | כָּנָף | עוֹף | כָּל | וְאֵת |
|---|---|---|---|---|---|---|---|---|
| good | as | God (Elohim) | and had seen (completed action) | to kind or by kind (singular) | winged (singular, but of plural effect) (due to the "all") | flyer | all of | and + dir. obj. marker |

Look carefully at the English translations below the Hebrew of Genesis 1:20-21. There is a progression from singular words in Genesis 1:20 to a plural meaning using the **same** singular words in Genesis 1:21. The singular words are הַחַיָּה נֶפֶשׁ "nephesh the living" and עוֹף "flyer." The plural in Genesis 1:21 comes about by the action of כָּל "all" at the beginning of line (4) and the plural "by kinds" at the end of line (4).

Line (5) has the same pattern. The word כָּל "all of" precedes the singular words "flyer" and "kind." The "all" continues the effect of the plural word "kinds" at the end of line (4) The many singular "flyer" and "kind" of each individual type of "flyer" combine to constitute the plural "all." Remember that each "kind" is composed of many individual creatures of that "kind."

The two verses in sequence indicate the following: Initially, a single type (kind) of שֶׁרֶץ "swarming" creature and a single type (kind) of עוֹף "flyer" were commanded to exist. Then the numbers of the individual types of "swarming" creatures and of "flying" creatures increased, resulting in the use of the plural word "by kinds."

**These verses attribute the increase in the number of the individual "kind" to the creative (bara) action of God. This is not Darwinism.** God acted directly to create the additional kinds. Because "bara" carries the connotation of "new," this indicates God acted in producing new additional kinds. The specific methods which God used to accomplish these actions are **not** specified.

Genesis 1:21 also mentions creatures called הַתַּנִּינִם "the tanniym." The plural word הַתַּנִּינִם is translated phonetically as the "*tanniym*" which references the root word in the manner used by *Strong's Concordance*. These are referenced in the plural and are said to be "great" or "large." The root word "tanniym" is translated "dragon" 21 times by the KJV. This is the same word which is used to describe the creature that the rod of Moses turned into during a confrontation of the Pharaoh.

The KJV translates "tanniym" as serpent only in those passages. The meaning intended for the word in Genesis 1:21 is not known. Translations of whale and monster have been used in attempts to give a suitable sense of meaning to the word in the absence of adequate knowledge.

A "Good English" translation of Genesis 1:20-22 will be presented for easy reference. The pluperfect translation "and God had seen *it* as good" was selected to agree with how this phrase is translated in other verses. The KJV translation "and God saw *it* as good" is equally appropriate in this verse.

Genesis 1:20-22 "Good English" Translation:

20. And God said, The waters shall swarm with a swarming "air breathing" creature and a "flying thing" shall fly above the land across the face of the sky of the heavens.

21. And God created (new things) the great "dragons," and all the "kinds" of the creeping "air breathing" creatures that swarmed in the waters, and all the "kinds" of winged "flying things"; and God had seen it as good.     (KJV: "and God saw that *it was* good")

22. And God blessed them saying, Be fruitful and multiply and fill the waters in the seas, and the "flying things" shall multiply on the land.

The creation sequence is:

1. God commands into existence a single "kind" of air breathing, water dwelling creature and a single "kind" of flying thing." The "flying thing" may have been an insect or some totally unknown "flying thing." Genesis 1:21 states that it is God who had created (bara) the creatures.

2. Then God creates (bara) more new "kinds" of "air breathing" water dwelling creatures which are described as "the creeping." God also creates (bara) additional "kind" of "flying things." The "kind" are approximately analogous to our major species divisions, i.e., cats, dogs, whales, etc. The word "bara" indicates that these "kinds" were new.

   The additional use of the word "wing" indicates an expansion of the "kind" within the "flying thing" category. The two Hebrew words עוֹף כָּנָף translated "winged flying thing" are used in Psalm 78:27 to refer to the birds which were sent to feed the children of Israel in the desert after the Exodus. The "flying things" in these two verses may represent creatures ranging from insects to birds. On the basis of the text, even pterodactyals cannot be excluded.

   Because the creative "yom" have been shown to be long periods of time, the possibility of the plural "tanniym" being a reference to the dinosaurs cannot be excluded. A reference to large crocodiles seems more likely because they were common creatures at the time of Moses.

   No statement is made of the "**when**" for the creation of any of the many "kind." The creation sequence is not given. Nothing is said about fish, or any water dwelling life that is not "air breathing". The critics' objection that Genesis has mammals and fish first appearing at the same time is found to have no basis in the text. The information given in Genesis One is not sufficient to agree or disagree with the sequence of "air breathing" life appearances recorded in the fossil record.

**The fossil record does not contradict Genesis One. Genesis One does not contradict the fossil record.**

3. The situation is viewed by God as "good." In the KJV this is translated as "and God saw *that it was* good." Some commentators have placed great emphasis on their own interpretation of the meaning of "and God saw it was good." Here the events of Genesis 1:20-22 are seen "as good" **before** the events of the fifth creative "yom" are completed. Genesis 1:22 informs us that after it was seen as "good" an extensive multiplication of the individual members of the "kinds" took place. Any valid interpretation using the "as good" must be consistent with the placement of the "as good" in Genesis 1:21.

**Any interpretation which represents the "as good" as implying completion or perfection fails.**

## The Methods Used by God to Introduce Plants, Air Breathing Life, and Fill the Waters

Now the third question for this section will be considered. **"What methods did God use to introduce plant life and animal life?**

The answer to this question has considerable importance for defending the Bible against the assumptions of Darwinism. The book *Darwin's God* [67] points out the emphatic assumptions and statements about God made by Darwinists. These statements are about what God has done, could have done, or could not have done. These statements are fundamental to their arguments. Their technique is to set up a view of God which meets their needs. The god they present is not the God of the Bible.

Understanding what the Bible says about the methods God used in accomplishing His purposes is a requirement for knowing how to respond to Darwinist distortions of Genesis. The following analysis presents what the Bible records as the methods which God did use. Understanding these methods will help the reader to recognize distortions.

**The Methods:**

(1) Genesis 1:11-12 indicate one method used in the introduction of land plants. The land (KJV "earth") is **commanded** to bring forth the specified plants. The response is that the land (KJV "earth") does bring forth the specified plants. The same root word דֶּשֶׁא "sprout" is used in the command and then again as "דֶּשֶׁא plant" in the command and in the response.

"Good English" Translation:
Genesis 1:11      And God said, The land תַּדְשֵׁא shall bring forth דֶּשֶׁא plant, עֵשֶׂב grass yielding seed, . . .
Genesis 1:12      And the land **had brought** forth דֶּשֶׁא plant, עֵשֶׂב grass yielding seed . . .

In these verses the commanded result is produced by means of an **intermediate agent**. The הָאָרֶץ (erets) which means land, ground, or earth is the agent used. The command is for the הָאָרֶץ ( the erets) to act, and the response is that the הָאָרֶץ (the erets) did act to accomplish the commanded action. **Method (1) is use of an intermediate agent.**

(2) Genesis 1:20 and Genesis 1:21 provide another example where the result is brought about by a different means, the direct action of God.

**Genesis 1:20**      And God said, The waters shall swarm with a swarming "air breathing" creature . . .
**Genesis 1:21**      And God created (new things) the great "dragons," and all the "kinds" of . . .

The command in this case is for the result to come into existence. The waters are not commanded to produce the result. The result is brought about by God who acts directly to create (bara) the desired "kinds" of creatures. **Method (2) is "direct action" by God.** The specific methods which God used to accomplish these actions is **not** specified. The Bible is silent about the specific methods or things used in accomplishing the creative actions of Genesis 1:21. Direct action is also used in the creation (bara) of Adam and Eve.

(3) God uses a third method when he issues a command to the creatures of Genesis 1:20-21, adaptive change within the "kind."

KJV Genesis 1:22      And God blessed them, saying, Be fruitful, and multiply, and fill the waters in the seas, and let fowl multiply in the earth (land).

Genesis 1:22

| וַיְבָרֶךְ | אֹתָם | אֱלֹהִים | לֵאמֹר | פְּרוּ | וּרְבוּ | וּמִלְאוּ | אֶת | הַמַּיִם |
|---|---|---|---|---|---|---|---|---|
| and had blessed ("waw"+ Piel imperfect) | them | God (Elohim) | saying (infinitive) | be fruitful | and multiply | and fill | dir. obj. marker | the waters |

| בַּיָּמִים | וְהָעוֹף | יִרְב | בָּאָרֶץ |
|---|---|---|---|
| in seas | and the flyer | multiply | in land |

The blessing and the command פְּרוּ וּרְבוּ וּמִלְאוּ "be fruitful multiply and fill" are the same as given to Adam and Eve in Genesis 1:28. The command in Genesis 1:28 makes it is possible to understand method (3).

The question is, "What actions are included in "be fruitful and multiply and fill . . ..?"

The Bible is clear in its statement that all of mankind is descended from Adam and Eve. In response to the command "Be fruitful and multiply and fill" mankind has spread over the surface of the Earth and has developed "racial types." All of this started from the first genetically nearly identical pair. The different racial types and characteristics are a consequence of genetic change with time. This is often termed "adaptive change" or "micro-evolution." The term "micro-evolution" refers to adaptive change within the individual "kind" but does not extend to the production of new "kinds." For example, some have proposed that the different skin colors are an adaptive long-term response to climate. The different racial types and skin colors are observable fact. The consequence derivable from this known result is that "Be fruitful and multiply and fill" permits and includes adaptive genetic modification of the "kinds." **Method (3) is adaptive change or micro-evolution within the "kind."**

In summary, the Bible indicates that God used three methods in accomplishing his commands:

1. Use of an intermediate agent.
2. Direct action.
3. Adaptive change or micro-evolution within the "kind."

**All of the methods listed above are in contradiction to Darwinism.**

All the methods involve the action of God, or action at the direction of God, during the natural history of planet Earth. Typically, the advocates of Darwinism will not accept a God who actively acts within what they call the natural history of planet Earth. The contradiction to Darwinism does not depend on which one of the specific methods was used or the purpose for which it was used.

In response to Darwinism some Christian commentators have also placed restrictions on the actions of God in creating and making. They have often done this indirectly by assuming that each account is complete as to the method used for the described actions of creating and making. The story of creation in Genesis One is the briefest of summaries; it does not give an account of everything that happened. When events are said to have occurred using one of the three methods, use of another of the three methods as a part of the process is **not** excluded.

God is not restrained from the use of any or all of the three methods. The Bible has indicated use of three methods, therefore it is improper for readers to assert a limitation on when any of the three the methods may have been used by God during the creative time periods of Genesis One. The God of the Bible is sovereign in His choice of actions and in His choice of the account which He provides to mankind.

The final verse of the fifth creative "yom" is a repetition of the phrase previously discussed extensively showing that it refers to a long period of time.

Genesis 1:23   וַיְהִי עֶרֶב וַיְהִי בֹקֶר יוֹם חֲמִישִׁי
and *there* had been   evening   and *there* had been   morning   yom   fifth

The "Good English" translation of Genesis 1:20-23 is found on page 142.

## Choices:

Two sections follow which provide additional information about words appearing in Genesis 1:21-22. A reader who does not require this additional information may prefer to fast forward to page 121 which begins the study of the sixth creative "yom."

The sections are entitled: "More About the Words שרץ "swarm" and רמש (ramas) "creep," and

"More About the Words עוֹף (owpf), צִפּוֹר (tsippor), and כָּנָף (kanaph)."

## More About the Words שרץ "swarm" and רמש (ramas) "creep"

The first word to be studied is the consonantal word שרץ, a word which **confusingly** has had several English translations. The word שרץ "swarm" or "teem" is used in the Old Testament 15 times as a noun (שֶׁרֶץ "sherets") and 14 times as a verb (שָׁרַץ "sharats"). The word is applied to living creatures as a noun and is applied to the behavior of these creatures when used as a verb. As a noun, the word שֶׁרֶץ "swarm" is used to refer to frogs, insects, grasshoppers, locusts, crocodiles, lizards, a mole, and the mouse. The noun refers to creatures which move in a manner that sometimes is correctly described by the verb "swarm." As a verb, the word שָׁרַץ "swarm" is also translated by a form of the word "move." The KJV differs from many other translations by translating שֶׁרֶץ "sherets" and שָׁרַץ "sharats" by some form of the word "creep" 19 times. The KJV also translates "bring forth abundantly" where other translations use "swarm."

The important point is that the KJV and other versions also translate another consonantal word ( רמש ) using forms of the word "creep." The words are different. The KJV translation of both שרץ and רמש by the same English word "creep" leads to confusion and a loss of information. The YLT has removed the confusion of the KJV by consistently translating שרץ by a form of "teem" in all 29 uses of the word in its noun or verb form. This has the advantage of informing the English reader that a specific Hebrew word appears in all these instances. The translations which translate שרץ "swarm" or "teem" interpret שרץ as referring to the motion of creatures in a collective group. This view is consistent with the application of שָׁרַץ "sharats" as a verb to describe the children of Israel in Exodus 1:7. Exodus 1:7 uses וַיִּשְׁרְצוּ which is the word יִשְׁרְצוּ "shall swarm" used in Genesis 1:20 prefixed by ו (waw) meaning "and." Here the KJV translates וַיִּשְׁרְצוּ as "increased abundantly."

KJV Exodus 1:7   And the children of Israel were fruitful, and וַיִּשְׁרְצוּ increased abundantly, and multiplied, and waxed exceeding mighty; and the land was filled with them.

Exodus 8:3 is a good example of the use of the word שֶׁרֶץ "swarm." The verse describes a situation that can be paraphrased as "Frogs! Frogs! Frogs everywhere!" Portions of three versions are shown for comparison.

KJV Exodus 8:3   And the river שָׁרַץ "**shall bring forth**" frogs "**abundantly**," which shall go up and come into thine house, and into thy bedchamber, and upon thy bed, and into the house of thy servants, and upon thy people, and into thine ovens, and into thy kneadingtroughs:

YLT Exodus 8:3   and the River שָׁרַץ **hath teemed** {with} frogs, and they have gone up and gone . . .

NAS Exodus 8:3   And the Nile will שָׁרַץ **swarm** with frogs, which will come up and go into your house . .

Other verses which illustrate the use of the word שֶׁרֶץ "swarm" are shown below. There is some uncertainty regarding the identification of the creatures other than the mouse.

KJV Leviticus 11:29   These also *shall be* unclean unto you among the בַּשֶּׁרֶץ **creeping things** that הַשֹּׁרֵץ *creep* upon the earth; the weasel, and the mouse, and the tortoise after his kind,

NAS Leviticus 11:29   'Now these are to you the unclean among the בַּשֶּׁרֶץ **swarming things** which הַשֹּׁרֵץ **swarm** on the earth: the mole, and the mouse, and the great lizard in its kinds,

Genesis 1:21 (line 4) uses both הָרֹמֶשֶׂת "the creeping" and שָׁרְצוּ "had swarmed" or "had teemed."

| לְמִינֵהֶם | הַמַּיִם | שָׁרְצוּ | אֲשֶׁר | הָרֹמֶשֶׂת | הַחַיָּה | נֶפֶשׁ | כָּל | (4) Genesis 1:21 |
|---|---|---|---|---|---|---|---|---|
| by kinds | the waters | "had swarmed" | which | the creeping | "the living" | "nephesh" | all | |

As translated, Genesis 1:21 (4) uses the word הָרֹמֶשֶׂת "the creeping" to identify a restricted subgroup of the air breathing creatures "the living nephesh." These creatures also "had swarmed the waters," which indicates they had existed in great number. Creatures which רמשׂ "creep" do not necessarily swarm in the waters. The verb רָמַשׂ "ramas" occurs 17 times and is usually translated by a form of the word "creep" by the YLT and the KJV. Fourteen of the 17 occurrences refer to "creeping" on the אֶרֶץ "land" or on the אֲדָמָה (adamah) "cultivated ground." Genesis 7:14 and Genesis 6:20 are representative examples of the use of the verb רָמַשׂ "ramas" and the noun רֶמֶשׂ "remes." These verses refer to the account of Noah.

YLT Genesis 7:14   They, and every living creature after its kind, and every beast after its kind,
and every הָרֶמֶשׂ creeping thing that הָרֹמֵשׂ is creeping on the הָאָרֶץ earth (land)
after its kind, and every fowl after its kind, every bird -- every wing.

YLT Genesis 6:20   Of the fowl after its kind, and of the cattle after their kind,
of every רֶמֶשׂ creeping thing of הָאֲדָמָה the ground (i.e., cultivated ground)
after its kind, two of every {sort} they come in unto thee, to keep alive.

Leviticus 11:46 shows an application of רמשׂ "creep" which is not restricted to the land. Here רמשׂ is translated "moving" but could just as well have been translated "creeping." The translation "moving" reflects a translator's choice which may not be correct. There are air breathing creatures which move on legs and live in the water; otters are an example. There are also non-air breathing creatures which live and walk on legs in the water; lobsters and crayfish are examples.

YLT Leviticus 11:46   This {is} a law of the beasts, and of the fowl, and of every living creature
which is הָרֹמֶשֶׂת moving (creeping) in the waters,
and of every creature which is הַשֹּׁרֶצֶת teeming on the הָאָרֶץ earth (land),

Now three additional verses will be considered. They illustrate the limitation of our knowledge of רמשׂ "creep" and the definitions of the biblical Hebrew categories. Leviticus 11:41-42 shown below identifies שֶׁרֶץ "swarmer" with things that have many feet.[68] This brings to mind centipedes and caterpillars of all kinds.

YLT Leviticus 11:41-42   And every הַשֶּׁרֶץ teeming thing which is הַשֹּׁרֵץ teeming on the earth is an
abomination, it is not eaten; any thing going on the belly, and any going on four,
unto every multiplier of feet, to every הַשֶּׁרֶץ teeming thing which is הַשֹּׁרֵץ teeming
on the earth -- ye do not eat them, for they {are} an abomination;

Leviticus 20:25 tells us that not all creatures תִּרְמֹשׂ "creeping" on the ground are unclean.

YLT Leviticus 20:25   And ye have made separation between the pure beasts and the unclean, and between
the unclean fowl and the pure, and ye do not make yourselves abominable by beast or
by fowl, or by anything which creepeth {on} the ground which I have separated to
you for unclean;

Genesis 9:3 is a statement to Noah and precedes the dietary restrictions of the Law of Moses in Leviticus.

YLT Genesis 9:3-4   Every רֶמֶשׂ creeping thing that is alive (air breathing), to you it is for food; as the green
herb I have given to you the whole; only flesh in its life -- its blood -- ye do not eat.

As a group, these verses tell us that רמשׂ "creep" and שׁרץ "teem" ("swarm") are different and should not be translated with the same word. These verses also illustrate that we do not fully comprehend the categories underlying the use of these words. A creeping thing may or may not be a swarming thing (teeming thing). The categorization is different, albeit incompletely known.

# More About the Words עוֹף (owpf), צִפּוֹר (tsippor), and כָּנָף (kanaph)

An important question raised by Genesis 1:20 is, "What does the word עוֹף "flyer" mean" in Genesis 1:20?"
The word עוֹף (owpf), in its most general meaning, corresponds to "a thing that flies." In most instances עוֹף (owpf), which appears 71 times, refers to birds. The KJV translates it as fowl (which includes insects!) 59 times and as "bird" 9 times. The restriction to "bird" is often accomplished by adding הַשָּׁמַיִם "the heavens" to generate the phrase הַשָּׁמַיִם עוֹף "flyer of the heavens." This phrase, in one of its forms, appears in the Bible 37 times. By use in context, it can be determined that עוֹף הַשָּׁמַיִם "flyer of the heavens" refers to birds.

That the word עוֹף (owpf) means "thing that flies" can be demonstrated by reference to Leviticus 11:21-22 where insects are placed into the categories of הָעוֹף "the flyer" and the שֶׁרֶץ "teeming" thing. Several specific edible insects are mentioned.

YLT Leviticus 11:21-22    'Only -- this ye do eat of any שֶׁרֶץ teeming thing which is הָעוֹף flying,
which is going on four, which hath legs above its feet, to move with them on the earth (land); these of them ye do eat: the locust after its kind, and the bald locust after its kind, and the beetle after its kind, and the grasshopper after its kind;

The word עוֹף (owpf) used in Genesis 1:20 is not restricted by attached qualifying words. Genesis 1:20 specifies where the "flyer" will fly, i.e., over the land and across the face the sky of the heavens. The nature of the flyer is not specified. It is not called "a flyer of the heavens" which refers to air breathing creatures. Because of this, the עוֹף (owpf) referred to in Genesis 1:20 could be a flying insect. Recall that Genesis 1:20 refers to a singular עוֹף "flyer."

Another way that the word עוֹף (owpf) is restricted to indicate birds is to use the word כָּנָף "wing." Psalm 78:27 refers to the birds which were sent to feed the children of Israel in the desert after the Exodus. The YLT is shown in the examples below because it follows the Hebrew word order; the KJV often alters the word order.

YLT Psalm 78:27    And He raineth on them flesh as dust, And as sand of the seas -- winged fowl,

| כָּנָף | עוֹף | יַמִּים | וּכְחוֹל | שְׁאֵר | כֶּעָפָר | עֲלֵיהֶם | וַיַּמְטֵר | Psalm 78:27 |
|---|---|---|---|---|---|---|---|---|
| winged | flyer | seas | and like sand of | flesh | like dust | on them | and he had rained | |

Genesis 7:14 qualifies the word הָעוֹף "the flyer" to mean "bird" by using two words, צִפּוֹר "bird" and כָּנָף "wing."

YLT Genesis 7:14    they, and every living creature after its kind, and every beast after its kind, and
every creeping thing that is הָרֹמֵשׂ creeping on the earth (land) after its kind,
and every הָעוֹף "fowl" after his kind, every צִפּוֹר "bird" -- every כָּנָף "wing."
                                        the flyer                           bird

The use of צִפּוֹר "bird" and כָּנָף "wing" together occurs in five other verses, three of which are given below as examples. Ezekiel 17:23 and Ezekiel 39:4 are the two verses not quoted. Deuteronomy 4:17 also makes clear the association of עוֹף הַשָּׁמַיִם "flyer of the heavens" with both "winged" and "bird."

YLT Deuteronomy 4:17    a form of any beast which {is} in the earth -- a form of
כָּל־צִפּוֹר כָּנָף any winged bird which תָּעוּף בַּשָּׁמַיִם flieth in the heavens --
  wing  bird  all                                             in heavens  flieth

YLT Psalm 148:10    The wild beast, and all cattle, creeping thing, וְצִפּוֹר כָּנָף and winged bird,

The verses shown above indicate that the plural kind of כָּנָף עוֹף "winged flyer" in Genesis 1:21 must include birds. Other flying creatures must be also allowed because of the inclusion of the "bat" among the עוֹף (owpf). Leviticus 11:19 and Deuteronomy 14:18 forbids the eating of bats. The list beginning in Leviticus 11:13 lists many birds.

# The Sixth Creative "Yom": Genesis 1:24-31     Land Animals and the Creation of Adam

Creative "yom" six is the grand finale for which the entire story has been preparing.

In Genesis 1:2 the future creation of Adam was foreshadowed by the phrase "tohu and bohu." The clear meaning of "tohu and bohu" was that the Earth was unsuitable for, and was devoid of, human life. By the start of the sixth creative "yom" the environment has become suitable for the introduction of land mammals. After their introduction, the absence of human life is rectified by the creation of "Adam," male and female.

The events of creative "yom" six are described in six verses plus a verse repeating the closing phrase. The events focus first on the introduction of creatures which populate the land, then on the creation of Adam, and finally on the relationship between Adam (male and female) and the land creatures. The verses will be considered one by one in sequence. The first two verses describe the land mammals in categories which are different from modern categories. These categories and their meaning with respect to "Adam" will be clarified as the analysis proceeds.

## The Land Animals

KJV Genesis 1:24     And God said, Let the earth bring forth the נֶפֶשׁ חַיָּה living creature after his kind, cattle, and creeping thing, and beast of the earth after his kind: and it was so.

Genesis 1:24

| וַיֹּאמֶר | אֱלֹהִים | תּוֹצֵא | הָאָרֶץ | נֶפֶשׁ | חַיָּה | לְמִינָהּ |
|---|---|---|---|---|---|---|
| and had said | God (Elohim) | shall bring forth | the land (erets) | nephesh | living | of kind |
| | | | | ("air breathing creatures") | | |

| בְּהֵמָה | וָרֶמֶשׂ | וְחַיְתוֹ | אֶרֶץ | לְמִינָהּ | וַיְהִי | כֵן |
|---|---|---|---|---|---|---|
| cattle | and creeper | and life of | land | of kind | and *it* did come to pass | so |

נֶפֶשׁ חַיָּה "nephesh living" is translated "air breathing creatures." Genesis 1:24 states that the land is to bring forth "air breathing creatures," then it specifies three subcategories of "air breathing creatures." There is another phrase regarding life forms which must also be considered carefully in this verse. This is the phrase חַיְתוֹ אֶרֶץ which is literally "land life" or "living thing *of the* land."

The phrase חַיְתוֹ אֶרֶץ which the KJV translates "beast of the earth" is used three times in Genesis One. The word חַיְתוֹ is translated in the Septuagint by the Greek word θηρία (thera) which means wild animal. Because of this translation language, authorities often say חַיְתוֹ אֶרֶץ refers to wild animals. There is another related phrase חַיַּת הַשָּׂדֶה which in Hebrew literally means "field life" or "living thing *of the* field." This phrase is not used in Genesis One but is used to describe the animals which Adam named. Both of these phrases are traditionally translated in English using "beast" for חַיְתוֹ and for חַיַּת.[69] The traditional translation "beast" presents a difficulty for the modern American reader. "Beast" is typically interpreted as meaning a large creature. At the time of the KJV translation "beast" referred to any animal, except man, and was even used to refer to insects.[70]

Because biblical Hebrew has a small vocabulary, the two phrases must have had different meanings to Moses. Not being able to clearly understand the difference in meaning reflects present day ignorance. Both "land life" and "field life" refer to living creatures. A consideration of all the verses which use the two phrases has lead to proposing that:

(1)     "Land life" is a category which refers generally to some kind of wild animal life as contrasted with domesticated animals.

(2)     "Field life" is a smaller category of wild animals which are in some way associated with the cultivated fields.

(3)     All "field life" are "land life" (wild animals), but not all "land life" are in the category "field life."

Consider the following example:
Lion and zebra and giraffe are all wild animals (land life). But zebra and giraffe are wild animals which eat plants (wild herbivores), a class of wild animals which does not include the lion (a wild carnivore).

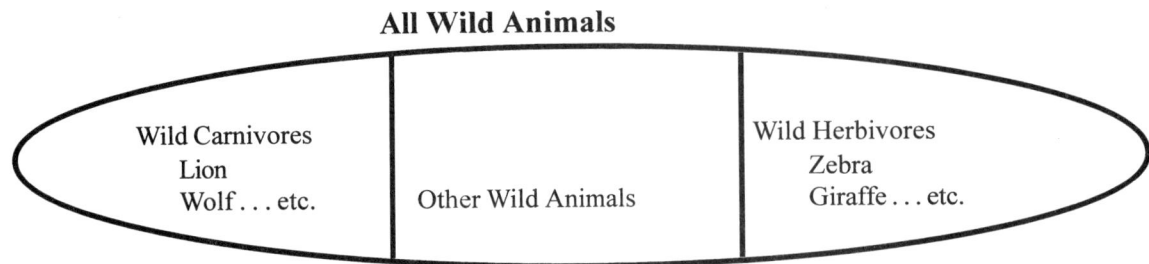

The phrases חַיַּת הָאָרֶץ and חַיְתוֹ אֶרֶץ will be translated as "land life" or "wild land animals" in future consideration of the verses. We do not know how biblical Hebrew classified the difference between the phrases חַיְתוֹ אֶרֶץ "land life" and חַיַּת הַשָּׂדֶה "field life."

KJV Genesis 1:25  And God made the beast of the earth (wild land animals) after his kind, and cattle after their kind, and every thing that creepeth upon the earth (cultivatable land) after his kind: and God saw that *it was* good.

| הַבְּהֵמָה | וְאֶת | לְמִינָהּ | חַיַּת הָאָרֶץ | אֵת | אֱלֹהִים | וַיַּעַשׂ | Genesis 1:25 |
|---|---|---|---|---|---|---|---|
| the cattle | and + dir. obj. marker | of kind | the land life of (*wild land animals*) | dir. obj. marker | God (Elohim) | and had made | |

| לְמִינָהּ | וְאֶת | כָּל | רֶמֶשׂ | הָאֲדָמָה | לְמִינֵהוּ | וַיַּרְא | אֱלֹהִים | כִּי טוֹב |
|---|---|---|---|---|---|---|---|---|
| of kind | and + dir. obj. marker | all | creeper | the **cultivatable** land | of kind | and had seen | God (Elohim) | good as |

Genesis 1:24 ends with the phrase "and *it did come to pass so*," and is followed by Genesis 1:25 which is a partial repetition of Genesis 1:24. The repetition indicates that Genesis 1:25 goes back in time, giving additional details of the events relating to Genesis 1:24. These are events completed before the "and *it did come to pass so*" of Genesis 1:24. In English, the usual way to indicate events already completed in the past is to use the pluperfect. The translation "had made" indicates that Genesis 1:25 takes place before the "and *it did come to pass so*" of Genesis 1:24.

In this verse the word אֲדָמָה "adamah" is encountered for the first time. This word refers to cultivatable or arable land. The KJV translates this word "earth," concealing the shift in focus. Other translations often use "ground" and obscure the connection to cultivatable land. The focus has progressed from planet Earth as a whole, to a view of the land as a whole, and now introduces the cultivatable land which man inhabits. The וָרֶמֶשׂ "creeping things" of Genesis 1:24 were creeping things having the broader geographical distribution of anywhere on the land. In Genesis 1:25 the geographical distribution is restricted to areas near the cultivatable land. This restriction of location also has the effect of restricting the types of creeping things. When Adam is mentioned in the next verse, the geographical distribution of the creeping things over which he is given dominion refers to all of the dry land.

The introduction of this word אֲדָמָה "adamah" is also important because אָדָם "Adam," the word for mankind, is closely related to the word for cultivatable land. "Adam" appears in the next verse. אֲדָמָה "adamah" is also closely related to Adam's assignment to cultivate the Garden.

The completed action phrase "and God (Elohim) had seen *it* as good" tells us that the preparation for the introduction of Adam (mankind) was satisfactory. Adam becomes the focus of the next four verses.

# Adam: Male and Female

KJV Genesis 1:26   And God said, Let us make man in our image, after our likeness:
and let them have dominion over the fish of the sea, and over the fowl of the air,
and over the cattle, and over all the earth (land),
and over every creeping thing that creepeth upon the earth (land).

**Genesis 1:26**

| הַיָּם | בִּדְגַת | וְיִרְדּוּ | כִּדְמוּתֵנוּ | בְּצַלְמֵנוּ | אָדָם | נַעֲשֶׂה | אֱלֹהִים | וַיֹּאמֶר |
|---|---|---|---|---|---|---|---|---|
| the sea | over fish of | and (Adam) shall rule | like our likeness | in our image | Adam | we shall make | God (Elohim | and had said |

| הָאָרֶץ | עַל | הָרֹמֵשׂ | הָרֶמֶשׂ | וּבְכָל | הָאָרֶץ | וּבְכָל | וּבַבְּהֵמָה | הַשָּׁמַיִם | וּבְעוֹף |
|---|---|---|---|---|---|---|---|---|---|
| the land (erets) | on | the creeping | the creeper | and over all | the land (erets) | and over all | and over cattle | the heavens | and over flyer of |

In Genesis 1:26 there are two verbs which will be considered first. The first of these verbs is נַעֲשֶׂה, the third word of the verse. The verb נַעֲשֶׂה (asah) is in the Qal imperfect third person referring to a plural subject "we." The prefix נ "nun" indicates the imperfect and the plural "we." The translation is "we shall make" as indicated above. The KJV has translated this verb in the jussive as "let us make." The Hebrew form for the jussive in this case is identical to the imperfect. The translator chooses between the imperfect and the jussive based upon his view of the meaning of the passage, or because of style preference.

The verb עָשָׂה "asah" is the same root word translated "making" or "yielding" in Genesis 1:12 for plants yielding seed. The word occurs 2,633 times in the Bible and is translated by the KJV as "do" (1,333 times) and as "make" (653 times), plus various other translations. Genesis 6:14 is an example of עָשָׂה used in the ordinary sense of make.

KJV Genesis 6:14   Make עָשָׂה thee an ark of gopher wood; rooms shalt thou make in the ark,
and shalt pitch it within and without with pitch.

Note that the word בָּרָא "bara" is not used in Genesis 1:26. The word "bara" is used three times in the next verse and the significance of the difference in words will be discussed there.

In Genesis 1:26 God (Elohim) says that אָדָם "Adam" is said to be made both בְּצַלְמֵנוּ "in our image" and כִּדְמוּתֵנוּ "like our likeness." The "our" is indicated in each word by the plural suffix נוּ, and כְּ is the preposition meaning "like." The passage is given emphasis by using two different but very similar words. The prepositions בְּ "in" and כְּ "like" are also different but are of similar meaning. Being made in the **image** and in the **likeness** of God is of great importance! This is **not** a casual statement. It is this which distinguishes "Adam" from all the other living creatures which God had created. Attempts to go beyond the reading of emphasis have been made, but fail, because of the lack of additional information in the Bible. In Genesis 5:3 the same two words are used to describe Seth as the offspring of Adam. The attached prepositions are used in the reverse order of their use in Genesis 1:26. The significance of this passage is unclear but, even so, a sense of importance concerning the birth of Seth is conveyed.

The next verb וְיִרְדּוּ is a singular imperfect (incomplete action) form preceded by a וְ. The singular shows that the verb refers to the type of creature called אָדָם "Adam." For this verb the jussive is spelled the same way as it is for the imperfect. If the verb is taken as the jussive, the וְ is the conjunction "and." In this case, the verb retains the imperfect (incomplete action) sense. If the verb is taken as an imperfect, the action of the וְ is to make the action of the verb completed "and had ruled." Only the jussive is consistent with the preceding verb and the actions of the next verse. The correct choice is made clear by the context.

KJV Genesis 1:27   So God created (bara) man in his *own* image,
in the image of God created (bara) he him;
male and female created (bara) he them.

| | | | | | | Genesis 1:27 |
|---|---|---|---|---|---|---|
| אֱלֹהִים | בְּצֶלֶם | בְּצַלְמוֹ | הָאָדָם | אֵת | אֱלֹהִים | וַיִּבְרָא |
| God (Elohim) | in image of noun msc. sing | in his image noun 3p msc. sing | the Adam | dir. obj. marker | God (Elohim) | and had created (bara) (completed action) |

| אֹתָם | בָּרָא | וּנְקֵבָה | זָכָר | אֹתוֹ | בָּרָא |
|---|---|---|---|---|---|
| them dir. obj. marker + 3p msc. plural suffix | he had created (bara) (completed action) | and female | male | him dir. obj. marker +3p msc. sing suffix | he had created (bara) (completed action) |

This verse emphasizes that the type of creature called Adam was created "in image of God." It does this by using the word for "in image" two times, in sequence. That "Adam" refers to a type of creature is clearly indicated by the statement that Adam was created "male and female." The word used for the creation of Adam is the word "bara," a word which includes the idea of the creation of a new thing. All three uses of the verb "bara" indicate completed action. The verb בָּרָא "he had created" is in the Qal perfect (completed action) form. The three repeated uses of "bara" places great emphasis on the finished nature of Adam and on the newness of Adam.

This great emphasis also tells us that Adam is not to be confused with any other creature which God has created. **Adam is different from the other creatures God created.** The meaning of "in the image" has been the subject of much opinion and discussion. The Bible is very clear that God is a spirit and does not have a body[71]. This important fact is often ignored, by secular and religious persons alike. "In image" must refer to the spiritual nature of Adam. Today this could be viewed as somewhat analogous to computer hardware (the body) and computer software. The spiritual part of the person would be analogous to the software which runs on the computer hardware, but which is not identical with the hardware.

Is the great emphasis given in order to prevent confusion? If so, the question arises as to what other creatures would have an appearance that could be confused with the appearance of "Adam."

The discovery of the remains of the Neanderthal has shown that at least one other hominid (i.e., man-like creature) existed in geologically recent times. Studies of Neanderthal physiology and DNA have shown that modern man is **not** closely related to and is **not** descended from the Neanderthal.[72] Anthropological digs indicate that creatures having the skeletal structure of modern man, and the Neanderthal, existed at the same time about 30,000 years ago. Modern skeletal remains are not sufficient to identify the creatures as Adam who was created "in *the* image of God." The Bible makes this clear because being "in the image of God" must refer to Adam's spiritual nature.

This assertion will be puzzling to most non-Christians as well as to many Christians. The assumption made by the modern scientific community, and often repeated in our schools and media, is that similarity of skeletal structure is sufficient to make an identification. Everyone must be open to the concept that skeletal bones, which look like those of the present species of mankind, may not be the bones of "Adam." They **may** be the remains of a different modern-looking hominid which is **not** ancestral to mankind. This is a radical thought made possible by the determination that the creative "yom" certainly span long periods of time.

Secular anthropology will be aghast when it fully realizes that bones are not sufficient evidence to indicate the ancestry of mankind as defined by the Bible. Archeology has revealed the sudden appearance of agriculture in the Middle East about 10,000 - 15,000 years ago. This was a sudden and substantial change. This is consistent with Genesis when the creative "yom" are recognized as being long periods of time. The sudden appearance of the agricultural economy is a drastic challenge to the evolutionary secular worldview. The evidence developed by the secular world indicates that modern man is a recent arrival. The Bible indicates that "Adam" is a fairly recent creation. "Adam" as defined by the Bible appears with language, farmed crops, herded animals, and sacrificial worship. The Bible's definition of "Adam" includes and requires more than "modern" looking skeletal bones.

YLT Genesis 1:28    And God blesseth them, and God saith to them, 'Be fruitful, and multiply,
and fill (KJV replenish) the earth, and subdue it, and rule (KJV have dominion) over fish of the sea,
and over fowl of the heavens, and over every living thing that is creeping upon the earth. '

**Genesis 1:28**

| וַיְבָרֶךְ | אֹתָם | אֱלֹהִים | וַיֹּאמֶר | לָהֶם | אֱלֹהִים | פְּרוּ | וּרְבוּ |
|---|---|---|---|---|---|---|---|
| and had blessed | dir. obj. marker + them | God (Elohim) | and had said | to them | God (Elohim) | bear fruit (Qal imperative) | and multiply |

| וּמִלְאוּ | אֶת | הָאָרֶץ | וְכִבְשֻׁהָ | וּרְדוּ | בִּדְגַת | הַיָּם | וּבְעוֹף |
|---|---|---|---|---|---|---|---|
| and fill (Qal imperative) | dir. obj. marker | the land | and subdue *it* (Qal imperative) | and rule (Qal imperative) | over fish | the sea | and flyer |

| הַשָּׁמַיִם | וּבְכָל | חַיָּה | הָרֹמֶשֶׂת | עַל | הָאָרֶץ |
|---|---|---|---|---|---|
| the heavens (sky) | and over all | live | the creeping | upon | land |

The YLT has been used as the English translation because, in this verse, the KJV has translated the word מלא as "replenish" even though it has translated this word "fill" in other verses (107 times). There is a considerable difference between fill and replenish. "Fill" is the better translation in this verse since Adam has just been created and had not previously filled the land. Also, the KJV translation of "the earth" for" הָאָרֶץ "erets" is clearly not correct because mankind lives upon the land which is a part of planet Earth. Adam would populate the land, not the waters.

Five of the verbs used in this verse are in the Qal imperative. They are commands which God (Elohim) spoke to Adam and to Eve. That the commands are spoken to both is indicated by the לָהֶם "to them." This is quite different from the impersonal statements of command which were given to the land (erets) and to the waters. Here the different nature of "Adam" is revealed in that there is personal communication from God to Adam and to Eve. Because of the subsequent use of "good" in Genesis 1:30 it can be inferred that the commands are given prior to the "Fall." Recall that Adam was placed in the Garden of Eden prior to the Fall to cultivate and keep it.

The verb כָּבַשׁ , translated "subdue," is used to describe conquering. Conquering implies resistance. The implication is that the subduing of the land will require effort. An example of its use is given below.

KJV 2 Samuel 8:10-11    Then Toi sent Joram his son unto king David, to salute him, and to bless him,
because he had fought against Hadadezer, and smitten him: for Hadadezer had
wars with Toi. And *Joram* brought with him vessels of silver, and vessels of gold,
and vessels of brass:
Which also king David did dedicate unto the LORD, with the silver and gold that
he had dedicated of all nations which he כִּבֵּשׁ subdued;

Also note that דָּגָה "dagâ" (fish) are referenced only in Genesis 1:26 and in Genesis 1:28. Adam and Eve are commanded to rule over the "dagâ" of the sea. The word "dagâ" is traditionally translated "fish." The range of meanings which the Hebrew word דָּגָה "dagâ" can represent may not be identical with that of the English word "fish." Recall that biblical Hebrew has a very small number of words. These words often have a broad range of possible meaning which is narrowed by the context. Here דָּגָה "dagâ" may represent a broader category including water dwelling creatures which the English word "fish" would not ordinarily include. The dominion may include water dwelling air-breathing creatures as well as "fish" and other water dwelling creatures. English also sometimes uses the word "fish" in a broader sense. A "fish market" will generally sell edible water dwelling creatures which are not "fish." A "fish market" can be expected to sell crab, octopus, oysters and perhaps whale meat; all of which are not strictly "fish" as a salmon is a "fish." The full range of meaning of the Hebrew word דָּגָה "dagâ" needs further scholarly study. Genesis One does not specify when "fish" or דָּגָה "dagâ" were created. The air-breathing creatures created in Genesis 1:20-21 are not referred to as "fish" or דָּגָה "dagâ."

Now consider Genesis 1:29 in which God (Elohim) tells Adam, male and female, about plants which have been provided to be food for them.

the first type of plants which are mentioned are עֵשֶׂב (eseb). This is the word which was translated "grass" in the discussion of Genesis 1:11. The issue of how to correctly translate this word also arises in this verse. Clearly, the seeds of grasses are an important food source for man. But man eats plants other than the seeds of grasses and the fruits of trees. Should the term עֵשֶׂב be translated more generally as "plants" or as "herbs"? The solution lies in noting that the assignment of the seed of עֵשֶׂב "grass" as food is not an exclusive assignment. The text does not say that foods other than עֵשֶׂב "grass" seed and the fruits of trees do not exist. Nor are other foods forbidden. Once the non-exclusivity of the food assignment is recognized the translation of עֵשֶׂב as "grass" becomes clearly appropriate. The grain grasses which man plants and processes are one of mankind's most significant food sources. The other food source which is identified in Genesis One is the fruit of the fruit trees. In the previous discussion of the word עֵץ (tree) it was shown that this word had a very broad definition. Even the grape is included in the definition of the fruit of a fruit tree (i.e., the vine).

KJV Genesis 1:29   God said, Behold, I have given you every herb (grass) bearing seed,
which *is* upon the face of all the earth, and every tree, in the which *is* the fruit
of a tree yielding seed; to you it shall be for meat (*food*).

**Genesis 1:29**

(1) וַיֹּאמֶר אֱלֹהִים הִנֵּה נָתַתִּי לָכֶם אֶת כָּל עֵשֶׂב
and had said | God (Elohim) | behold | I have given (completed action) | to you | dir. obj. marker | all | grass

(2) זֹרֵעַ זֶרַע אֲשֶׁר עַל פְּנֵי כָל הָאָרֶץ וְאֶת כָּל הָעֵץ
seeding | seed | which | over | face | all | land | and + dir. obj. marker | all | the tree

(3) אֲשֶׁר בּוֹ פְרִי עֵץ זֹרֵעַ זֶרַע לָכֶם יִהְיֶה לְאָכְלָה
which | in it | fruit of | tree | seeding | seed | to you | shall be | for food

The Hebrew in line (3) describing the fruit of the fruit tree is somewhat difficult to translate into English. The two consecutive words פְרִי עֵץ , "fruit" followed by "tree", are in the "construct" state. This is a method by which the Hebrew expresses the "of" of English. The word "of" does not exist in biblical Hebrew. In the construct state, the word "of " is implied, and is inserted into the English, leading to KJV "the fruit of a tree."

The next difficulty in line three is the words זֹרֵעַ זֶרַע. Without the added vowel markings the two words זרע זרע are identical. The non-vowel marked word זרע may be the word "seed," or the active participle "seeding." Seeding is sometimes translated sowing. The New KJV has abandoned the word sequence of the Hebrew and translates these words as "every tree whose fruit yields seed." This is a clearer representation of the meaning than that obtained by using all the Hebrew words and retaining the Hebrew word order.

Now consider Genesis 1:30. The YLT follows the Hebrew more closely than does the KJV.

KJV Genesis 1:30   And to every beast of the earth, and to every fowl of the air, and
to every thing that creepeth upon the earth, wherein *there is* life, ("breath" not translated)
*I have given* every green herb (grass) for meat: and it was so.

YLT Genesis 1:30   and to every beast of the earth (land), and to every fowl of the heavens,
and to every creeping thing on the earth (land), in which {is} breath of life,
every green herb (grass) {is} for food: and it is so.

**Genesis 1:30**

| וְלְכָל | חַיַּת הָאָרֶץ | וּלְכָל | עוֹף | הַשָּׁמַיִם | וּלְכָל | רוֹמֵשׂ | עַל | הָאָרֶץ |
|---|---|---|---|---|---|---|---|---|
| and to all *of* | the land life of *(the wild animals)* | and to all *of* | *the* flyer | the heavens (skies) | and to all | creeping | on | the land |

| אֲשֶׁר | בּוֹ | נֶפֶשׁ | חַיָּה | אֵת | כָּל | יֶרֶק | עֵשֶׂב | לְאָכְלָה | וַיְהִי | כֵן |
|---|---|---|---|---|---|---|---|---|---|---|
| which | in | breath of | life | dir. obj. marker | all *of* | *the* green | plants (grass) | for food | and it did come to pass | so |

Part of this verse was discussed when studying the phrase "breath of life" in the section on the fifth creative "yom." For Genesis 1:30 עֵשֶׂב "eseb" will be translated as "plants." In Genesis 1:29 עֵשֶׂב "eseb" was translated "grass." The translation "plants" in Genesis 1:30 is based on the context of "all the wild animals." These animals include those which can subsist on grass that has not yielded seed, and on parts of trees that are not the fruit. Cows, with their complex stomach, can process cellulose, a material which man's digestive system cannot use as a food source. In fact, cows process resources which man cannot eat into products which man can eat. The choice of "plants" in this verse is consistent with the Hebrew requirement that word meaning be chosen depending on the context. This is another example of the ambiguity of biblical Hebrew.

The text does not say that every kind of animal is to eat every kind of plant. It only states that God (Elohim) has provided food for the animals. The text does not go into specific dietary assignments for each kind of animal. The entire food chain for animal life (predators included) is based upon the consumption of plant life as the primary food source. A carnivore merely consumes the energy derived from plant life in an indirect manner.

The food assignment does bring into question the meaning of the phrase חַיַּת הָאָרֶץ "life of the land." Does this phrase include carnivorous predators? The phrase חַיַּת הָאָרֶץ "life of the land" is used in ten verses, five of which are in Genesis. Four of the verses which are not in Genesis refer to the חַיַּת הָאָרֶץ "life of the land" as eating the carcasses of people who have already been killed. No verse indicates that the חַיַּת הָאָרֶץ "life of the land" had killed the people or that the חַיַּת הָאָרֶץ are predators. The food assignment of Genesis 1:30 is evidence that the creatures referred to as חַיַּת הָאָרֶץ "life of the land" are not normally carnivorous. This observation, if correct and applied to Genesis 1:30, results in Genesis One containing no reference to large carnivorous predators. The number of words in biblical Hebrew are so few that specific phrases which have the effect of expanding the vocabulary must be considered to carry different meanings.

Any theological speculation based on including carnivorous predators within the category חַיַּת הָאָרֶץ "life of the land" should not be accepted without additional convincing evidence from the biblical text.

Genesis 1:31 concludes the sixth creative "yom" and is considered on the next page.

KJV Genesis 1:31   And God saw (had seen) every thing that he had made, and, behold, *it was* very good.
And the evening and the morning were the sixth day.

(1) Genesis 1:31  וַיַּרְא   אֱלֹהִים   אֶת   כָּל   אֲשֶׁר   עָשָׂה   וְהִנֵּה   טוֹב   מְאֹד
and had seen   God (Elohim)   dir. obj.   all *of*   which   he had made   and behold   good   much
(completed action)           marker                        (completed action)

(2)  וַיְהִי   עֶרֶב   וַיְהִי   בֹקֶר   יוֹם   הַשִּׁשִּׁי
and had been   morning   and had been   evening   "yom"   the sixth

The verb עָשָׂה (asah) in this verse is in the Qal perfect which indicates completed action. The verb עָשָׂה is not the verb "bara" for the creating of new things, but rather is the verb which means "to make," "to form," or "to fashion." עָשָׂה (asah) was the verb used in Genesis 1:26 when God (Elohim) said "We shall make Adam in our image." The next verse used "bara" three times, emphasizing the newness of this creation. As a consequence, Adam (male and female) are included in the things which God had created (bara) and in the things God had made (asah). The word עָשָׂה (asah) is also used in reference to the making of "the heavens," "the two great lights," and by inference, "the stars" and the "land animals." Because of the breadth of the use of the word עָשָׂה (asah), the "all he had made" is generally taken to refer to everything created, or commanded to be produced, which precedes this statement.

It is then stated that God "had seen all *of* which he had made." This completed action is followed by "and behold much good." Then this is followed by a version of the concluding phrase.

Now consider the two sequential statements which are quoted from the Study Translations under the Hebrew of Genesis 1:30-31. The first (1) is the final two words of Genesis 1:30. The second (2) is the first line of Genesis 1:31 above.

(1)   "and *it* did come to pass so."
(2)   "And God had seen all which he had made and behold much good."

Statement (1) is the statement of the completion of all the preceding commanded actions. Because (2) follows (1), statement (2) could be a statement which also includes actions completed in verses before those related during the sixth creative time. Considered in this manner, the verse would be a summarizing (adding up) of all the individual times that God had seen results "as good." The word מְאֹד would then refer to the number of times or the total quantity of "good" seen. The "seeing" of good would include more than "seeing" the good of the events of the sixth creative "yom." Notice that Genesis 1:31 does not use the phrase כִּי טוֹב "as good" of the previous "seeings." The "all *of* which he had made" includes things made in all the preceding creative times. The question is "when" were each of these things seen as good.

This study does not translate Genesis 1:31 as indicating that the "much good" includes, or represents, a sum of all the preceding "and God had seen it as good" statements. This verse comes after the conclusion of all the described creative events. Because of this, interpreting it as a reference to the total of what had already been related is not clearly established. The translation "much" has been adopted instead of the KJV "very" to leave the interpretation of this verse open for further consideration. The KJV translates מְאֹד as "much" ten times.

A "Good English" translation is presented on the next page.

## A "Good English" Translation of Genesis 1:24-31

Genesis 1:24      And God said, The land shall bring forth "air breathing" creatures of their kind,
cattle, and creeping things, and land life of their kind;
and *it* did come to pass so.      (KJV "and it was so," this does not imply immediate fulfillment.)

Back in time before { Genesis 1:25      And God had made the land life of their kind, and the cattle of their
" and it did come kind, and all the creeping things of the cultivatable land of their kind;
to pass so" " and God had seen *it* as good.

Genesis 1:26      And God said, We shall make man (Adam) in our image and like our likeness,
and they shall rule over the fish of the sea, the flyer of the heavens,
and over the cattle, and over all of the land,
and over all of the creeping creeping things on the land.

Genesis 1:27      And God created (bara) the man in his image,
in the image of God he created (bara) him;
male and female he created (bara) them.

Genesis 1:28      And God blessed them and God had said to them,
Be fruitful and multiply and fill the land and subdue it,
and rule over the fish of the sea, and the flyer of the heavens,
and over all the life creeping upon the land.

Genesis 1:29      And God said, Behold,
I have given to you all grass yielding seed which is on the surface of the land,
and all the trees yielding fruit which has in it its seed, for you it shall be food.

Genesis 1:30      And to all the land life, and to all of the flyers of the heavens, and to all that creeping on the land
in which there is the breath of life, all of the green plants for food;
and *it* did come to pass so.      (KJV "and it was so," this does not imply immediate fulfillment.)

Genesis 1:31      And God had seen all which He had made, and behold much good,
and *there* was evening and *there* was morning, the sixth time.

# The Seventh "Yom": Genesis 2:1-4             The Ceasing of the Seventh Time

Genesis One concludes with the four verses Genesis 2:1 through Genesis 2:4. These verses are properly the concluding verses of the narrative on Genesis 1:1-31. The Hebrew text of Genesis does not have chapter divisions. These four verses were placed in the second chapter as the result of an arbitrary division of the Bible into chapters which was made in about 1200.[73] Genesis 2:4 is simultaneously a final reference to the preceding account of the creation and a pointer to the following expanded account of the events of the sixth creative time. Consider Genesis 2:1:

KJV Genesis 2:1    Thus the heavens and the earth were finished, and all the host of them.

| Genesis 2:1 | וַיְכֻלּוּ | הַשָּׁמַיִם | וְהָאָרֶץ | וְכָל | צְבָאָם |
|---|---|---|---|---|---|
| | and had been finished | the heavens | and the earth | and all | hosts |

The first word וַיְכֻלּוּ is a verb which means "finished," with the included sense of completed or totally finished. This word is often translated "consumed" when it refers to something which is totally used up in a destruction or by burning. The verb וַיְכֻלּוּ is a plural passive imperfect form prefixed by וַ resulting in the meaning of completed action. The plural indicates that the heavens, the earth, and the hosts all receive the action of being finished. The final word צְבָאָם "hosts" has been generally taken by commentators to refer to **all** the results of the creative actions which precede this verse. It is important to note that Genesis 2:1 says that **all** that has occurred before this verse is completed, totally finished. This completion must be kept in mind when considering the Hebrew of the next verse, Genesis 2:2.

Genesis 2:2, in Hebrew, consists of two lines; each line has seven words. Both lines discuss actions of God regarding the seventh "yom."

KJV Genesis 2:2      And on the seventh "yom" God ended his work which he had made;
                        and he rested on the seventh "yom" from all his work which he had made.

YLT Genesis 2:2      And God completeth by the seventh "yom" His work which He hath made,
                        and **ceaseth** by the seventh "yom" from all His work which He hath made.

| Genesis 2:2 | וַיְכַל | אֱלֹהִים | בַּיּוֹם | הַשְּׁבִיעִי | מְלַאכְתּוֹ | אֲשֶׁר | עָשָׂה |
|---|---|---|---|---|---|---|---|
| | and *(he)* had finished | God (Elohim) | in "yom" | the seventh | work | which | he had done |
| | וַיִּשְׁבֹּת | בַּיּוֹם | הַשְּׁבִיעִי | מִכָּל | מְלַאכְתּוֹ | אֲשֶׁר | עָשָׂה |
| | and *(he)* had ceased (completed action) | in yom | the seventh | from all | work (business) | which | he had done |

In isolation, Genesis 2:2 can be understood in two ways. It can be read that God "ceased" at the dawn of the "yom." It can also be read as indicating that some work was done on "yom" seven and then the work was "ceased." The Septuagint translation uses the Greek τῇ ἕκτῃ "the sixth" instead of "the seventh" of the Hebrew text. It has been argued that the Septuagint translation was done to maintain the correct meaning. The Greek aorist tense used in the Septuagint can be understood as a continuing past action or as a completed past action. A continuing past action would not be the meaning of the Hebrew text. The use of "the sixth" instead of "the seventh" avoids the misunderstanding that the "making" continued on any part of "the seventh."

What was the "work which he had made" and when was the "work" ceased?

This verse is clear regarding the "work which he had made." The "work which he had made" is all the work, or works, of creation made during the first six "yom." The two lines of this verse do **not** say that God did **no** work on the seventh "yom." They say that God did not do the works of the first six "yom" on the seventh "yom." This understanding is required for the verses Genesis 2:1-3 to be consistent as a whole. The translation difficulty has involved the correct translation of בַּיּוֹם הַשְּׁבִיעִי "in yom" "the seventh" in both lines.

Young's Literal Translation has solved the translation problem by translating the preposition בְּ as "by." "In," "at," or "by" are the three most common meanings assigned to the preposition בְּ. The translation "by" does not permit work of the first six creative "yom" to take place on the seventh "yom." Cassuto, in defending the Masoretic text, avoids misunderstanding by translating "And since God was finished . . . ."[74] This preserves the completed action nature of the verb but requires the insertion of an additional word not explicitly found in the Hebrew text. This translation is justified by reference to other verses using "and had finished" in the Books of Moses. Young's solution seems to be the most straightforward.

Another issue to be addressed concerns the correct translation of the verb וַיִּשְׁבֹּת in the second line of Genesis 2:2. This "waw-consecutive" verb וַיִּשְׁבֹּת = שָׁבַת + יִ + וַ has been translated "ceased" in YLT and "rested" in the KJV. How should this verb be translated? As a starting point, the reader should be advised that the KJV translates the root word שָׁבַת (shabat) as "cease" (55 times) and as "rest" (11 times). We can easily misunderstand the KJV due to changes in the connotation of the English word "rest" since the 1611 translation of the KJV. In many cases the English translation "rest" is actually used to express a ceasing of work. The meaning of וַיִּשְׁבֹּת is better translated "cease" because the action required is to "not work." Nehemiah 6:3 is a verse which clearly illustrates this meaning using an imperfect verb form word of the word שָׁבַת (shabat). This Qal imperfect verb is formed by prefixing ת to the verb root שָׁבַת. The imperfect is the verb which we have been translating using "shall." The KJV here uses "should" to express the "shall," which leads to the translation "should . . . . . . cease." Nehemiah 6:3 refers to rebuilding of the wall of Jerusalem.

KJV Nehemiah 6:3   And I sent messengers unto them, saying, I *am* doing a great work,
   so that I cannot come down: why should the work תִּשְׁבַּת cease,
   whilst I leave it, and come down to you?

In today's English, it would normally have been said, "Why should the work stop?" "Cease" is equivalent to "stop." Had a person said, "Why should the work rest?," a listener would have understood that rest was used as an equivalent to stop. Translations which translate תִּשְׁבֹּת "rest" should be understood with "stop" or "cease" as the intended meaning for the word "rest".

Consider Exodus 23:12 where the KJV translates the imperfect form תִּשְׁבֹּת = שָׁבַת + תִּ as "you shall rest." This verse also uses the word יָנוּחַ translated "he shall rest" and the "rest' is a consequence of the "ceasing." The word נוּחַ (nuah) means "rest." Both words appear in line (2) of the Hebrew shown below.

KJV Exodus 23:12   Six days thou shalt do thy work, and on the seventh day
   thou shalt rest (*cease*): that thine ox and thine ass may rest,
   and the son of thy handmaid, and the stranger, may be refreshed (*take breath*).

| | הַשְּׁבִיעִי | וּבַיּוֹם | מַעֲשֶׂיךָ | תַּעֲשֶׂה | יָמִים | שֵׁשֶׁת | (1) | Exodus 23:12 |
|---|---|---|---|---|---|---|---|---|
| | the seventh | and in "yom" | your work | you shall do | "yoms" | six of | | |

| וְהַגֵּר | אֲמָתְךָ | בֶּן | וְיִנָּפֵשׁ | וַחֲמֹרְךָ | שׁוֹרְךָ | יָנוּחַ | לְמַעַן | תִּשְׁבֹּת | (2) |
|---|---|---|---|---|---|---|---|---|---|
| and the stranger | maid servant | son of | and shall take breath | and your ass | your ox | he shall rest | in order that | you shall cease | |

The meaning of תִּשְׁבֹּת is better translated "cease" because the action required is to "not work." When the work is stopped (ceased), the ox that is plowing and the ass that is carrying burdens cease these activities. If rest is understood as only the owner taking a personal rest, a taking of his personal leisure, then the work of servants and animals could continue. The rest of the ox and the ass require a ceasing of the work. This similarly applies to the "son of the maid servant" and the "stranger."

The next verse, Genesis 2:3, is a verse which tells of God "blessing" the seventh "yom." The action of blessing is a completed action as is the action of sanctifying (setting apart). The reason for the sanctification and blessing are given in the remainder of Genesis 2:3.

**KJV Genesis 2:3**  And God blessed the seventh "yom," and sanctified it:
because that in it he had rested *(ceased)* from all his work which God created and made.

**YLT Genesis 2:3**  And God blesseth the seventh day, and sanctifieth it,
for in it He hath ceased from all His work which God had prepared *(created)* for making.

| Genesis 2:3 | וַיְבָרֶךְ | אֱלֹהִים | אֶת | יוֹם | הַשְּׁבִיעִי | וַיְקַדֵּשׁ | אֹתוֹ |
|---|---|---|---|---|---|---|---|
| | and had blessed | God (Elohim) | dir. obj. marker | "yom" | the seventh | and had sanctified | dir. obj. marker + it |

| כִּי | בוֹ | שָׁבַת | מִכָּל | מְלַאכְתּוֹ | אֲשֶׁר | בָּרָא | אֱלֹהִים | לַעֲשׂוֹת |
|---|---|---|---|---|---|---|---|---|
| for (because) | in it | he had ceased (Qal perfect) | from all | work (business) | which | had created (Qal perfect) | God (Elohim) | for making, to make, to do (Qal infinitive) |

Genesis 2:3 also uses the word שָׁבַת "had ceased" in the second line. The KJV has translated this "had rested" and the YLT has translated this as "hath ceased." The translation "had ceased" is in agreement with the translation of this word as "cease" in Genesis 2:2 i.e., תִּשְׁבֹּת = "you shall cease."

The second line of Genesis 2:3 is of considerable interest because it uses both the verb בָּרָא "had created" and the infinitive לַעֲשׂוֹת "for making." Genesis 2:3 shows that the word "bara" (create) is not equivalent to the word "asah" (make). The writer of Genesis has illustrated the difference in this verse. The word בָּרָא "bara" is the verb translated "had created" in Genesis 1:1. The verb is the Qal perfect completed action verb. The word לַעֲשׂוֹת = ל + עֲשׂוֹת, is based on the infinitive form עֲשׂוֹת "making" of the verb עשה "asah" (make). The ל is the prefix meaning "for" or "to" when indicating purpose.

The word עשה "asah" is the verb which has been consistently translated "make" throughout Genesis One. The KJV does not translate the infinitive as "making" nor does the KJV translate the prefix "for." The KJV translates "and made."[75] The preposition ל is **not** the preposition ו meaning "and" as translated in the KJV. The YLT translates the infinitive as "for making" because the infinitive עֲשׂוֹת is prefixed by ל meaning "for" or "to." The YLT is a correct translation because it includes the preposition ל "for" and by translating the verb as "making" provides an equivalent of the infinitive "to make." The translation of the KJV is derived from the Latin Vulgate. The Latin Vulgate uses the verb "faceret" which translates as "made." The Septuagint uses the verb ποιῆσαι which is an infinitive form of the verb ποιέω meaning to make or to do.

For Genesis 2:3 the translation of this study is:

Genesis 2:3  And God had blessed the seventh "yom" and had sanctified it: because in it
He had ceased from all His work which God had created *for making*."

The two Hebrew verbs translated "had ceased" and "had created" are both in the Qal perfect form indicating completed action. The "making" which is indicated by the word "asah" takes place after the completed action "had created." Note that this ordering does not depend on the translation "had created." This ordering is also apparent in this study's modified KJV translation where the word "asah" is translated "*for making*." This modified KJV is given below. The meaning of the verse becomes apparent.

**KJV Genesis 2:3 "modified":**    And God blessed the seventh day, and sanctified it: because that in it
he had rested from all his work which God created *for making*.

As shown in the above, Genesis 2:3 clearly shows that the word "asah" is used to refer to actions taken by God to additionally modify or perfect things which God already "had created." The "making" (asah) is a subsequent action and is **not** equivalent to the creating indicated by the word "bara." Note: Translating לַעֲשׂוֹת "to make" or "to do" leads to the same meaning. The 1611 KJV has a margin note, "Hebr. created to make."[75]

Note: It is the writer of Genesis who uses the words in a manner that distinguishes between things created (bara) and things subsequently modified by making (asah). The difference in the meaning of "bara" and "asah" are considered further in the section "Analysis of Exodus 20:11" (page 28) and in the section 'More About "Bara," "Asah," and "Yatsar" (page 32).

The final verse which will be considered as part of this study is Genesis 2:4.

| KJV Genesis 2:4 | These are the generations of the heavens and of the earth when they were created, in the "yom" that the LORD God made the earth and the heavens, |
|---|---|
| YLT Genesis 2:4 | These {are} births of the heavens and of the earth in their being prepared, in the day of Jehovah God's making earth and heavens; |

Genesis 2:4

| אֵלֶּה | תוֹלְדוֹת | הַשָּׁמַיִם | וְהָאָרֶץ | בְּהִבָּרְאָם |
|---|---|---|---|---|
| these *are* | generations of | the heavens | and the earth | in his creating |

| בְּיוֹם | עֲשׂוֹת | יְהוָה | אֱלֹהִים | אֶרֶץ | וְשָׁמָיִם |
|---|---|---|---|---|---|
| in "yom" ( at the time) | (*of*) making | Yahweh | Elohim | earth | and heavens |

The singular בְּיוֹם "in yom" is used here to refer to the entire sequence of six creative "yom" in the preceding verses.

The word תוֹלְדוֹת (toldot) translated "generations" is a word which is used 11 times in Genesis as a marker between topical sections. The words "these are the generations" are usually followed by other words in the same sentence which refer to the preceding topical section. The words may be repetitions of words used in the preceding passage or they may refer, in some way, to the person who was the main subject of the preceding passage. In some cases the transition may also include several additional sentences which continue the referenced events. Then another subject or "story" is started.

In this verse, the phrases and words which refer back to the preceding verses are:

1. The phrase הַשָּׁמַיִם וְהָאָרֶץ "the heavens and the earth" (from the first verse of Genesis).

2. The word בְּהִבָּרְאָם which is a form of בָּרָא "create" (from the first verse and used another four times in other verses).

3. The word עֲשׂוֹת "making" (a word used for the activities of God many times in Genesis One).
   In the Hebrew the making is referred to "earth (land) and heavens" not "the heavens and the earth"; thereby **not** including Genesis 1:1 in the making.

By use of the two words, בָּרָא "create" and עֲשׂוֹת "making," reference is made to **all** of God's actions of "creating" and "making" in Genesis One. The "He" who is the agent causing the "creating" is אֱלֹהִים "Elohim," the name used in the first verse and throughout Genesis One.

Genesis 2:4 also performs an important function by stating that יְהוָה "Yahweh" and אֱלֹהִים "Elohim" are the same Person. This is important because the next topical section almost always uses the double title "Yahweh Elohim." In many English Bibles this is translated "Lord God," "Lord" being the translation of Yahweh. This verse makes the identification of Yahweh as Elohim clear by its consistent referencing to the creative events of **all** six of the preceding creative "yom." This is done before the next section begins.

The change in the name used for God was part of the basis of the **now discredited** "Documentary Hypothesis." [76] Cassuto, in his treatments of the underlying assumptions of the "Documentary Hypothesis," explains that the name used for God in the Books of Moses depends upon the nature of the actions being discussed.[77] Actions of a personal nature toward Israel, or the ancestors of Israel, generally use "Yahweh." Actions of an impersonal nature, or towards non-Israel, generally use "Elohim."

Below is a summary "Good English" translation of Genesis 2:1-4, translating the completed action verbs using had."

**"Good English" Translation of Genesis 2:1-4**

Genesis 2:1   And the heavens and the earth and all hosts had been finished.

Genesis 2:2   And God had finished by the seventh time the work which He had made,
and He had ceased in the seventh time from all the work He had made.

Genesis 2:3   And God had blessed the seventh time and had sanctified it,
because in it He had ceased from all the work which God had created for making.

Genesis 2:4   These *are* the generated results of the heavens and the earth in His creating (bara),
at the time of Yahweh God (Elohim) making the earth and the heavens.

# Concluding Remarks

This study reached a number of conclusions about the "when" of the events related in Genesis One. Some of these conclusions are:

1. Genesis One does not specify an age for the Universe or planet Earth.

2. Genesis One does not indicate the length of the six creative time periods or the total interval of time required for their completion.

3. Genesis One indicates that the cause of the creative acts is God.

4. Genesis One does not indicate that the creative acts are completed "instantaneously" and does not indicate the specific means and steps by which the creative actions were brought to completion.

These conclusions are not new. They were well known in the early 1900's. To many readers the results of *Reading Genesis One* will be surprising. To others the results will be familiar but the biblical basis for the results will have not been presented to them in the detail offered by this study.

At the present time there is among Evangelical Christians a degree of confusion about Genesis One. The confusion has arisen from the advocacy of a "Young Earth" reading of Genesis One. This advocacy has come to prominence mainly within the past forty years. It is the opinion of the author that this rise to prominence has been aided and abetted by the Darwinists themselves. The opposition to Darwinism of the Young Earth advocates serves the Darwinists because it avoids the need to mount a scientific defense of Darwinism. Instead, the Darwinist can attack the claims and assertions of the Young Earth advocates, assertions which are not in accord with the Hebrew of Genesis One. The Bible cannot be effectively defended nor can the Gospel be effectively proclaimed by asserting things which the Bible does not say.

This confusion has now reached the point where *some* people think that fundamental Christianity and the writers of *The Fundamentals*[78] were Young Earth believers. Nothing could be farther from the truth. The writers of *The Fundamentals* did not hold Young Earth views; they accepted an Old Earth view and opposed Darwinism. Because of this confusion a brief review the views of those who wrote in *The Fundamentals* will be given.

**The Fundamentalists and the Age of the Earth**

By the early 1900's the issue of the age of the Earth had been considered and it was widely known and held that the Bible did not give an age for the Earth and did not assert that the Earth was young. In the years 1909-1917 a set of booklets entitled *The Fundamentals* were published which set forth the Christian faith. These booklets, or articles, were edited and published in four volumes which a still available today.[78]

Those who wrote in *The Fundamentals* defended Evangelical Christianity and presented the Gospel of Jesus Christ. With respect to Darwinism, they did not view the old Earth as the issue; they recognized that the essence of Darwinism was a denial of design and thereby a denial of a creator God.

Three of the writers, C. I. Scofield, Benjamin B. Warfield, and James Orr, all opponents of Darwinism, were well known for their acceptance of an Old Earth. These writers and others who wrote in opposition to Darwinism were opposed on the basis of theology and presented arguments citing evidence of design. Today it is the implicit evidence of design in the complex structure of life that is the basis of a very effective opposition to Darwinism. These arguments speak to the scientific evidence. Argument from design has confronted advocates of Darwinism with scientific evidence which does not support the claims of Darwinism. Books like *Darwin's Black Box*[79] and *Darwin on Trial*[80] have altered the terms of the confrontation with Darwinism.

Those who are opposed to the theological message of the Bible find it useful to promote or assert interpretations of Genesis which lead to apparent conflict with scientific knowledge. James Orr, in the article "Science And Christian Faith" in *The Fundamentals* said of Genesis One and the supposed conflict with science:

> "There is no violence done to the narrative in substituting in thought "aeonic" days -- vast cosmic periods--for "days" on our narrower, sun-measured scale. Then the last trace of apparent conflict disappears."

A second statement by James Orr reports a confusion that still exists today.

> "Much of the difficulty on this subject has arisen from the unwarrantable confusion of identification of evolution with *Darwinism*."

The word "evolution" refers to "change with the passage of time." Darwinism or Darwinian Evolution includes more than mere change with time. Darwinian Evolution **excludes God** as a source and a cause of the change with time.

Those who are opposed to the theological message of the Bible exploit this confusion to their advantage. The term "Darwinian" is dropped and the term used becomes merely "Evolution." By this ploy, any observable change with time can be offered to the unwary as evidence for Darwinian evolution.

This book's discussion of Genesis 1:20-23 pointed out that change with time is not in opposition to the Bible's account of creation. The writers of *The Fundamentals* knew that change with time is not in opposition to the Bible's account of creation. The Rev. Dyson Hague in the article "The Doctrinal Value of the First Chapter of Genesis" presented a powerful exposition of the theological message of Genesis One. It is the theological message which instigates an opposition which employs Darwinism as a advocacy. With respect to Darwinism, Hague wrote:

> " The Bible stands openly against the evolutionary development of man, and his gradual ascent through indefinite aeons from the animal. Not against the idea of the development of the plans of the Creator in nature, or a variation of species by means of environment and processes of time. That is seen in Genesis, and throughout the Bible, and in this world."[78]

One attacker of Creationism, Tim M. Berra, actually offers the successive improvements made in the Chevrolet Corvette as an illustration of descent with modification.[81] Four photographs of successive models are included as evidence. This illustration immediately follows a statement that the "hominid fossils" are evidence of evolution. The relevance of the teams of engineering designers in purposely choosing and introducing changes to modify the Corvette is seemingly lost.

Automobiles have "evolved" though time from the early 1905 types to the present day types through the active design efforts of automotive engineers. This "change with time" is not "Darwinian Evolution." The changes were made purposefully by intelligent agents. Darwinism excludes "intelligent design" as a cause. Because it is to their advantage, Darwinists often assert that the existence of "change with time" is a proof of Darwinian Evolution.

Benjamin B. Warfield, Professor at the Princeton Theological Seminary, wrote the article "The Deity of Christ" in *The Fundamentals*. He held an Old Earth view and opposed Darwinism. In the 1911 *Princeton Theological Review* he wrote concerning the interpretation of the days of Genesis as 24-hours: [82]

> " There was thus created the appearance of conflict between Biblical statements and the findings of scientific investigators, and it became the duty of theologians to investigate the matter. The asserted conflict proves, however, to be entirely factitious. The Bible does not assign a brief span to human history: this is done only by a particular mode of interpreting the Biblical data, which is found on examination to rest on no solid basis. Science does not demand an inordinate period for the life of human beings on earth: this is done only by a particular school of speculative theorizers, the validity of whose demands on time exact investigators are more and more chary of allowing. As the real state of the case has become better understood the problem has therefore tended to disappear from theological discussion, till now is pretty well understood that theology as such has no interest in it."

When *The Fundamentals* were published in book form in 1917, the advocacy of Darwinian Evolution was so in eclipse that two articles which addressed Darwinism were entitled "The Passing of Evolution" and "The Decadence of Darwinism."

C. I. Scofield, editor of the *Scofield Reference Bible*, wrote an article "The Grace of God" in *The Fundamentals*. Scofield held an Old Earth view of Genesis One. The 1909 and the 1917 Scofield Reference Bibles contained a footnote for Genesis 1:1 which read in part: "The first creative act refers to the dateless past, and gives scope for all the geologic ages."

R. A. Torrey, an editor of *The Fundamentals* and a noted evangelist, wrote the article "The Place of Prayer in Evangelism." Torrey held an Old Earth view. In another book, he wrote concerning the 24 hour interpretation of the "days" of Genesis One: [83]

> "Anyone who is at all familiar with the Bible and the way the Bible uses words, knows that the use of the word day is not limited to twenty-four hours. It is frequently used to denote a period of time of entirely undefined length."

> And again later in the same passage; "There is no necessity whatsoever for interpreting the days of Genesis 1 as solar days of twenty-four hours length."

The issue of how the early commentators on Genesis One interpreted Genesis will not be considered here. Readers interested in additional information would be well advised to consult the book *Reason, Science and Faith*.[84] Two sections are of particular interest. Chapter 7, *Genesis Through History* reviews the interpretations from the first century through Augustine. Chapter 8, *Interpreting Genesis Today*, reviews the history of the past 150 years.

Augustine did not consider the 24-hour day interpretation valid. Augustine clearly states this in *The Literal Meaning of Genesis*, a work finished in about 415 A. D. There he says, regarding the normal 24-hour day which we experience:

> " . . . one day is constituted by the course of the sun from its rising to its setting, but we must bear in mind that these days indeed recall the days of creation, but without in any way being really similar to them."[85]

The message of Genesis One is primarily theological. It informs the descendents of Adam (mankind) about their origin and about their relationship to their Creator. The message is that God is the creator of Adam (mankind) and that mankind has a responsibility toward God and is accountable to God. The modern attacks on Genesis One have, as their basis, a wish to discredit this theological message and to assert freedom from accountability.

Some of the theological content of Genesis One escapes our attention today because the sun and moon are not presently viewed as gods. At the time of Moses, Genesis One expressed powerful theological contradictions of the religions of Egypt, Canaan, and Babylon. Some of these contradictions are:

One creator God, not many gods.
The sun and moon are created objects, not gods.
The animals are created and are not gods. (The Egyptians worshipped many creatures.)

Because the theological message that the sun and moon are not gods is not significant in our time, it is possible to mistake Genesis One as being a description of the physical and biological history of planet Earth. Genesis One does make statements about the physical and biological development, but does so as a subsidiary to the theological message against the pagan gods worshiped at the time of Moses. The statements are true, but the statements are an incomplete description of the events that transpired.

At the present time the opposition to the theological message of Genesis One is opposition to a Creator God who acts in history and in time. The tactic is to interpret the "when" and the "creative acts" in a way that introduces conflict between the interpretation and the observable geological record. The Darwinist assumes a God that does not act in history or geologic time, or assumes there is no God at all. The Bible reveals a God that **does** act in history and geologic time.

## Things Genesis One Does and Does Not Say (A partial list):

Genesis One does **not** specify an age for the Earth or an age for the Universe.

Genesis One **does** say that there was a beginning to the Universe and planet Earth.
Genesis One **does** say that God created the heavens and the Earth.

Genesis One **does** say that planet Earth was not always as it is now; changes have occurred.
Genesis One **does** say that God acted to bring the present condition of the Earth into being.

Genesis One does **not** say that the creative times (yom) are 24 hours in duration.
Genesis One does **not** say that the creative times (yom) followed immediately one after another.
Genesis One does **not** say that the commands of God were fulfilled immediately, like a bolt of lightening.

Genesis One **does** say that God acted and issued commands for changes in the physical environment.
Genesis One **does** say that God commanded the land to bring forth plants.

Genesis One does **not** mention algae, diatoms, or any microscopic plant or creature.
Genesis One does **not** categorize "life" in agreement with the modern categorization of "life."
Genesis One does **not** say when fish appeared or how they were brought into being.

Genesis One **does** say that God commanded the appearance of air-breathing creatures in the water.
Genesis One **does** say that God commanded and created air-breathing animals of the land.
Genesis One **does** say that God created Adam (mankind).

Genesis One does **not** say that the creation of Eve was accomplished quickly.

This Page Intentionally Blank

# Chapter Five   The Translations of Genesis One

**Introduction**

The foregoing study has determined the "when" of the actions described by the verbs in Genesis One, using only the pluperfect to translate completed action Hebrew verbs. However, the resulting translation is not suitable for general use. Therefore, the results of this study will now be presented in the usual manner using both the past tense and the pluperfect tense. The use of the two tenses will provide the time ordering information expected by readers of an English translation and will be in a form more suitable for use by Bible readers and teachers.

There will follow two English translations presented on facing pages. These translations have been produced by modifying two translations. One translation is a modification of the well-known KJV; the other is a modification of the translations which appeared in this study under the Hebrew verses of Genesis One. The use of facing pages is to facilitate comparison of the translations. The translations are titled "This Study's Good English Translation" and "Modified KJV Translation (KJV-M)." These are described more fully below.

**About the "Good English" Translation**

This translation started with the translations which appeared under the Hebrew verses of Genesis One. Then pluperfect forms using "had" were replaced with the simple past tense whenever the actions of the narrative events were advancing in time. When the pluperfect form using "had" was used exclusively, the time ordering function of the pluperfect was not effective. When the simple past tense was again introduced, the time ordering function of the pluperfect was made effective again. This meant that the insertion of a past tense verb often required the replacement of additional pluperfect verb forms. The additional replacements were necessary if the translation was to indicate the correct time ordering of the events and actions. This process was somewhat different than that of modifying the KJV. The KJV almost exclusively used the past tense.

**The Modified KJV Translation (KJV-M)**

The Modified KJV Translation (KJV-M) was produced by replacing some past tense verb forms with pluperfect forms. This generated a translation which also indicated the time location of the events and actions found in this study. These changes are identified by an underlining of the entire pluperfect verb. Other word changes were also made to express more accurately the meaning of the translated Hebrew words or phrases. These changes are those found in the foregoing study. For example, "sky" replaces the "firmament" of the KJV. "Flyer" replaces "fowl," "air breathing creature" replaces "living creature," and "land life" replaces "beast of the earth." These word changes are also identified by underlining. Words to be omitted are indicated by strikethru or otherwise indicated. Bracketed words are sometimes inserted to identify the root Hebrew word being translated. Examples are create (bara), make (asah), earth (land), or earth (erets). The modifications are the minimum changes thought necessary to reflect the findings of this study.

**The phrase <u>and *it* did come to pass so</u>  KJV "and it was so"**

"And it was so" is the KJV translation of וַיְהִי כֵן the six times it is used in Genesis One. The change in translation is to indicate that the completion of the commands is not indicated to take place immediately. "And it was so" could be properly understood, but is able to be misunderstood, because of prior training to read it as immediate completion. The KJV also translated וַיְהִי כֵן as "and so it came to pass" in 2 Kings 15:12, a verse where the completion occurs over four generations. This was discussed on page 95. The change in translation in this case avoids misunderstanding.

The KJV-M is intended to serve as a model for study helps or margin notes which readers may wish to add to the text of their preferred translations of the Bible. It also serves the function of illustrating the minimal change required to express the "when" of the actions.

# This Study's "Good English" Translation

Genesis 1:1   In *the* beginning God **had created** the heavens and the Earth.

Genesis 1:2   And the Earth had existed unsuitable for human life (*tohu*), and empty (*bohu*) of human life,
and darkness was on the surface of the deep,
and the Spirit of God moving over the surface of the water(s).

Genesis 1:3   And God said, Light shall exist; and light existed.

Genesis 1:4   And God had seen the light as good;
and God had separated between the light and between the dark.

Genesis 1:5   And God called the light "daytime" and the darkness he had called "nighttime";
and *there* was evening and *there* was morning, one time.

Genesis 1:6   And God said, *There* shall be a sky in the midst of the waters
and *there* shall be a separating between *the* waters to *the* waters.

Genesis 1:7   And God made the sky, and separated between the waters under the sky,
and between those waters off of the sky; and *it* did come to pass so.
        (KJV "and it was so")

Genesis 1:8   And God called the sky *a part of the* heavens;
and *there* was evening and *there* was morning, a second time.

Genesis 1:9   And God said, The waters under the heavens shall be gathered together unto one place,
and the dry shall be seen; and *it* did come to pass so.   (KJV "and it was so")

Genesis 1:10   And God **had called** the dry "land",
and the gathering together of the waters he **had called** Seas;
and God had seen *it* as good.   (KJV "and God saw that *it was* good.")

Genesis 1:11   And God said, The land shall bring forth plant, grass yielding seed,
*and* fruit tree yielding fruit after its kind, whose seed *is* in itself,
upon the land; and *it* did come to pass so.
        (KJV "and it was so")

Genesis 1:12   And the land **had brought** forth plant, grass yielding seed after its kind,
and tree bearing (making) fruit, whose seed *was* in itself, after its kind:
and God had seen *it* as good.   (KJV "and God saw that *it was* good)

Genesis 1:13   And *there* was evening and *there* was morning, a third time.

# Modified KJV Translation ( KJV-M) of GENESIS ONE

KJV-M Genesis 1:1      In the beginning God **had created** the heaven and the earth.

KJV-M Genesis 1:2      And the earth was **<u>unsuitable for human life (*tohu*), and empty (*bohu*) of human life</u>,**
and darkness *was* upon the face of the deep.
And the spirit of God moved upon the face of the waters.

KJV-M Genesis 1:3      And God said, Let there be light: and there was light.

KJV-M Genesis 1:4      And God **had seen** the light **as good**:
and God **had** divided the light from the darkness.

KJV-M Genesis 1:5      And God called the light **daytime**, and the darkness he **had called nighttime**.
And evening **was** and morning **was, one time.** †

> KJV 1611 margin note. (Quoted as written.)
> "† *Hebr. and euening was and morning was &c.*"

KJV-M Genesis 1:6      And God said, Let there be a **sky** in the midst of the waters,
and let *there* divide the waters from the waters.

KJV-M Genesis 1:7      And God made the **sky**, and divided the waters which *were* under the **sky**
from the waters which *were* **off of** the **sky**: **and *it* did come to pass so** .
                   (KJV "and it was so")

KJV-M Genesis 1:8      And God called the **sky a part of the Heavens**.
And evening **was** and morning **was, a second time.**

KJV-M Genesis 1:9      And God said, Let the waters under the heaven be gathered together unto one place,
and let the dry ~~land~~ appear: **and *it* did come to pass so** .  (KJV "and it was so")

KJV-M Genesis 1:10      And God **had called** the **dry** "**land** ";  (KJV "Earth" has been omitted.)
and the gathering together of the waters **he had called** Seas:
and God saw that *it was* good.

KJV-M Genesis 1:11      And God said, Let the earth (land) bring forth grass, the herb **(grass)** yielding seed,
*and* the fruit tree yielding fruit after his kind, whose seed *is* in itself, upon the earth (land):
**and *it* did come to pass so** .
     (KJV "and it was so")

KJV-M Genesis 1:12      And the earth (land) **had brought forth** grass, *and* herb **(grass)** yielding seed
after his kind, and the tree yielding fruit, whose seed *was* in itself, after his kind:
and **<u>God had seen it as good.</u>**

KJV-M Genesis 1:13      And evening **was** and morning **was, a third time.**

# This Study's "Good English" Translation

Genesis 1:14   And God said, *There* shall be lights in the sky of the heavens
to separate between the daytime and the nighttime,
and *they* will be for signs, and for seasons, and for days, and years.

Genesis 1:15   And *they* will be for lights in the sky of the heavens
for giving light upon the land; and *it* did come to pass so.
(KJV "and it was so")

Genesis 1:16   And God **had made (prepared)** the two great lights;
the great for rule of the daytime and the small for rule of the nighttime, and the stars.

Genesis 1:17   And God **had given (set)** them in the sky of the heavens
for giving light upon the land,

Genesis 1:18   And for ruling in the daytime and in the nighttime, and to separate between
the light and the dark: and God had seen it as good.   (KJV "and God saw that *it was* good.")

Genesis 1:19   And *there* was evening and *there* was morning, a fourth time.


Genesis 1:20   And God said, The waters shall swarm with a swarming air breathing creature
and a "flying thing" shall fly above the land
across the face of the sky of the heavens.

Genesis 1:21   And God created (bara) the great dragons,
and all the kinds of the creeping air breathing creatures
that swarmed in the waters, and all the kinds of winged
flying things, and God had seen it as good.      (KJV "and God saw that *it was* good)

Genesis 1:22   And God blessed them saying, Be fruitful and multiply and fill the waters in the seas,
and the flying things shall multiply on the land.

Genesis 1:23   And *there* was evening and *there* was morning, a fifth time.


Genesis 1:24   And God said, The land shall bring forth air breathing creatures of their kind,
cattle, and creeping things, and land life of their kind;
And *it* did come to pass so.
 (KJV "and it was so")

Genesis 1:25   And God **had made** the land life of their kind and the cattle of their kind,
and all the creeping things of the cultivatable land of their kind;
and God had seen *it* as good.         (KJV "and God saw that *it was* good)

Genesis 1:26   And God said, We shall make Man (Adam) in our image and like our likeness,
and they shall rule over the fish of the sea, the flyer of the heavens,
and over the cattle, and over all of the land (erets),
and over all of the creeping creeping things on the land.

# Modified KJV Translation ( KJV-M) of GENESIS ONE

KJV-M Genesis 1:14     And God said, Let there be lights in the firmament of the heaven to divide the **daytime** from the **nighttime**; and let them be for signs, and for seasons, and for days, and years:

KJV-M Genesis 1:15     And let them be for lights in the **sky of the heavens** to give light upon the earth (land): **and *it* did come to pass so**.
(KJV "and it was so")

KJV-M Genesis 1:16     And God **had made (prepared)** two great lights; the greater light to rule the **daytime**, and the lesser light to rule the **nighttime: and the stars**.

KJV-M Genesis 1:17     And God **had set** them in the **sky of the heavens** to give light upon the earth,

KJV-M Genesis 1:18     And to rule over the **daytime** and over the **nighttime**, and to divide the light from the darkness: and God saw that *it was* good.

KJV-M Genesis 1:19     And evening **was** and morning **was, a fourth time.**

KJV-M Genesis 1:20     And God said, Let the waters bring forth abundantly **a swarming air breathing creature**, and **a flyer shall fly** above the earth (land) **across the face of the sky of the heavens.**

KJV-M Genesis 1:21     And God created (bara) the great **dragons**, and **all the kinds of the creeping air breathing creatures that swarmed in the waters, and all the kinds of winged flying things,** and God saw that *it was* good.

KJV-M Genesis 1:22     And God blessed them, saying, Be fruitful, and multiply, and fill the waters in the seas, and let **flying things** multiply **on** the earth (land).

KJV-M Genesis 1:23     And evening **was** and morning **was, a fifth time.**

KJV-M Genesis 1:24     And God said, Let the earth (land) bring forth the **air breathing creatures** after his kind, cattle, and creeping thing, and **land life** after his kind: **and *it* did come to pass so**.
(KJV "and it was so")

KJV-M Genesis 1:25     And God **had made** the **land life** after **their** kind, and cattle after their kind, and every thing that creepeth upon the earth (land) after his kind: and God saw that *it was* good.

KJV-M Genesis 1:26     And God said, Let us make man in our image, after our likeness: and let them have dominion over the fish of the sea, and over **the flyer of the heavens**, and over the cattle, and over all the earth (erets), and over every creeping thing that creepeth upon the earth (land).

# This Study's "Good English" Translation

Genesis 1:27  And God created (bara) the man in his image,
in the image of God he created (bara) him;
male and female he created (bara) them.

Genesis 1:28  And God blessed them and God said to them,
Be fruitful and multiply and fill the land and subdue it,
and rule over the fish of the sea, and the flyer of the heavens,
and over all the life creeping upon the land.

Genesis 1:29  And God said, Behold,
I have given to you all grass yielding seed which is on the surface of the land,
and all the trees yielding fruit which has in it its seed,
for you it shall be food.

Genesis 1:30  And to all the land life and to all of the flyers of the heavens
and to all that creeping on the land in which there is the breath of life,
all of the green plants for food;
and *it* did come to pass so .
(KJV "and it was so")

Genesis 1:31  And God had seen all which he had made, and behold much good,
and *there* was evening and *there* was morning, the sixth time.


Genesis 2:1  And the heavens and the earth and all hosts had been finished.

Genesis 2:2  And God had finished by the seventh time the work which he made,
and he had ceased in the seventh time from all the work he had made.

Genesis 2:3  And God had blessed the seventh time and had sanctified it,
because in it he had ceased from all the work which God had created for making.


Genesis 2:4  These *are* the generated results of the heavens and the earth of his creating (bara),
at the time of Yahweh God making the earth and the heavens.

# Modified KJV Translation ( KJV-M) of GENESIS ONE

KJV-M Genesis 1:27     So God created (bara) man in his *own* image,
in the image of God created (bara) he him; male and female created (bara) he them.

KJV-M Genesis 1:28     And God blessed them, and God said, unto them, Be fruitful, and multiply,
and **fill** the earth (land), and subdue it: and have dominion over the fish of the sea,
and over **the flyer of the heavens**,
and over every living thing that **creeps** upon the earth.

KJV-M Genesis 1:29     And God said, Behold, I have given you every herb bearing seed,
which *is* upon the face of all the earth (land), and every tree, in the which *is*
the fruit of a tree yielding seed; to you it shall be for **food**.

KJV-M Genesis 1:30     And **to all the land life**, and to **all of the flyers of the heavens**,
and to every thing that creepeth upon the earth (land), wherein *there is* the **breath of life**,
*I have given* every green herb for **food**: **and *it* did come to pass so.**
                               (KJV "and it was so")

KJV-M Genesis 1:31     And God **had seen** every thing that he had made (asah), and, behold, **much** good.
And evening **was** and morning **was**, **the sixth time.**

KJV-M Genesis 2:1     Thus the heavens and the earth **had been** finished, and all **hosts**.

KJV-M Genesis 2:2     And **by** the seventh day God **had finished** his work which he had made (asah);
and he **had ceased** on the seventh day from all his work which he had made (asah).

KJV-M Genesis 2:3     And God blessed the seventh day, and sanctified it: because that in it
he had rested from all his work which God **had created** (bara) *for making*† (asah).
                               († **KJV 1611 note:** "Hebr. created to make.")

KJV-M Genesis 2:4     These *are* the generations of the heavens and of the earth **of his creating** (bara),
**at the time** that the LORD God made (asah) the earth and the heavens.

# This Study's "Good English" Translation of Genesis One With Strong's Numbers for the Translated Hebrew Words

Genesis 1:1    In *the* beginning God **had created** the heavens and the Earth.
07225    0430    01254    08064    0776

Genesis 1:2    And the Earth had existed unsuitable (*tohu*) for human life, and empty (*bohu*) of human life,
0776    01961    08414    0922

and darkness *was* on the surface of the deep,
02822    06440    08415

and the Spirit of God moving over the surface of the waters.
07307    0430    07363    05921    06440    04325

Genesis 1:3    And God said, Light shall exist; and light existed.
0430    0559    0216    01961    0216    01961

Genesis 1:4    And God had seen the light, as good;
0430    07200    0216    3588    02896

and God had separated between the light and between the dark.
0430    0914    0996    0216    0996    02822

Genesis 1:5    And God called the light "daytime" and the darkness he had called "nighttime";
0430    07121    0216    03117    02822    07121    03915

and *there* was evening and *there* was morning, one time.
01961    06153    01961    01242    0259    03117

Genesis 1:6    And God said, *There* shall be a sky in the midst of the waters
0430    0559    01961    07549    08432    04325

and *there* shall be a separating between *the* waters to *the* waters.
01961    0914    04325    04325

Genesis 1:7    And God made the sky, and separated between the waters under the sky,
0430    06213    07549    0914    04325    08478    07549

and between those waters off of the sky; and *it* did come to pass so.
04325    07549    01961    03651

Genesis 1:8    And God called the sky *a part of the* heavens;
0430    07121    07549    08064

and *there* was evening and *there* was morning, a second time.
01961    06153    01961    01242    08145    03117

Genesis 1:9    And God said, The waters under the heavens shall be gathered together unto one place,
0430    0559    04325    08064    06960    0413    0259    04725

and the dry shall be seen; and *it* did come to pass so. (KJV "and it was so")
03004    07200    01961    03651

# This Study's "Good English" Translation of Genesis One
# With Strong's Numbers for the Translated Hebrew Words

Genesis 1:10　　And God　**had called**　the dry　"land",
　　　　　　　　　　0430　　07121　　　　03004　　0776

　　　　　　　　and the gathering together of　the waters　he **had** called　Seas;
　　　　　　　　　　　　　04723　　　　　　　　04325　　　07121　　　03220

　　　　　　　　and God　had seen　*it* as　good.　(KJV: and God saw that *it was* good)
　　　　　　　　　0430　　07200　　　　　　02896

Genesis 1:11　　And God　said,　The land　shall bring forth　plant,　grass　yielding　seed,
　　　　　　　　　0430　0559　　0776　　　　01876　　　　01877　06212　02232　　02233

　　　　　　　　*and*　fruit　tree　yielding　fruit　after its kind,　whose　seed *is* in itself,
　　　　　　　　　　06529　06086　06213　　06529　　04327　　　　0834　　02233

　　　　　　　　upon the land;　and it did come to pass　so.　(KJV "and it was so")
　　　　　　　　　　0776　　　　　　　01961　　　　　　03651

Genesis 1:12　　And the land　**had brought** forth　plant,　grass　yielding　seed　after its kind,
　　　　　　　　　　0776　　　　03318　　　　　01877　　06212　02232　02233　　　04327

　　　　　　　　and　tree　yielding　fruit,　whose　seed　*was* in itself,　after its kind:
　　　　　　　　　　06086　06213　　08802　　0834　　02233　　　　　　　　　　04327

　　　　　　　　and God　had seen　*it* as　good.　(KJV "and God saw that *it was* good.")
　　　　　　　　　0430　　7200　　　　　　02896

Genesis 1:13　　And *there* was　evening　　and *there* was　morning, a third　time.
　　　　　　　　　　01961　　06153　　　　　　01961　　　01242　　07992　　03117

Genesis 1:14　　And God　said,　*There* shall be　lights　in the sky of　the heavens
　　　　　　　　　0430　　0559　　　　　　　　03974　　　07549　　　08064

　　　　　　　　to separate between　the daytime　　and the nighttime,
　　　　　　　　　　0914　　　　　　　03117　　　　　　03915

　　　　　　　　and *they* will be　for signs,　and for seasons,　and for days,　and years.
　　　　　　　　　　　　　　　　　　0226　　　　　04150　　　　　　03117　　　08141

Genesis 1:15　　And *they* will be　for lights　in the sky of　the heavens
　　　　　　　　　　　　　　　　　03974　　　07549　　　　08064

　　　　　　　　for giving light　upon　the land;　and it did come to pass　so.　(KJV "and it was so")
　　　　　　　　　　0776　　　　　　　0776　　　　　　　01961　　　　　　03651

Genesis 1:16　　And God　**had made**　the two　great　lights;　the great　for rule of　the daytime,
　　　　　　　　　0430　　06213　　　　08147　01419　03974　　01419　　　04475　　　03117

　　　　　　　　and the small　for rule　of the nighttime, and the stars.
　　　　　　　　　　06996　　　04475　　　　03915　　　　　　03556

Genesis 1:17　　And God　**had given (set)** them　in the sky of　the heavens
　　　　　　　　　0430　　　05414　　　　　　　　07549　　　　08064

　　　　　　　　for giving light　upon　the land,
　　　　　　　　　　0215　　　　　　　0776

# This Study's "Good English" Translation of Genesis One With Strong's Numbers for the Translated Hebrew Words

Genesis 1:18    And for ruling    in the daytime    and in the nighttime,
                    04910              03117                03915

and  to separate   between   the light   and the dark:
       0914                    0216         02822

and God    had seen   *it* as   good.    (KJV "and God saw that *it was* good)
 0430       07200               02896

Genesis 1:19    And *there* was evening    and *there* was  morning, a fourth   time.
                     01961   06153              01961    01242    07243    03117

Genesis 1:20    And God    said,  The waters   shall swarm   with a swarming   "air breathing" creature
                    0430    0559      04325        08317           08318              05315 + 02416

and a "flying thing"   shall fly   above   the land   across   the face of   the sky of   the heavens.
       05775             05774      05921    0776                 06440          07549        08064

Genesis 1:21    And God    created (bara)   the great    "dragons,"
                    0430       01254           01419       08577

and all   the kinds   of the creeping   "air breathing" creatures
            04327          07430             05315  +  02416

that   swarmed   in the waters,   and all   the kinds   of winged   "flying things,"
         08317         04325                  04327         03671         05775

and God    had seen   *it* as   good.    (KJV "and God saw that *it was* good)
 0430       07200               02896

Genesis 1:22    And God    blessed them   saying,  Be fruitful   and multiply   and fill    the waters
                    0430      01288          0559      06509          07235         04390      04325

in the seas,   and the "flying things"   shall multiply   on the land.
   03220                05775                  07235           0776

Genesis 1:23    And *there* was evening    and *there* was  morning, a fifth   time.
                     01961   06153              01961    0124    02549   03117

Genesis 1:24    And God    said,  The land   shall bring forth   "air breathing" creatures of   their kind,
                    0430    0559    0776          03318              02416 + 05315                  04327

cattle,   and creeping things,   and land    life    of their kind;
 0929           07431              0776     02416        04327

and *it* did come to pass       so.    (KJV "and it was so")
        01961                  03651

Genesis 1:25    And God   **had made**   the land   life of   their kind  and   the cattle of   their kind,
                    0430      06213        0776     02416       04327                0929          04327

and all    the creeping things of    the cultivatable land of    their kind;
              07431                         0127                    04327

and God    had seen   *it* as   good.    (KJV "and God saw that *it was* good)
 0430       07200               02896

# This Study's "Good English" Translation Genesis One
# With Strong's Numbers for the Translated Hebrew Words

Genesis 1:26     And God said, We shall make Man (Adam) in our image and like our likeness,
                  0430   0559       06213     0120         06754             01823

             and they shall rule over the fish of the sea, the flyer of the heavens,
                   07287        01710     03220     05775       08064

             and over the cattle, and over all of the land,
                         0929               0776

             and over all of the creeping creeping things on the land.
                           07430       07431        0776

Genesis 1:27     And God created (bara) the man in his image,
                  0430    01254        0120     06754

             in the image of God he created (bara) him; male and female he created (bara) them.
                  06754     0430     01254          02145      05347     01254

Genesis 1:28     And God blessed them and God said to them,
                  0430    01288         0430   0559

             Be fruitful and multiply and fill the land and subdue it,
                  06509      07235     04390   0776       03533

             and rule over the fish of the sea, and the flyer of the heavens,
                  07287        01710       03220        05775      08064

             and over all the life creeping upon the land.
                          02416    07430        0776

Genesis 1:29     And God said Behold,
                  0430   0559   02009

             I have given to you all grass yielding seed which is on the surface of the land,
                  05414           06212    02232    02233          06440      0776

             and all the trees yielding fruit which has in it its seed, for you it shall be food.
                  06086    02232    06529            02233          01961   0402

Genesis 1:30     And to all the land life and to all of the flyers of the heavens
                       0776    02416            05775      08064

             and to all that creeping on the land in which there is the breath of life,
                          07430     0776                  02416 + 05315

             all of the green plants for food; and *it* did come to pass so.    (KJV "and it was so")
                  03418   06212    0402          01961        03651

Genesis 1:31     And God had seen all which he had made, and behold much good,
                  0430    07200       0834      06213              03966   02896

             and *there* was evening and *there* was morning, the sixth time.
                      01961   06153        01961   01242       08345   03117

## This Study's "Good English" Translation of Genesis One With Strong's Numbers for the Translated Hebrew Words.

| Genesis 2:1 | And the heavens and the earth and all hosts had been finished. |
|---|---|
| | 08064  0776  06635  03615 |

Genesis 2:2   And God  had finished  by the seventh  time  the work  which  he made,
                              0430     06213            07637    0311    04399           06213

                        and he had ceased   in the seventh  time   from all   the work   he had made.
                            07673        07637   03117          04399     06213

Genesis 2:3   And God  had blessed  the seventh  time  and had sanctified it,
                            0430     01288     07637    03117     06942

                        because  in it  he had ceased  from all  the work  which  God  had created  for making.
                        03588      07673          04399         0430    01254      6213

Genesis 2:4   These *are* the generated results of  the heavens  and the earth of  his creating (bara),
                            0428        08435         08064         0776       01254

                        at the time of  Yahweh  God  making  the earth  and the heavens.
                          03117     03068   0430   06213   0776      08064

# APPENDIXES

# AND

# VERSE

# INDEXES

# Appendix 1:

# English Transliterations Used in the Text for Hebrew Words

The transliterations are listed in the order they first occur by verses of first occurrence. The transliterations used in the text are not identical to Strong's, and in many cases their use preceded the transliterations favored by Strong.

| English Transliterations used in text | Hebrew root word | Root meaning, (Translation in verse) (of first use.) | Strong's number | First Use | Strong's English Transliterations | Strong's Phonetic Pronunciation |
|---|---|---|---|---|---|---|
| Elohim | אֱלֹהִים | God | 430 | 1:1 | 'elohiym | el-o-heem' |
| bara | בָּרָא | create (had created) | 1254 | 1:1 | bara' | baw-raw' |
| shamayim | שָׁמַיִם | heavens (the heavens) | 8064 | 1:1 | shamayim | shaw-mah'-yim |
| erets | אֶרֶץ | land, earth, ground (and the Earth) | 776 | 1:1 | 'erets | eh'-rets |
| haya | הָיָה | be, exist, become (had existed) | 1961 | 1:2 | hayah | haw-yaw |
| tohu | תֹהוּ | tohu (unsuitable for human life) See discussion pages 43-46. | 8414 | 1:2 | tohuw | to'-hoo |
| bohu | בֹהוּ | bohu (empty of human life) See discussion pages 43-46. | 922 | 1:2 | bohuw | bo'-hoo |
| tehom | תְהוֹם | deep | 8415 | 1:2 | t@howm | teh-home' |
| ore | אוֹר | light | 216 | 1:3 | 'owr | ore |
| tob | טוֹב | good | 2896 | 1:4 | towb | tobe |
| yom | יוֹם | daytime and time, "time" in the concluding phrases See discussions pages 60-70. | 3117 | 1:5 | yowm | yome |
| ereb | עֶרֶב | evening | 6153 | 1:5 | `ereb | eh'-reb |
| boqer | בֹּקֶר | morning | 1242 | 1:5 | boqer | bo'-ker |
| raqia | רָקִיעַ | sky | 7549 | 1:6 | raqiya` | raw-kee'-ah |
| asah | עָשָׂה | make, fashion (had made) | 6213 | 1:7 | `asah | aw-saw' |
| dasha | דָּשָׁא | shall sprout | 1876 | 1:11 | dasha | daw-shaw' |
| deshe' | דֶּשֶׁא | grass | 1877 | 1:11 | deshe' | deh'-sheh |
| 'eseb | עֵשֶׂב | grass (plants) | 6212 | 1:11 | `eseb | eh'seb |

| English Transliterations used in text | Hebrew root word | Root meaning, (Translation in verse) (of first use.) | Strong's number | First Use | Strong's English Transliterations | Strong's Phonetic Pronunciation |
|---|---|---|---|---|---|---|
| 'ets | עֵץ | tree | 6086 | 1:11 | `ets | ates |
| min | מִין | kind | 4327 | 1:11 | miyn | meen |
| sharats | שָׁרַץ | swarm, teem; a verb (shall swarm) | 8317 | 1:20 | sharats | shaw-rats' |
| sherets | שֶׁרֶץ | swarm, teem: a noun (swarmer) | 8318 | 1:20 | sherets | sheh'-rets |
| nephesh | נֶפֶשׁ | nephesh | 5315 | 1:20 | nephesh | neh'-fesh |
| ḥayyâ | חַיָּה | living (The Word Book of the Old Testament lists this as the root of Strong's "chay" below.) | 2416 | 1:20 | pronounce "khay-yah" or chay-ya (Strong's) | |
| ḥay or chay | חַי | living (This is the same word as "chay-yah" listed above.) | 2416 | 1:20 | khay or chay (Strong's) | khah'-ee |
| 'owpf | עוֹף | flyer | 5775 | 1:20 | `owph | ofe |
| 'owpf | עוּף | shall fly (verb of 5775) | 5774 | 1:20 | `uwph | oof |
| tanniym | תַּנִּים | "tanniym" | 8577 | 1:21 | tanniym | tan-neen' |
| ramas | רָמַשׂ | creep or creeping i.e., a verb | 7430 | 1:21 | ramas | raw-mas' |
| remes | רֶמֶשׂ | creeper or creeping thing, i.e., a noun | 7431 | 1:24 | remes | reh'-mes |
| adamah | אֲדָמָה | cultivatable land | 127 | 1:25 | adamah | ad-aw-maw' |
| adam | אָדָם | adam | 120 | 1:26 | 'adam | aw-dawm' |
| dag, or dagah | דָּג, or דָּגָה | fish | 1710 | 1:26 | dagah | daw-gaw' |
| shabat | שָׁבַת | cease (and had ceased) | 7673 | 2:2 | shabath | shaw-bath' |
| Yahweh | יְהוָה | Yahweh | 3068 | 2:4 | Y@hovah | yeh-ho-vaw' |
| yatsar | יָצַר | See discussion pages 32-36. | 3335 | not used | yatsar | yaw-tsar' |

## Table of Hebrew Letters with Name and Strong's Articulation

Note: Some Hebrew letters are written using a modified form when the letter appears as the final letter of a word.

|    | Hebrew Letter | Name of Letter | Strong's Phonetic Pronunciation |
|----|---|---|---|
| 1  | א | 'Aleph | aw'-lef |
| 2  | ב | Bêyth | bayth |
| 3  | ג | Gîymel | ghee'-mel |
| 4  | ד | Dâleth | daw'-leth |
| 5  | ה | Hê' | hay |
| 6  | ו | Vâv | vawv |
| 7  | ז | Zayin | zah'-yin |
| 8  | ח | Chêyth | khayth |
| 9  | ט | Têyth | tayth |
| 10 | י | Yôwd | yode |
| 11 | כ | Kaph | caf |
| 12 | ל | Lâmed | law'-med |
| 13 | מ ( final ם ) | Mêm | mame |
| 14 | נ ( final ן ) | Nûwn | noon |
| 15 | ס | Çâmek | saw'-mek |
| 16 | ע | 'Ayin | ah'-yin |
| 17 | פ or פ (final ף ) | Pê' or Phê' | pay or fay |
| 18 | צ ( final ץ ) | Tsâdêy | tsaw-day' |
| 19 | ק | Qôwph | cofe |
| 20 | ר | Rêysh | raysh |
| 21 | שׂ or שׁ | Sîyn or Shîyn | seen or sheen |
| 22 | ת or ת | Thâv or Tâv | thawv or tawv |

# Appendix 2:
# Strong's Numbers and Hebrew Root Word Phonetic Representations

This listing of the Strong's numbers for words used in Genesis One is to facilitate the reader's access to other information. The words and numbers are listed in order of first occurrence in Genesis One. Note that there are, in some cases, more than one Strong's number for an individual Hebrew root word.

| Strong's number | Verse of first occurrence | Hebrew Root Word | Meaning in text (Text's First Translation) | Strong's English Transliteration of Hebrew Root Word | Strong's Phonetic Pronunciation of Hebrew Root Word |
|---|---|---|---|---|---|
| 7225 | 1:1 | רֵאשִׁית | beginning, (In beginning) | re'shiyth | ray-sheeth' |
| 430 | 1:1 | אֱלֹהִים | God | 'elohiym | el-o-heem' |
| 1254 | 1:1 | ברא | create, (had created) | bara' | baw-raw' |
| 853 | 1:1 | אֵת | (direct object marker) | 'eth | ayth |
| 8064 | 1:1 | שָׁמַיִם | heavens, (the heavens) | shamayim | shaw-mah'-yim |
| 776 | 1:1 | אֶרֶץ | land, earth;(and the Earth) | 'erets | eh'-rets |
| 1961 | 1:2 | הָיָה | be, exist, become; (had existed) | hayah | haw-yaw |
| 8414 | 1:2 | תֹּהוּ | tohu, (tohu) | tohuw | to'-hoo |
| 922 | 1:2 | בֹּהוּ | bohu, (bohu) | bohuw | bo'-hoo |
| 2822 | 1:2 | חֹשֶׁךְ | darkness | choshek | kho-shek' |
| 6440 | 1:2 | פָּנִים | surface or "face of", (surface) | paniym | paw-neem' |
| 8415 | 1:2 | תְּהוֹם | deep | t@howm | teh-home' |
| 7307 | 1:2 | רוּחַ | spirit | ruwach | roo'-akh |
| 7363 | 1:2 | רָחַף | moving | rachaph | raw-khaf' |
| 5921 | 1:2 | עַל | over | `al {al} | |
| 4325 | 1:2 | מַיִם | waters | mayim | mah'-yim |
| 559 | 1:3 | אָמַר | said | 'amar | |
| 216 | 1:3 | אוֹר | light | 'owr | ore |
| 7200 | 1:3 | רָאָה | see, (had seen) | ra'ah | raw-aw' |
| 3588 | 1:4 | כִּי | as | kiy | kee |
| 2896 | 1:4 | טוֹב | good | towb | tobe |
| 914 | 1:4 | בָּדַל | separate, (had separated) | badal | baw-dal' |
| 996 | 1:4 | בֵּין | between | beyn | bane |
| 7121 | 1:5 | קָרָא | call, name; (had called) | qara' | kaw-raw' |
| 3117 | 1:5 | יוֹם | "daytime" also "time" as in Genesis 1:5 | yowm | yome |
| 3915 | 1:5 | לַיִל | "nighttime" | layil | lah'-yil |
| 6153 | 1:5 | עֶרֶב | evening | 'ereb | eh'-reb |
| 1242 | 1:5 | בֹּקֶר | morning | boqer | bo'-ker |
| 259 | 1:5 | אֶחָד | one | 'echad | ekh-awd' |
| 7549 | 1:6 | רָקִיעַ | sky | raqiya` | raw-kee'-ah |
| 7225 | 1:1 | רֵאשִׁית | beginning, (In beginning) | re'shiyth | ray-sheeth' |
| 6213 | 1:7 | עָשָׂה | had made | `asah | aw-saw' |
| 834 | 1:7 | אֲשֶׁר | those or "which" | 'asher | ash-er' |
| 8478 | 1:7 | תַּחַת | from under | tachath | takh'-ath |
| 3651 | 1:7 | כֵּן | between | ken | kane |
| 8145 | 1:8 | שֵׁנִי | second | sheniy | shay-nee' |
| 413 | 1:9 | אֶל | into | 'el | ale |

| Strong's number | Verse of first occurrence | Hebrew Root Word | Meaning in text (Text's First Translation) | Strong's English Transliteration of Hebrew Root Word | Strong's Phonetic Pronunciation of Hebrew Root Word |
|---|---|---|---|---|---|
| 4725 | 1:9 | מָקוֹם | place | maqowm | maw-kome' |
| 3004 | 1:9 | יַבָּשָׁה | dry | yabbashah | yab-baw-haw' |
| 4723 | 1:10 | מִקְוֶה | *the* gathered | miqveh | |
| 3220 | 1:10 | יָם | sea | yam | yawm |
| | | | (the plural is יָמִים "seas") | | |
| 1876 | 1:11 | דָּשָׁא | shall sprout | dasha | daw-shaw' |
| 1877 | 1:11 | דֶּשֶׁא | grass | deshe' | deh'-sheh |
| 6212 | 1:11 | עֵשֶׂב | grass (plants) | `eseb | eh'seb |
| 2232 | 1:11 | זָרַע | yielding | zara` | zaw-rah' |
| 2233 | 1:11 | זֶרַע | seed (seeding) | zera` | zeh'-rah |
| 6529 | 1:11 | פְּרִי | fruit | p@riy | per-ee' |
| 6086 | 1:11 | עֵץ | tree | `ets | ates |
| 4327 | 1:11 | מִין | kind | miyn | meen |
| 3318 | 1:12 | יָצָא | had brought forth | yatsa' | yaw-tsaw' |
| 799 | 1:13 | שְׁלִישִׁי | third | sh@liyshiy | shel-ee-shee' |
| 397 | 1:14 | מָאוֹר | lights, light source | ma'or | maw-ore' |
| 226 | 1:14 | אוֹת | signs | 'owth | oth |
| 4150 | 1:14 | מוֹעֵד | seasons | mow‘ed | mo-ade' |
| | | or מֹעֵד | | mo‘ed | mo-ade' |
| 8141 | 1:14 | שָׁנָה | years | shana | shaw-neh' |
| 215 | 1:15 | אוֹר | give light | 'owr | ore |
| 8147 | 1:16 | שְׁתַיִם | two | sh@nayim | shen-ah'-yim |
| 1419 | 1:16 | גָּדוֹל | lights | gadowl or gadol | gaw-dole' |
| | | or גְּדֹלָה | | | |
| 4475 | 1:16 | מֶמְשָׁלָה | rule | memshalah | mem-shaw-law' |
| 6996 | 1:16 | קָטָן | small | qatan or qaton | kaw-tawn' |
| | | or קָטֹן | | | kaw-tone' |
| 3556 | 1:16 | כּוֹכָב | stars | kowkab | ko-kawb' |
| 5414 | 1:17 | נָתַן | had given (set) | nathan | naw-than' |
| 7243 | 1:19 | רְבִיעִי | fourth | r@biy`iy | reb-ee-ee' |
| 8317 | 1:20 | שָׁרַץ | shall swarm | sharats | shaw-rats' |
| 8318 | 1:20 | שֶׁרֶץ | swarm | sherets | sheh'-rets |
| 5315 | 1:20 | נֶפֶשׁ | nephesh | nephesh | neh'-fesh |
| 2416 | 1:20 | חַי | living | chay | khah'-ee |
| 5775 | 1:20 | עוֹף | flyer | `owph | ofe |
| 5774 | 1:20 | עוּף | shall fly (verb of 5775) | uwph | oof |
| 8577 | 1:21 | תַּנִּים | "tanniym" | tanniym | tan-neen' |
| 7430 | 1:21 | רָמַשׂ | creeping (creep) | ramas | raw-mas' |
| 3671 | 1:21 | כָּנָף | wing | kanaph | kaw-nawf' |
| 1288 | 1:22 | בָּרַךְ | had blessed (bless) | barak | baw-rak' |

| Strongs number | Verse of first occurrence | Hebrew Root Word | Meaning in text (Text's First Translation) | Strong's English Transliteration of Hebrew Root Word | Strong's Phonetic Pronunciation of Hebrew Root Word |
|---|---|---|---|---|---|
| 6509 | 1:21 | פָּרָה | be fruitful | parah | paw-raw' |
| 7235 | 1:22 | רָבָה | multiply (increase) | rabah | raw-baw' |
| 4390 | 1:21 | מָלֵא | fill | male' | maw-lay' |
| 2549 | 1:23 | חֲמִישִׁי | fifth | chamiyshiy | kham-ee-shee' |
| 7431 | 1:24 | רֶמֶשׂ | creeper (creeping thing) | remes | reh'-mes |
| 929 | 1:24 | בְּהֵמָה | cattle | b@hemah | be-hay-maw' |
| 127 | 1:25 | אֲדָמָה | cultivatable land | adamah | ad-aw-maw' |
| 120 | 1:26 | אָדָם | adam | 'adam | aw-dawm' |
| 6754 | 1:26 | צֶלֶם | image | tselem | tseh'-lem |
| 1823 | 1:26 | דְּמוּת | likeness | d@muwth | dem-ooth' |
| 7287 | 1:26 | רָדָה | shall rule (rule) | radah | raw-daw' |
| 1710 | 1:26 | דָּגָה | fish | dagah | daw-gaw' |
| 2145 | 1:27 | זָכָר | male | zakar | zaw-kawr' |
| 5347 | 1:27 | נְקֵבָה | female | n@qebah | nek-ay-baw' |
| 3533 | 1:28 | כָּבַשׁ | subdue | kabash | kaw-bash' |
| 2009 | 1:29 | הִנֵּה | behold | hinneh | hin-nay' |
| 402 | 1:29 | אָכְלָה | food | 'oklah | ok-law' |
| 3418 | 1:30 | יֶרֶק | green | yereq | yeh'-rek |
| 3966 | 1:31 | מְאֹד | much | m@`od | meh-ode' |
| 8345 | 1:31 | שִׁשִּׁי | sixth | shishshiy | shish-shee' |
| 3615 | 2:1 | כָּלָה | had been finished | kalah | kaw-law' |
| 6635 | 2:1 | צָבָא or בָאָה | hosts | tsaba' or orts@ba'ah | tsaw-baw' |
| 7637 | 2:2 | שְׁבִיעִי or שְׁבִעִי | seventh | sh@biy`iy or sh@bi`iy | sheb-ee-ee' |
| 4399 | 2:2 | מְלָאכָה | work or business | m@la'kah | mel-aw-kaw' |
| 7673 | 2:2 | שָׁבַת | cease or "and had ceased" | shabath | shaw-bath' |
| 6942 | 2:3 | קָדַשׁ | sanctified or "and had sanctified" | qadash | kaw-dash' |
| 428 | 2:4 | אֵלֶּה | these *are* | 'el-leh | ale'-leh |
| 8435 | 2:4 | תּוֹלְדָה or תֹּלְדָה | generations | towl@dah or tol@dah | to-led-aw' |
| 3068 | 2:4 | יְהוָה | Yahweh | Y@hovah | yeh-ho-vaw' |

157

# Index of the Hebrew Text of Genesis 1:1 - Genesis 2:4

| Verse | Page of appearance of Hebrew verse | Verse | Page of appearance of Hebrew verse | Verse | Page of appearance of Hebrew verse |
|---|---|---|---|---|---|
| Genesis 1:1 | 15 | Genesis 1:13 | 101 | Genesis 1:25 | 122 |
| Genesis 1:2 | 24 | Genesis 1:14 | 102 | Genesis 1:26 | 123 |
| Genesis 1:3 | 54 | Genesis 1:15 | 103 | Genesis 1:27 | 124 |
| Genesis 1:4 | 56 | Genesis 1:16 | 104 | Genesis 1:28 | 125 |
| Genesis 1:5 | 58-59, 74-77 | Genesis 1:17 | 104 | Genesis 1:29 | 126 |
| Genesis 1:6 | 90 | Genesis 1:18 | 105 | Genesis 1:30 | 127 |
| Genesis 1:7 | 91 | Genesis 1:19 | 108 | Genesis 1:31 | 128 |
| Genesis 1:8 | 94 | Genesis 1:20 | 110, 113, 114 | Genesis 2:1 | 130 |
| Genesis 1:9 | 96 | Genesis 1:21 | 114 | Genesis 2:2 | 130 |
| Genesis 1:10 | 96 | Genesis 1:22 | 116 | Genesis 2:3 | 29, 132 |
| Genesis 1:11 | 97 | Genesis 1:23 | 117 | Genesis 2:4 | 61, 133 |
| Genesis 1:12 | 97 | Genesis 1:24 | 121 | | |

# Index of Referenced Verses  (Not the verses of Genesis 1:1-Genesis 2:4)

| Verse | Page where verse appears | Verse | Page where verse appears | Verse | Page where verse appears |
|---|---|---|---|---|---|
| Genesis 2:7 | 111 | Leviticus 8:33-35 | 85 | Jeremiah 2:13 | 167 |
| Genesis 2:17 | 61 | Leviticus 11:21-22 | 120 | Jeremiah 4:23-28 | 21 |
| Genesis 2:19 | 113 | Leviticus 11:29 | 118 | Jeremiah 15:9 | 165 |
| Genesis 2:23 | 68 | Leviticus 11:41-42 | 119, 168 | Jeremiah 52:3 | 48 |
| Genesis 2:24-25 | 25 | Leviticus 11:46 | 119 | | |
| Genesis 3:1 | 25 | Leviticus 20:25 | 119 | Ezekiel 15:2-3 | 100 |
| Genesis 3:2 | 25 | Leviticus 23:27 | 67 | Ezekiel 30:3 | 62 |
| Genesis 4:1 | 37 | Leviticus 23:27-32 | 85 | | |
| Genesis 4:2 | 37 | Leviticus 23:32 | 67, 84 | Amos 5:14 | 95 |
| Genesis 6:14 | 123 | Leviticus 25:2 | 77 | Amos 9:11 | 63 |
| Genesis 6:20 | 119 | Leviticus 25:2-8 | 165 | Amos 9:12 | 63 |
| Genesis 7:4 | 82 | | | | |
| Genesis 7:11 | 81, 83 | Deuteronomy 6:4 | 161 | 2 Maccabees 7:28 | 51 |
| Genesis 7:12 | 81, 82 | Deuteronomy 17:3 | 58 | | |
| Genesis 7:14 | 119, 120 | Deuteronomy 31:17 | 63 | Matthew 4:2 | 62 |
| Genesis 7:17 | 81, 82, 93 | Deuteronomy 32:2 | 100 | | |
| Genesis 7:24 | 81, 82 | | | Luke 18:7 | 165 |
| Genesis 8:3 | 83 | Joshua 2:6 | 100 | | |
| Genesis 8:6 | 83 | | | John 1:1 | 20, 50 |
| Genesis 9:3-4 | 119 | Judges 6:37 | 95 | John 1:1-3 | 50 |
| Genesis 9:10 | 112 | Judges 6:38 | 95 | John 4:24 | 168 |
| Genesis 10:10 | 19 | Judges 9:12 | 101 | | |
| Genesis 10:25 | 163 | | | Acts 2:20 | 165 |
| Genesis 16:1 | 38 | Samuel 8:10-11 | 125 | Acts 9:24 | 165 |
| Genesis 16:2 | 38 | | | | |
| Genesis 18:1 | 64 | 1Kings 11:16 | 162 | Galatians 4:9-11 | 103 |
| Genesis 18:10 | 12 | | | | |
| Genesis 18:14 | 12 | 2Kings 15:12 | 72, 95 | Colossians 1:15 | 168 |
| Genesis 19:26 | 47 | | | Colossians 2:16-17 | 65 |
| Genesis 19:33-34 | 85 | Nehemiah 1:6 | 66 | | |
| Genesis 19:37 | 64 | Nehemiah 4:9 | 66 | 1 Timothy 1:17 | 168 |
| Genesis 21:1 | 12, 13, 39 | Nehemiah 6:3 | 131 | | |
| Genesis 21:2 | 39 | Nehemiah 13:15-17 | 86 | Hebrews 4:9-11 | 65 |
| Genesis 21:34 | 165 | Nehemiah 13:19 | 87 | Hebrews 8:4-5 | 65 |
| Genesis 22:1-4 | 165 | Nehemiah 12:46 | 162 | Hebrews 10:1 | 65 |
| Genesis 26:19 | 167 | | | Hebrews 11:3 | 50, 51 |
| Genesis 24:64 | 93 | Esther 4:16 | 66 | | |
| Genesis 28:10 | 71 | | | 2 Peter 3:8 | 62, 165 |
| Genesis 28:11 | 71 | Job 1:1 | 20 | | |
| Genesis 29:34 | 68 | Job 38:9 | 55, 107 | | |
| Genesis 40:6-7 | 64 | | | | |
| | | Psalm 1:1 | 30, 36 | | |
| Exodus 1:7 | 118 | Psalm 78:27 | 120 | | |
| Exodus 3:5 | 93 | Psalm 90:3-6 | 68 | | |
| Exodus 8:3 | 118 | Psalm 90:4 | 62, 165 | | |
| Exodus 9:23-24 | 47 | Psalm 148:7 | 18 | | |
| Exodus 10:6 | 64 | Psalm 148:10 | 120 | | |
| Exodus 10:21 | 90 | Psalm 115:15 | 18 | | |
| Exodus 12:6 | 84 | Psalm 115:16 | 18 | | |
| Exodus 12:18 | 84 | | | | |
| Exodus 12:38 | 79 | Proverbs 8:23 | 52 | | |
| Exodus 13:21 | 66 | | | | |
| Exodus 15:5 | 161 | Ecc. 3:11 | 52 | | |
| Exodus 15:10-12 | 161 | | | | |
| Exodus 16:12-13 | 49 | Isaiah 11:10-11 | 63 | | |
| Exodus 16:26 | 78 | Isaiah 23:15 | 63 | | |
| Exodus 20:11 | 28, 76 | Isaiah 34:8 | 61 | | |
| Exodus 23:12 | 131 | Isaiah 41:4 | 52 | | |
| Exodus 23:19 | 19 | Isaiah 43:6 | 35 | | |
| Exodus 31:16 | 77 | Isaiah 43:7 | 35 | | |
| Exodus 31:17 | 77 | Isaiah 45:7 | 30, 36 | | |
| Exodus 34:10 | 34, 35 | Isaiah 46:10 | 52 | | |
| Exodus 34:28 | 61 | Isaiah 40:21 | 52 | | |
| | | Isaiah 51:10 | 161 | | |
| | | Isaiah 65:17 | 34 | | |

**End Notes:**

1. R. H. Kennett, *A Short Account of the Hebrew Tenses* (Cambridge, Massachusetts: At the University Press, 1901), page 1.

2. Chinese is an example of a present day language where the verb form does not express tense. Modern Hebrew is based on the Hebrew of the Mishna, circa. 200 A.D. Mishnaic Hebrew had become tensed. By this time Israel had been under the influence of Greek culture and language for about 500 years. Modern Hebrew differs from biblical Hebrew by having tensed verb forms and a different word order in the sentence.

3. James Strong, *Strong's Exhaustive Concordance of the Bible* (New York: 1894) (Tulsa, Oklahoma: American Christian College, no date).

4. R. L. Harris, et al., *Theological Word Book of the Old Testament* (Chicago, Illinois: Moody Press, 1980). In two volumes. This book also lists 514 Aramaic words, resulting in a total word list of 3,067 numbered words. If the Hebrew root words and the Aramaic are considered together, the number of biblical root words could be described as about 3,100. It is the effect of the small number of words which is of importance, not the precise number.

5. *Merriam-Webster's Collegiate Dictionary,* 10th ed. (Springfield, Massachusetts: Merriam-Webster, Inc., An Encyclopaedia Britannica Company, 1999). The claim on the back cover of the dictionary is, "Entries present correct spellings for more than 160,000 words and phrases." The back cover claim was used at face value for the illustration. It provides a reasonable qualitative sense of the size of the languages. The actual total English language is several times larger than the number of words in this dictionary.

6. The date range in the text is approximate. Waltke and O'Connor provide a good review.

    Bruce K. Waltke and M. O'Connor, *An Introduction to Biblical Hebrew Syntax* (Winona Lake, Indiana: Eisenbrauns, 1990). The chapter entitled "History of the Study of Hebrew Grammar," pages 31-43, provides the review.

7. In this case there is an "assumed" three-letter root שמה which is then indicated to have dropped the final ה. Assumed roots are indicated in the *Theological Wordbook of the Old Testament* for some words which have no clear attestation of a three-letter root in biblical Hebrew. The assumed root seemingly allows the word to be systematized within the three-letter word root system ascribed to biblical Hebrew by grammarians.

8. In קל , the ל is roughly equivalent to the English "L." The ק is usually represented by the English "Q" and has a sound roughly equivalent to the English "K." This results in קל being pronounced like "call" The other Hebrew verb patterns are usually described by the additions which are made to the Hebrew root קטל (QTL) in the making of those forms. For example, the Niphal for the third person masculine singular of קטל is נקטל. The third person masculine singular represents a "he" acting. The prefixed נ is the letter "nun," which corresponds to the "N" in Niphal. C. L. Seow's *A Grammar for Biblical Hebrew* (Nashville, Tennessee: Abingdon Press, 1995) can be consulted for details. This study will not attempt to explain the formation of the verb forms, but will often identify such forms. They will be identified when it is important for the reader to know that something other than simple direct action is being described.

9. Menahem Mansoor, *Biblical Hebrew Step-by-Step,* Vol. 1, 2nd ed. (Grand Rapids, Michigan: Baker House, 1979), page 70. Mansoor suggests that this word be translated "study." When contrasted with the more usual translation "learn," it provides an example of the nuance which can be added by a translator's choice of words. The word לָמַד also means "teach" when used in the Piel verb form. The KJV translates לָמַד as "teach" (56 times) and as "learn" (22 times).

10. Chinese is one example. Elements of the Slavic language system are another example. Waltke and O'Connor, op.cit, page 348, state, "Hebrew aspectual marking is similar to the Slavic imperfective/perfective system, ... . "

11. W. D. Mounce, *Basics of Biblical Greek* (Grand Rapids, Michigan: Zondervan Publishing House, 1993), pages 119, 145, 177.

12. The punctiliar aspect is not usually discussed in English grammars. It is a kind of action considered under the categories of aspect and aktionsart. The punctiliar is important in the translation of biblical Greek and is discussed in grammars of biblical Greek. An internet search of "punctiliar Greek" will yield a considerable number of responses.

13. W. D. Mounce, *Basics of Biblical Greek* (Grand Rapids, Michigan: Zondervan Publishing House, 1993), page 190 (section 22.2), pages 118-119 (section 15.6-7).

14. Robert Young, *Young's Literal Translation of the Bible* (Grand Rapids, MI: Baker Book House Company, reprinted 1995, originally published 1898).

    Robert Young, *Young's Analytical Concordance to the Bible*, first published 1879, presently available as a reprint edition published by Hendrickson Publishers, Peabody, MA.

15. In connection with the Trinity, it is interesting to consider the Hebrew of Deuteronomy 6:4:

    **Deuteronomy 6:4**

    | אֶחָד | יְהוָה | אֱלֹהֵינוּ | יְהוָה | יִשְׂרָאֵל | שְׁמַע | ← Hebrew starts here. |
    |---|---|---|---|---|---|---|
    | one | Yahweh (singular) | our Elohim (plural) | Yahweh (singular) | Israel | Hear | ← Start English here. |

    The word אֱלֹהֵינוּ is the word אֱלֹהִים modified by replacing the suffix ם with נו to indicate the plural pronoun "our." In the KJV the singular יְהוָה (Yahweh) is translated LORD and the plural אֱלֹהֵינוּ (our Elohim) is translated "our GOD" yielding:

    Deuteronomy 6:4  Hear, O Israel: *The* LORD our God *is* one LORD:
                                                (singular)   (plural)   (singular)

16. R. L. Harris, et al., *Theological Word Book of the Old Testament* (Chicago, Illinois: Moody Press, 1980), vol. 2: page 935, word number 2407.

17. תְּהוֹם "deep" (teh-home') is used 36 times in the Bible. In Genesis 1:2 it is used in "face of the deep." The word "deep" refers to bodies of water and to the sea. Exodus 15:5 is an example describing the drowning of Pharaoh's army following the crossing of the sea. תְּהֹמֹת is a form of the Hebrew word תְּהוֹם "deep."

    KJV Exodus 15:5  The depths (תְּהֹמֹת) have covered them; they sank into the bottom as a stone.

    Following Exodus 15:5 there is another of the rare uses of "erets" used in a manner including the surface waters, the sea, and the deep. After Pharaoh's army has been said to have sunk in "mighty waters" they are again in poetic parallel said to have been swallowed by the Earth (erets).

    KJV Exodus 15:10    Thou didst blow with thy wind, the sea covered them:
                                    they sank as lead in the mighty waters.

    KJV Exodus 15:11    Who *is* like unto thee, O LORD, among the gods? who *is* like thee, glorious in
                                    holiness, fearful *in* praises, doing wonders?

    KJV Exodus 15:12    Thou stretchedst out thy right hand, the אֶרֶץ earth swallowed them.

    The equivalency of deep and water is again clear in Isaiah 51:10.

    KJV Isaiah 51:10    *Art* thou not it which hath dried the sea, the waters of the great תְּהוֹם deep;
                                   that hath made the depths of the sea a way for the ransomed to pass over?

18. That the translators of the Septuagint (LXX) sometimes translated meaning-for-meaning can be seen in Genesis 2:2 where their translation (in English) is:

    LXX (in English) Genesis 2:2    And God finished on the **sixth** day his works which he made,

    KJV Genesis 2:2    And on the seventh day God ended his work which he had made;

    YLT Genesis 2:2    and God completeth by the seventh day His work which He hath made,

    Arguably, translating the "sixth day" instead of the "seventh day" had purpose. The argued purpose being to avoid the possibility of a Greek reader inferring, from the Greek aorist tense, that God had started to work on the seventh day and then had ceased working. Recognizing that this type of translation exists in the Septuagint, the Septuagint translation of Genesis 1:2 becomes understandable. In the Septuagint the words "tohu and bohu" are translated by the words "unseen and unformed." The word translating the Hebrew "erets" is the Greek word γη which has the meanings of ground, land, and earth. Earth is one of the four Greek elements of fire, water, air, and earth. The ancient Greeks viewed these as being combined to form the different substances which we can see and touch.

19. The verses which refer to the crossings are: Exod. 14:16, Exod. 14:22, Exod. 14:29, Exod. 15:19, Jos. 4:22, Neh. 9:11, and Ps. 66:6. The word יַבָּשָׁה "dry" appears in these verses as בַּיַּבָּשָׁה which has the prefix בַּ translated "on." The word יַבָּשָׁה (Strongs # 3004) is the word יָבֵשׁ "dry" to which the feminine singular ending ה has been added.

    Other appearances of יַבָּשָׁה "dry" as הַיַּבָּשָׁה "the dry" (the word appearing in Genesis 1:9) occur in Exodus 4:9, Jonah 1:9, Jonah 1:13, and Jonah 2:10. Jonah 1:13 and Jonah 2:10 refer to the shore where the land rises out of the water of the sea. Exodus 4:9 refers to water which Moses was to take from the Nile and pour it out upon "the dry." The agriculture of Egypt was based on crops grown on land that was flooded by the Nile every year. The crops were grown on this land as it subsequently dried.

20. In other verses the KJV does not insert "in" into the translation of כִּי שֵׁשֶׁת "for six." This is shown in the example of 1 Kings 11:16. Only the first six Hebrew words are shown below. The translation below the Hebrew word שֵׁשֶׁת is "six of" because this word is in the construct relationship with respect to the following word חֳדָשִׁים "months." The KJV English translation does not include the "of."

    KJV 1 Kings 11:16   (For six months did Joab remain there with all Israel, until he had cut off every male in Edom:)

    | 1 Kings 11:16 | כִּי | שֵׁשֶׁת | חֳדָשִׁים | יָשַׁב | שָׁם | יוֹאָב |
    |---|---|---|---|---|---|---|
    | | For | six of | months | did remain | there | Joab |

    The preposition בְּ "in" does appear in the Hebrew of other verses. This shows that the word "in" is not to be inserted into a translation unless the preposition בְּ actually appears in the Hebrew. The example of Nehemiah 12:46 is shown below. The plural of the word יוֹם "yom" is יָמִים = יָמ + יִ , which in this case drops the final ם of the plural ending יִם and becomes יְמֵי . Only the first six Hebrew words of the verse are shown. The "of" again comes from the Hebrew construct relationship.

    KJV Nehemiah 12:46    **For in the days** of David and Asaph of old *there were* chief of the singers, and songs of praise and thanksgiving unto God.

    | Nehemiah 12:46 | (1) | כִּי | בִּימֵי | דָוִיד | וְאָסָף | מִקֶּדֶם | (רֹאשׁ) |
    |---|---|---|---|---|---|---|---|
    | | | For | in days of | David | and Asaph | of old | |

The following example of Genesis 10:25 is similar to that of Nehemiah 12:46. In this case the final ו of the בְיָמָיו word represents the pronoun "his."

KJV Genesis 10:25      (1) And unto Eber were born two sons: the name of one *was* Peleg;
(2) for in his days was the earth divided; and his brother's name *was* Joktan.

Genesis 10:25    (2)   כִּי   בְיָמָיו   נִפְלְגָה   הָאָרֶץ
                             for   in days his   was divided   the land

21. The 1611 KJV has a margin note "† Hebr. created to make." This means that the translators of the KJV were aware the Hebrew differed significantly from the English. The margin notes have generally been removed from the modern KJV Bibles.

22. Henry M. Morris, *The Genesis Record* (Grand Rapids, Michigan: Baker Books, 1976).

On page 42, Morris states ". . . , the primeval creation of heaven and earth in the beginning was the first act of the first day of the six days, . . . ".

23. Ziony Zevit, *The Anterior Construction In Classical Hebrew* (The Society of Biblical Literature, 1998), page 7.

24. While variations of this argument are made by various people, the sequence shown in the text can be found in the book *Unformed and Unfilled: A Critique of the Gap Theory*. The three points which are discussed are found in Chapter 3, "The Grammar of Genesis 1:2."

Weston W. Fields, *Unformed and Unfilled: A Critique of the Gap Theory* ( Collinsville, Illinois: Burgner Enterprises, 1976).

25. E. Kautzsch and A. E. Crowley, *Gesenius' Hebrew Grammar* (Oxford, England: Clarendon Press, 1910). Edited and enlarged by E. Kautzsch; 2nd English edition by A. E. Crowley.

26. Thomas O. Lambdin, *Introduction To Biblical Hebrew* (Charles Scribner's and Sons, New York, 1971). The discussion is in section 132, "Clauses joined with ו *we-*," pages 162 and 164.

27. S. R. Driver, *A Treatise on the Use of the Tenses in Hebrew and Some Other Syntactical Questions* (Oxford at The Clarendon Press, 1881), page 102, section 76. A reprint edition is currently available. This title and the reference location in it is: A Treatise on the Use of the Tenses in Hebrew and Some Other Syntactical Questions, S. R. Driver (Eerdmans Publishing Co., Grand Rapids, MI, 1998), (first pub. 1874), page 84, section 76.

28. Alveriero Niccacci, *The Syntax of the Verb in Classical Hebrew Prose*, W. G. E. Watson translator, Journal for the Study of the Old Testament Supplement series 86, Sheffield Academic Press, 1990.

29. In *Biblical Hebrew and Discourse Linguistics* the analysis of Genesis 1:1-2 and its relation to the narrative which starts with Genesis 1:3 is found in his second article, "Analysis of Biblical Narrative," on pages 182-184.

30. H. B. Swete, *The Old Testament in Greek According to the Septuagint* (Cambridge University Press, 1887). Available on the internet in digital facsimile edition in the Christian Classics Ethereal Library, Grand Rapids, MI. http:/www.ccel.org/s/swete/lxx1/htm/i.htm

Another commonly available source of the Greek Septuagint is: Alfred Rahlfs, ed., *LXT – LXX Septuaginta (LXT)* (Old Greek Jewish Scriptures) (Stuttgart, Germany: Wurttembergische Bibelstalt/Deutsche Bibelgesellschaft) (German Bible Society), copyright 1935.

31. Wm. Whiston, trans., *The Complete Works of Josephus* (W. Borradaile, New York, 1828). Also currently available online at the Wesley Center for Applied Theology, http://wesley.nnu.edu/josephus/
*The Complete Works of Josephus* can also be found in reprint editions. One of the most easily found is: Wm. Whiston, trans., *The Complete Works of Josephus* (Grand Rapids, Michigan: Kregel Publications, 1981), Book I, 25. In Antiquities of the Jews, Book 1, page 25.

    Other references are:
    The works of Flavius Josephus: comprising the antiquities of the Jews; A History of the Jewish Wars; and Life of Flavius Josephus, Josephus, Flavius (Porter & Coates, Philadelphia, 1870).

    *The genuine works of Flavius Josephus containing five books of the Antiquities of the Jews: to which are prefixed three dissertations*, Josephus, Flavius (Printed for Evert Duyckinck, John Tiebout, and M. & W. Ward, New-York, 1810).

32. See End Note 31 above.

33. J. W. Etheridge, trans., *The Targums of Onkelos and Jonathan Ben Uzziel On the Pentateuch With The Fragments of the Jerusalem Targum From the Chaldee*, First Published 1862. Currently available on the internet at http://www.tulane.edu/~ntcs/pj/psjon.htm

34. M. Aberbach and B. Grossfeld, *Targum Onkelos To Genesis* (Denver, CO: Ktav Publishing House, 1995), page 20.

35. See End Note 33 above.

36. John Calvin, *Commentary on Genesis,* trans. and ed. John King (Calvin Translation Society Edition, 1847), Volume 1, Chapters 1-23: Latin ed., 1554. 1st English ed. 1578.

    Note: The first six words have been purposely inserted in untranslated Latin. The Latin words are the words which Calvin used in his translation and in the commentary. Calvin wrote the commentary in Latin. John King, when translating the commentary, inserts the KJV "And the earth was without form and void" as a translation of "Terra autem erat informis et inanis." This could lead the English reader to think that Calvin endorsed the "formless" of the later versions and to not understand the remainder of the comment about "tohu" and "bohu."

37. Op. cit. See reference 36 above. The text of the edition (Grand Rapids, MI: Christian Classics Ethereal Library, 1999-11-10, v1.0, URL 1999-11-10 ) is currently available online at http://www.ccel.org/c/calvin/comment3/comm_vol01/htm/vii.htm

38  Jonathan A. Goldstein, *2 Maccabees*, The Anchor Bible, vol. 41a (Doubleday, 1984), page 83.

39. Edward J. Young, *Studies In Genesis One* (Phillipsburg, NJ: P&R Publishing, 1964), page 5.

    "A disjunctive accent marks a major, intermediate, or minor pause..." C. L. Seow, *A Grammar for Biblical Hebrew* (Nashville, Tennessee: Abingdon Press, 1995), page 64. Not all published Hebrew texts of the Bible contain all the accent markings which are in the ancient manuscripts.

40. Alexander Heidel, *The Babylonian Genesis* (U. Chicago Press, 1963 paperback ed.), page 92, and pages 89-96. Heidel noted that עוֹלָם "olam" (eternity) also appears without the article "ה," and is not in the construct sequence which indicates "of" in Hebrew sentences.

41. W. D. Mounce, *Basics of Biblical Greek* (Grand Rapids, Michigan: Zondervan Publishing House, 1993), page 4, and page 19.

42. C. D. Yonge, trans., *The Works of Philo Judaeus, the Contemporary of Josephus*, tr. from the Greek (London: H. G. Bohn, 1854). Note: The (i.e.,"six yom") is an explanatory insertion added by this book.

    This is more easily found in a reprint edition: C.D. Yonge, trans., *The Works of Philo* (Peabody, Massachusetts, Hendrickson Publishing, 1993), "On Creation," page 4.

43. Additional examples are given below. The ending ς is taken to be a genitive singular in these verses.

    KJV Luke 18:7    And shall not God avenge his own elect, which cry ἡμέρας (day) and νυκτός (night) unto Him, though he bear long with them?

    KJV Acts 9:24    But their laying await was known of Saul.
    And they watched the gates ἡμέρας (day) and νυκτὸς (night) to kill him.

The word ἡμέραν is also used in Acts 2:20 in a quotation from Joel 2:31 concerning "yom" of the Lord.

    KJV Acts 2:20    The sun shall be turned into darkness, and the moon into blood,
    before that great and notable ἡμέραν (day) of the Lord come:

44. Hipparchus was a Greek astronomer who is thought to have died in approximately 127 B.C. His introduction of the word (νυχθήμερον) "nuchthemeron" added explicitness in references to the 24-hour time cycle. We do this today with the English word "day" by using augmented terms such as "24-hour day" and "eight-hour day." The Greek word ἡμέρα "hemera" was used to refer to the "daytime," a 24-hour period, and to longer periods of "time." The use in 2 Peter 3:8 is not an explicit reference to a 24-hour day. ἡμέρα "hemera" is used in the same manner as the Hebrew word "yom" used in the parallel passage of Psalm 90:4. In Psalm 90:4 the Hebrew uses כְּיוֹם "like yom" which the KJV translates "as yesterday." The contrast is used to show that the eternal God does not view the passage of time as a limitation.

45. KJV Leviticus 25:2-8
    25:2    Speak unto the children of Israel, and say unto them, When ye come into the land which I give you, then shall the land keep a sabbath unto the LORD.
    25:3    Six years thou shalt sow thy field, and six years thou shalt prune thy vineyard, and gather in the fruit thereof;
    25:4    But in the seventh year shall be a sabbath of rest unto the land, a sabbath for the LORD: thou shalt neither sow thy field, nor prune thy vineyard.
    25:5    That which groweth of its own accord of thy harvest thou shalt not reap, neither gather the grapes of thy vine undressed: *for* it is a year of rest unto the land.
    25:6    And the sabbath of the land shall be meat for you; for thee, and for thy servant, and for thy maid, and for thy hired servant, and for thy stranger that sojourneth with thee,

46. Exodus 21:2; Deuteronomy 15:12-15

47. Leviticus 25:10; Leviticus 25:39-42

48. Jeremiah 15:9 uses יוֹמָם "by yom" either to indicate the daytime or a longer period of time.

    KJV Jeremiah 15:9    She that hath borne seven languisheth: she hath given up the ghost;
    her sun is gone down while *it was* yet day:
    she hath been ashamed and confounded: and the residue of them will I
    deliver to the sword before their enemies, saith the LORD.

49. E. A. Wallis Budge, *A Hieroglyphic Vocabulary to The Theban Recension of the Book of the Dead* (London: Kegan Paul, Trench, Trubner & Co., 1911), page 195. The four hieroglyphic words illustrating the effect of the determinatives are listed as equivalent to the English spelling "nu."

50. In Genesis 21:34 Abraham is said to sojourn in the vicinity of Beersheba, in the land of the Philistines. Then in Genesis 22:1-4 the journey of Abraham is related. The "crow's fly" distance from Beersheba to Jerusalem is about 44 miles, and the journey required three days. About 14 crow's fly miles per day. The offering of Isaac is usually considered to be on or near the Temple Mount in Jerusalem. The "crow's fly" distance from Beersheba to Bethel is about 55 miles, which leads to an estimate of four days for the journey of Jacob from Beersheba to Bethel. The KJV translation for Genesis 21:31 through Genesis 22:4 is given following.

KJV Genesis 21:31  Wherefore he called that place Beersheba; because there they sware both of them.
21:32  Thus they made a covenant at Beersheba: then Abimelech rose up, and Phichol the chief captain of his host, and they returned into the land of the Philistines.
21:33  And *Abraham* planted a grove in Beersheba, and called there on the name of the LORD, the everlasting God.
21:34  And Abraham sojourned in the Philistines' land many days.

KJV Genesis 22:1  And it came to pass after these things, that God did tempt Abraham, and said unto him, Abraham: and he said, Behold, *here* I *am*.
22:2  And he said, Take now thy son, thine only *son* Isaac, whom thou lovest, and get thee into the land of Moriah; and offer him there for a burnt offering upon one of the mountains which I will tell thee of.
22:3  And Abraham rose up early in the morning, and saddled his ass, and took two of his young men with him, and Isaac his son, and clave the wood for the burnt offering, and rose up, and went unto the place of which God had told him.
22:4  Then on the third day Abraham lifted up his eyes, and saw the place afar off.

51. If בדל (badal) were translated as "distinguished," a non-physical action, the verbs would translate in the simple past tense. The verb translations would be "saw" and "distinguished between." While "distinguished" is a possible translation, I know of no English translation which makes this translation. To make this interpretation would be a significant departure from the traditional translation. Genesis 1:6 and Genesis 1:7 also use a form of the the word בדל (badal), and do so when referring to a physical separation. Genesis 1:3-5 refers to the appearance of a physical state where there is a physical division between the lighted hemisphere of planet Earth and the night side. A translation "distinguished between" would interpret Genesis 1:4 as a part of the "naming" and not a reference to the physical separation.

52. Alveriero Niccacci, whom we quoted regarding the "waw + noun--perfect verb" word sequence as the pluperfect, considers Genesis 1:5 (1) an example of a statement made in contrast. The reference below gives examples of repeated actions and other actions connected with, and nearly contemporaneous with, the first verb of a sentence.

Alveriero Niccacci, *The Syntax of the Verb in Classical Hebrew Prose*, W. G. E. Watson translator, Journal for the Study of the Old Testament Supplement Series 86, Sheffield Academic Press, 1990, section 42., page 64.

53. Ziony Zevit, *The Anterior Construction In Classical Hebrew* (The Society of Biblical Literature, 1998). Anterior construction is Zevit's term for the "waw + noun--perfect verb" construction.

54. William Tyndale, trans., *Tyndale's Old Testament* (New Haven and London: Yale University Press, 1992), page 81.

55. When ויהי is considered as the Qal imperfect of יהוה prefixed by the ו, the verb can be a "waw-conjunctive" or a "waw-consecutive."

Interpreted as a "waw-conjunctive" ויהי would represent the command "There shall be." The command would be completed some time after the giving of the command.

Interpreting ויהי as a "waw-consecutive," the translation would be "and *there* was a dividing." This would indicate an already completed action. The verb ויהי has the same consonantal form as ויהי. The verb ויהי is translated "and *there* was" in Genesis 1:5 and Genesis 1:3 ( i.e., as a "waw-consecutive" completed action). The KJV also translates "haya," in the verb form ויהי, as "and it came to pass" 320 times. The consonantal form of the verb is the same differing only in the vowel marking which were added much later.

56. C. L. Seow, *A Grammar for Biblical Hebrew* (Nashville, Tennessee: Abingdon Press, 1995), chapter XVI, section 12, pages 188-189.

57. The word firmament is the English equivalent of the Latin word "firmamentum" used in the Vulgate. It is a word used in Latin to refer to a solid material. Outside of the Bible and studies commenting on the Bible, it was not used to refer to the sky. Speculation has been made that this word was chosen based on the word στερέωμα (stereoma) used to translate רָקִיעַ (raqia) in the Septuagint. The translation στερέωμα has been suggested to have been an accommodation made to avoid direct conflict with the Greek astronomy of Aristotle. The Greek astronomy described the heavens as a series of solid crystalline spheres.

From *Webster's Revised Unabridged Dictionary* (1913). Webster 1913 ARTFL Project:

Fir"ma*ment (?), n. [L. firmamentum, fr. firmare to make firm: cf. F. firmament. See Firm, v. & a.]

1. Fixed foundation; established basis. [Obs.] Custom is the ... firmament of the law. Jer. Taylor.
2. The region of the air; the sky or heavens.

And God said, Let there be a firmament in the mist of the waters, and let it divide the waters from the waters. Gen. 1. 6.

And God said, Let there be lights in the firmament. Gen. 1. 14.

&hand; In Scripture, the word denotes an expanse, a wide extent; the great arch or expanse over our heads, in which are placed the atmosphere and the clouds, and in which the stars appear to be placed, and are really seen.

58. Bruce K. Waltke and M. O'Connor, *An Introduction to Biblical Hebrew Syntax* (Winona Lake, Indiana: Eisenbrauns, 1990), page 382 (section 23.2.2).

59. S. R. Driver, *A Treatise on the Use of the Tenses in Hebrew and Some Other Syntactical Questions* (Oxford at The Clarendon Press, 1881) page 99, section 75. A reprint edition is currently available. This title and the reference location in it is: *A Treatise on the Use of the Tenses in Hebrew and Some Other Syntactical Questions*, S. R. Driver (Eerdmans Publishing Co., Grand Rapids, MI, 1998) first pub. 1874, page 81, section 75.

60. Ziony Zevit, *The Anterior Construction In Classical Hebrew* (The Society of Biblical Literature, 1998), page 69.

61. Randall Bluth, Methodological Collision Between Source Criticism and Discourse Analysis: The Problem of "Unmarked Temporal Overlay" and the Pluperfect/Nonsequential *wayyiatol*, Robert D. Bergen, editor, in *Biblical Hebrew and Discourse Linguistics in Summer Institute of Linguistics* (Winona Lake, Indiana: Eisenbrauns, 1994) page 138.

Also: W. J. Martin, *"Dischronologized" Narrative in the Old Testament*, Vestus Testamentum supplement 17, (Leiden: Brill, 1969), pages 179-186.

62. Bruce K. Waltke and M. O'Connor, *An Introduction to Biblical Hebrew Syntax* (Winona Lake, Indiana: Eisenbrauns, 1990), pages 551-552, chapter 32, sections 32.2.2 and 32.2.3.

63. Bruce K. Waltke and M. O'Connor, *An Introduction to Biblical Hebrew Syntax* (Winona Lake, Indiana: Eisenbrauns, 1990), page 435, chapter 27, particularly section 27.1e.

64. The KJV translations are: breath 17 times, blast 3 times, spirit 2 times, inspiration 1 time, souls 1 times: Total 24.

65. חַי (hay), pronounced "khah'-ee," is also used in the phrase מַיִם חַיִּים "living waters."
                                                             living  waters

The phrase can also mean "running water" and is applied to artesian wells. Examples are:

KJV Genesis 26:19    And Isaac's servants digged in the valley,
                       and found there a well of מַיִם חַיִּים springing water.

KJV Jeremiah 2:13    For my people have committed two evils; they have forsaken me
                       the fountain of מַיִם חַיִּים living waters, *and* hewed them out cisterns,
                       broken cisterns, that can hold no water.

66. The translation "a swarm of" considers the words שֶׁרֶץ נֶפֶשׁ חַיָּה to be a construct. The construct is a Hebrew construction which expresses "of." Hebrew does not have a word equivalent to the English word "of." J. Owens (in the *Analytical Key to the Old Testament*, volume 1, page 4) indicates the translation "swarms of" and marks the word as "construct?" (with the question mark). The KJV "the moving creature" and the YLT "teeming creature" also express a construct, but render the שֶׁרֶץ as a participle using the "-ing."

All three of the above words are singular. One of the issues considered regarding Genesis 1:20-23 is the transition from singular to plural in these verses. The conclusion that the creatures are air breathing is not altered by the singular or plural choice in the translation. All the English translations consider the שֶׁרֶץ (sherets) to be a word describing the נֶפֶשׁ חַיָּה "nephesh khay-yah."

67. Cornelius G. Hunter, *Darwin's God* (Grand Rapids, Michigan: Brazos Press, 2001).

68. KJV Leviticus 11:42  Whatsoever goeth upon the belly, and whatsoever goeth upon *all* four,
or whatsoever hath more feet among all creeping things that creep upon the earth,
them ye shall not eat; for they *are* an abomination.

ASV Leviticus 11:42  Whatsoever goeth upon the belly, and whatsoever goeth upon all fours,
or whatsoever hath many feet, even all creeping things that creep upon the earth,
them ye shall not eat; for they are an abomination.

YLT Leviticus 11:42  any thing going on the belly, and any going on four,
unto every multiplier of feet, to every teeming thing which is teeming on the earth
ye do not eat them, for they {are} an abomination;

69. The author has not found a good explanation for the difference in the spelling of these two words. Both of the words חַיְתוֹ and חַיַּת are translated in the same manner in the versions examined.

70. From *Webster's Revised Unabridged Dictionary* (1913).

Beast \ Beast \, n. [OE. best, beste, OF. beste, F. b[^e]te, fr. L. bestia.]
Any living creature; an animal; --including man, insects, etc. [Obs.] --Chaucer.
2.   Any four-footed animal, that may be used for labor, food, or sport; as, a beast of burden.

The reference to insects is not easily discerned in modern dictionaries. The *Merriam-Webster's Collegiate Dictionary* op cit. contains the following explanation: : "A four-footed mammal as distinguished from a human vertebrate, a lower vertebrate and an invertebrate." The insect is included in the classification "invertebrate."

71. KJV John 4:24  God *is* a Spirit: and they that worship him must worship *him* in spirit and in truth.

KJV Colossians 1:15  Who is the image of the **invisible God**, the firstborn of every creature:

KJV 1 Timothy 1:17  Now unto the King eternal, immortal, **invisible**, the only wise God,
*be* honour and glory for ever and ever. Amen.

72. Igor V. Ovchinnikov et. al., "Molecular analysis of Neanderthal DNA from the northern Caucasus," *Nature*, vol.404, pages 409-493, March 30, 2000.

73. Chapters were introduced by Stephen Langton, 1155-1228 A.D.

74. U. Cassuto, *A Commentary on the Book of Genesis*, trans. Israel Abrahams (Jerusalem: Magnes Press, 1998), pages 60-62. Part I: "From Adam to Noah." Genesis I – VI8.74.

75. The KJV 1611 does however have a margin note "Heb. created to make." The modern reader of the KJV would often not know this because many current versions do not include the margin notes.

76. R. K. Harrison provides a review of the development of the "Documentary Hypothsis" in the first chapter of his book *Introduction to the Old Testament.* He calls it the "Graf-Wellhausen Hypothesis." R. K. Harrison, *Introduction to the Old Testament* (Grand Rapids, Michigan: William B. Eerdmans Publishing Company, 1969), pages 495-541. Part 8j, Section 1. Available from Christian Books Distributors.

77. U. Cassuto, *The Documentary Hypothesis and Composition of the Pentateuch – Eight Lectures*, trans. Israel Abrahams (Jerusalem: Magnes Press, 1983), pages 60-62.

78. Rev. Dyson Hague in the article "The Doctrinal Value of the First Chapter of Genesis." The Fundamentals; R. A. Torrey, A. C. Dixon and Others Ed.; 4 volume set, 1917, reprinted 1988 by Baker House Co. ISBN 0-9010-8809-7.

    Some typical titles are:

    | | |
    |---|---|
    | The Early Narratives of Genesis | by Professor James Orr |
    | Decadence of Darwinism | by Rev. Henry H. Beach |
    | The Passing of Evolution | by Prof. George Frederick Wright |
    | The Grace of God | by C. I. Scofield |
    | Is There A God? | by Rev. Thomas Whitelaw |
    | The Deity Of Christ | by Prof. Benjamin B. Warfield |

    The articles "Decadence of Darwinism" and "The Passing of Evolution" do not oppose Darwinism on the basis of the age of the Earth. They accept an old Earth and present opposition to Darwinism on the basis of theology, argument for design, and the complexity of life.

79. Michael J. Behe, *Darwins Black Box* (New York, New York: Free Press, 1996).

80. Phillip E. Johnson, *Darwin On Trial* (Downers Grove, Illinois: Inter Varsity Press, 1991).

81. Tim M. Berra, *Evolution and the Myth of Creationism* (Stanford University Press, 1990).

82. Benjamin B. Warfield ,"On the Antiquity and the Unity of the Human Race," *Princeton Theological Review,* volume ix, 1911, pp. 1-25, Also in *Biblical and Theological Studies*, reprinted 1968.

83. R. A. Torrey, *Difficulties in the Bible*, Moody ,1907, chapter 4. This book is still in print. It is a defense of the Bible in answer to issues raised by critics of the Bible.

84. Roger Forster and Paul Marston, *Reason Science and Faith* (Eugene, Oregon: Wipf and Stock Publishers, 2001).

85. St. Augustine, *The Literal Meaning of Genesis*, Volume I, Paulist Press, 1982, page 135, John Hammond Taylor, S.J.,Translator. The passage is in Augustine's "book 4, chapter 27."

86. There is presently no clear uniformly adopted descriptive reference for this construction. Many grammars do not treat this construction. The terminology "waw + noun – perfect verb" closely parallels Niccacci's terminology of WAW–X– QATAL. QATAL is a reference to a perfect verb form. The "waw + noun – perfect verb" describes all the key elements of the construction in normal English terms. Because of this, it was adopted as a description to assist the reader. More information about the terminology appears on page 42.